smart
casual

smart casual

the transformation
of gourmet restaurant
style in america

alison
pearlman

The University of Chicago Press
Chicago and London

Alison Pearlman is a Los Angeles–based art historian and cultural critic who blogs under the name the Eye in Dining. She teaches modern and contemporary art and design history at Cal Poly Pomona and is the author of *Unpackaging Art of the 1980s*, also published by the University of Chicago Press.

The University of Chicago Press, Chicago 60637
The University of Chicago Press, Ltd., London

22 21 20 19 18 17 16 15 14 13   1 2 3 4 5

ISBN-13: 978-0-226-65140-8 (cloth)
ISBN-13: 978-0-226-02993-1 (e-book)

Library of Congress Cataloging-in-Publication Data
Pearlman, Alison, author.
    Smart casual : the transformation of gourmet restaurant style in America / Alison Pearlman.
        pages   cm
    Includes bibliographical references and index.
    ISBN 978-0-226-65140-8 (hardcover : alkaline paper) — ISBN 978-0-226-02993-1 (e-book) 1. Gastronomy— United States—History—20th century. 2. Gastronomy— United States—History—21st century. 3. Restaurants— United States—History—20th century. 4. Restaurants— United States—History—21st century. I. Title.
    TX633.P33 2013
    641.01'30973—dc23
                                        2012033126

♾ This paper meets the requirements of ANSI/NISO Z39.48-1992 (Permanence of Paper).

I dedicate this book to those whose help, in
disparate forms at different times, was decisive:

Ken Albala
Gary Allen
Malaga Baldi
Susan Bielstein
Homaro Cantu
Mary Cappello
Francis Itaya
Paula Itaya
Raymond Kampf
Pat Kuleto
John T. Lang
Jamisin Matthews
Daniel Pearlman
Sandra Pearlman
Scott Shaw
Rob Wilder

contents

introduction

Between 1975 and 2010, the style of gourmet dining in America transformed. Increasingly, restaurants of "fine" dining incorporated food, décor, and other elements formerly limited to the "casual" dining experience. Meanwhile, a growing number of venerated chefs opened informal eateries in addition to ceremonious venues. As a result of these boundary crossings, the gourmet field is replete with eroded hierarchies and pointed style contrasts, convergences of *haute* and ordinary.

The extent of this change may be gauged by the ascent of chef David Chang. In just a few years after he opened his first venue, Chang's New York City restaurants Momofuku Noodle Bar (2004–), Momofuku Ssäm Bar (2006–), and Momofuku Ko (2008) were bringing him top honors. He received multiple James Beard Foundation awards, Michelin stars, *New York Times* accolades, and recognition on San Pellegrino's list of the "world's 50 best restaurants."[1] These honors in turn aroused insatiable press interest in Chang's every culinary enthusiasm and industry alliance, making him one of the most celebrated and influential chefs in the United States.[2]

Of the restaurants that brought Chang this attention, only Ko has been explicitly labeled "fine dining."[3] Why the star treatment for restaurants not so named? Chang has successfully traded in upsetting restaurant hierarchies. Noodle Bar and Ssäm Bar have hybridized the high and the humble by turning out exceptional renditions of everyday foods. By boutique sourcing, carefully crafting, and creatively tweaking the likes of ramen, fried chicken, and pork buns, Chang and his *chefs de cuisine*, Tien Ho and Peter Serpico, have garnered the sort of praise once reserved for *haute cuisine*.

Chang's restaurant interiors have upended hierarchies as well. All his restaurants are irreverently basic. Plain wooden tables, walls, stools, and communal counters have become signatures. At Momofuku Ssäm Bar, the only real wall art is a framed poster of John McEnroe.

We might expect Ko, the first Chang restaurant to require reservations, to have elevated itself architecturally from the drop-in Noodle Bar and Ssäm Bar. It hasn't. Ko is a punk middle finger to fancy. Chang himself admits in his *Momofuku* cookbook (2009) that the *fuk-u* in *Momofuku* is intentional.[4]

It's provocative to open a temple of gastronomy that looks like a diner (fig. 1). It was unprecedented for the *Michelin* guide to honor such a place with two of its rare stars. Several feet into the tiny East Village storefront is Ko's main feature, an L-shaped blond-wood counter at which twelve people can sit on backless stools and peer into the stainless-steel maw of hissing cooktops. There are no tables, let alone tablecloths.

In August 2010, I lunched literally two feet from the two cooks and one sous-chef. They toiled to the boisterous beats of rock, rap, and other tie-looseners. No matter that no diner wore a tie. Patrons could have shown up for Ko's three-hour, sixteen-course extravagance in pajamas. The two cooks dressed in kind, donning not traditional toques but street-stylish blue "Momofuku" baseball caps. Scoring a reservation, notoriously competitive, was distinction enough.

An iconoclastic streak also ran through Ko's tasting menu. It appeared now and then, like a wake-up slap in between or as part of otherwise intricate and esoteric courses. At the precious and arcane end of the spectrum were a dish of pine nut brittle and Riesling *gelée* under a powdery blanket of grated frozen *foie gras*, and a wide plate featuring a narrow trail of fastidiously arranged exotic mushrooms.

1. Interior of Momofuku Ko in New York City. Photo by Noah Kalina, © momofuku.

By contrast, I recall a soulful pork rib for gnawing in hand. Another dish came with a beer chaser. My favorite lowbrow reference was a nod to the root beer float. A dessert course of onion and lavender ice cream with onion seltzer water might sound like a sophomoric prank dreamed up by a ten-year-old to taunt a younger sibling, but it was transporting in its subtle allium sweetness and pristine white cream. It's traditional in the finest places to give diners a parting gift of a box of house-made truffles or other *mignardises* (tiny sweet tidbits). Ko sent me off with house-made kimchi and pickles—a riff on delis.

For restaurants to mix the rarified and the commonplace, let alone heighten the contrast of the two to Ko's extent, would have been practically unheard of in the United States before 1975.[5] With few exceptions, the best restaurants, such as those with four stars from the *New York Times*, were modeled after the French restaurant Le Pavillon (Manhattan, 1941–72), considered the pinnacle of fine dining in the country from the 1940s through the mid-1960s.

Le Pavillon's 1960s descendants—New York City restaurants La Caravelle (1960–2004), Lutèce (1961–2004), and La Grenouille (1962–), among others—were not quite as formal. Gone, for example, was the strict *service à la Russe*, which, as Patric Kuh recalls in *The Last Days of Haute Cuisine* (2001), involved such contortions as first presenting an entire cake when a customer ordered only one slice.[6] Nevertheless, Le Pavillon's progeny did not stray too far from its motifs of décor. Abundant flower displays, chandeliers and/or sconces, velvet curtains and/or damask wall treatments, tablecloths, and formally structured place settings of fine china and crystal were still typical.[7] It's true that some restaurants simplified their décor in the 1970s. After chef André Soltner became full owner in 1973, the revered Lutèce may have gone the furthest—and, ironically, the most authentically French—in reducing its ornamentation.[8] But most still evoked lustrous, turn-of-the-twentieth-century hotels such as the Ritz or European grandeur of an even earlier era.

Under these circumstances, an unsophisticated diner would have been easy to spot. Imitators of Le Pavillon's peremptory *maitre d'hôtel*, Henri Soulé, would have seated one in the back, the established location of restaurant "Siberia." Sound levels were low enough to magnify not only the tink-tink of glasses and silver but also the manners *faux pas*. Many outsiders wouldn't have been able to read the menus, printed in French, or been familiar with their recurring repertoire of Continental classics. Failing the proper use in correct sequence of several layers of silver, these patrons were sure to expose themselves. If a gentleman arrived without jacket and tie, the *maitre d'* might dismiss him or put the gauche fellow in a lender.

In contrast, Ko's mixture of highbrow and lowbrow indicates a major change in what counts as sophisticated taste. It's best described as a shift toward what sociologists call omnivorousness—an elite appreciation of not simply formal "high" culture but rather a range of the "high" and the "low." In *Foodies: Democracy and Distinction in the Gourmet Foodscape* (2010), Josée Johnston and Shyon Baumann declare omnivorous taste a chief badge of distinction among contemporary gourmets known as "foodies."[9]

As an art and design historian, I wonder how omnivorousness evolved as an aspect of restaurant design. Also, what are the most significant omnivorous trends? Probing further, what new criteria of sophistication do those trends represent? And, finally, which hierarchies in American society do they reinforce? *Smart Casual* is my attempt to answer these questions.

This book contributes to writing on restaurant design in several ways. It treats design in an unusually expansive sense. It addresses styles and themes of food as well as décor and, when relevant, menus, websites, utensils, and service attire and performance—in other words, the full range of visible restaurant components. Consumers experience these aspects of gourmet dining in tandem, yet writers have tended to address each in isolation.

Finally, *Smart Casual* is the first book to identify the trends examined here as part of a pattern of changing tastes and social hierarchies in the United States. While the trends I discuss are not at all limited to these shores, their social significance in America is distinctive. The nation's history of restaurant types and the relatively late rise of its gourmet public provide a unique historical context.

*   *   *

Before I begin, a few words about contents, assumptions, and methods. Chapter 1 establishes how complicated the meaning of *fine dining* had become by 2010, and reviews the foundations of this state of affairs in the period between 1975 and 1985. Chapter 2 identifies the rise of new restaurant-industry tastemakers and the cultural changes underlying the transformation of gourmet restaurant style from 1975 through 2010. The next two chapters each observe patterns in the advancement of an especially enduring and pervasive design trend; analyze its style and themes; and identify the American social values they reinforce. Chapter 3 examines the pervasive phenomenon of kitchens being open to the dining room. Chapter 4 looks at leading chefs' borrowings from and transformations of humble or commonplace foods formerly excluded from *haute cuisine*. The conclusion assesses these trends' collective implications for the meaning of sophisticated taste in America.

My central premise—that aesthetic tastes express and enforce social hierarchies—is partly rooted in the history of the Western restaurant, born in Paris in the 1760s. Rebecca Spang's thorough study of the subject in *The Invention of the Restaurant* (2000) offers ample evidence that the association of restaurants with sophistication was there from the start. Their identification with cosmopolitanism had something to do with their proliferation in cities. Moreover, as they spread rapidly in Paris over the nineteenth century, their reputation as places requiring urbanity, proper conduct, and cultivation in a specifically French cuisine gained ground through popular literature, from guidebooks to novels.[10]

My understanding of the link between taste and social stratification in contemporary society is indebted to the sociology of taste. Its foundation is Pierre Bourdieu's influential *Distinction* of 1979.[11] From his vast empirical study of the cultural preferences of French people, he established a correlation between tastes and social-class positions, and persuasively argued that the class stratification of taste was reinforced by the upper classes' tendency to exclude those of lower rank. Through the social institutions they dominated, they made it difficult to obtain the "cultural capital"—education and sensibility—required to cultivate "good" taste.

Social scientists still largely accept Bourdieu's basic idea that taste and social strata are linked, and that those links are structurally reinforced. But they have legitimately questioned the post-1970s relevance of his view of classes as (1) uniform social groups and (2) the primary drivers of individual taste. Alan Warde, in *Consumption, Food and Taste* (1997), offers some compelling grounds for currently doubting Bourdieu's original model. Individual consumer choices have become complicated by factors other than class structure. The diversification of goods and services since the 1970s has transformed a once "mass" market into a more varied, subcultural field of targeted niche markets organized around lifestyle ideals. People of similar class standing can choose to differentiate themselves from one another according to special interests, information about which is ever more accessible through increasingly diverse global mass media.[12] In his seminal economic study of 1989, David Harvey described this as "the condition of postmodernity," a departure from the modern era dominated by mass industrial economies of scale and toward one ruled by socially segmented "economies of scope."[13]

I embrace the idea that contemporary taste distinctions are subcultural. I don't study the taste of elites as a whole but rather as that of a subset known as gourmets or foodies. They comprise the core and most influential consumers and audiences for the trends I explore. But I do attempt to link their tastes and values to their broader cultural context. Foodies, especially those who influence others, generally come from an elite social stratum. They tend to have the higher-than-average financial and cultural capital needed to afford regular travel and fine dining. While they may distinguish themselves by the extent of their knowledge of and passion for culinary art, I will point out the significant overlaps between their taste criteria and cultural ideals and those of other elite consumers of nonculinary arts.

Characterizations of elite taste have also evolved since Bourdieu's *Distinction*. In his study, the upper classes snobbishly expressed preference for highbrow culture—classical music, fine art—forms associated with formal education. Since 1992, sociologist Richard A. Peterson has conducted research showing that contemporary elites no longer fit Bourdieu's picture of highbrow snobbery. With evidence of historical shifts in American cultural-taste distinctions, he has concluded that late twentieth-century elites, especially from the 1980s onward, are "omnivorous."[14] In 2000, John Seabrook memorably coined the term *nobrow* to describe this very movement of American elites beyond the highbrow paradigm.[15]

The term *omnivorous* is an apt label for the restaurant-design trends I examine as well as the consumer tastes that have encouraged them. But it can be misleading. Although *omnivorous* suggests the opposite of *hierarchical*, such taste isn't as indiscriminate as it sounds. Johnston and Baumann point this out in their study of contemporary foodies. Through interviews with foodies and analysis of food writing, the authors show that their subjects are highly selective. Foodies have embraced humble, family-run street stalls and yet shunned the likes of the Cheesecake Factory, even though both are examples of everyday culture.[16]

In what follows, I try to understand what drives omnivorous restaurant-design trends and tastes. This might seem consistent with Johnson and Bauman's attempt to explain foodies' omnivorous culinary tastes. They argue that this group's taste is mainly an expression of "democracy and distinction." By this they mean that foodies' competitive desire for social distinction coexists with an equally strong, but contradictory, pull toward egalitarian ideals rooted in their increasingly pluralistic democratic society.

I accept Johnson and Baumann's conclusion that omnivorous taste is snobbery redefined, not lessened. Yet their "democracy" claim is unsatisfying. To arrive at it, they explicitly followed an insight of early sociology. Max Weber had argued that moral virtue, which he called "status honor," is a basis for social hierarchy distinct from, though often overlapping with, class. But the authors don't convince me that foodies' appreciation of the common cultural forms fine dining has appropriated, a trend I discuss in this book, necessarily has moral origins.[17]

Appeals to virtue drive some food-world tastes. Harvey Levenstein's *Paradox of Plenty* (originally published in 1993) is a thoroughly researched history of how, over the twentieth century, the cautions of an emerging nutrition science helped shape American health- and dieting-conscious food attitudes and tastes. More recently, impassioned exposés of industrial-scale food production such as Eric Schlosser's *Fast Food Nation* (2001) and Michael Pollan's *The Omnivore's Dilemma* (2006) have themselves, as best sellers, influenced food taste—for organics, locavorism, and Slow Food—on moral grounds.[18]

But what, then, to make of the attraction to the hamburger, as witnessed in the trend of *haute* burgers I address in chapter 4? I don't think egalitarian ethos can account for the discourse surrounding it. Such foods as hamburgers, appropriated by master chefs including Daniel Boulud, are recurrently labeled "comfort food." Whatever is comforting about hamburgers can't solely be a matter of ethics. If anything, as icons of the fast-food juggernaut Johnston and Baumann claim that foodies disdain, hamburgers might even be deemed the opposite of ethical. Whatever their appeal may be is one task of this book to unpack.

Like most histories, this one relies on archival research. I reviewed print and audiovisual materials from library databases and catalogues, menu collections, and websites—sources I credit in the acknowledgments. But in telling the story of a *living* culture, I also draw heavily on firsthand dialogue and participant observation. I conducted in-depth interviews with chefs, restaurateurs, and designers (also listed in the acknowledgments). I talked informally with countless others. Specifically with my research in mind, I dined between 2008 and 2011 at over one hundred establishments representing a range of trends, historical moments of influence, and regions. The appendix lists the restaurants, their location, and the dates of my visits.

Only limitations of time and money prevented me from visiting every culinary hot spot in the country. If the reader finds my discussion weighted toward certain cities, it's not out of snobbish disregard of others. Obviously, I can describe with greater authority and vividness the places I've actually experienced than those I've only heard about. Since the examples I raise are either trendsetting or broadly representative of the national (if not international) gourmet scene, I believe they do justice to a study of national scope. In any case, I make sure to acknowledge any restaurants of formative importance to the trends examined, regardless of region and whether or not I've personally visited them.

For each restaurant I observed, I took photographs of food and décor (flashless, per food-blogger etiquette, unless forbidden), collected menus (unless nonexistent), made notes, and, when necessary, noted significant alterations to décor or menus since the time of that place's greatest influence. My sample encompassed geographically diverse metropolitan sites of top culinary reputation and historical importance: Los Angeles, the San Francisco Bay Area and Napa Valley, Chicago, Washington, DC, and New York City. I produced additional documentation for roughly 30 percent of the restaurants I sampled. That subgroup represents a wide, and typical, stylistic range of display kitchens. For reasons that will become clear in chapter 3, I drew detailed diagrams of the open kitchens' structure and features or questioned various staff—chefs, cooks, servers, or hosts—about the location of food preparation stations or "prep" kitchens not visible to diners.

Aside from meals documented deliberately for this project, my own experience as a lifelong restaurant enthusiast inevitably marks these pages. Albeit from selective vantage points—having lived mainly in San Francisco from the mid-1970s through the 1980s, Chicago over the 1990s, and Los Angeles in the 2000s—I witnessed the rise of the trends I write about. I still have menus I began collecting as a teen in the 1980s. My stepfather and my mother, the latter an avid reader of *Gourmet*, brought me with infectious excitement to places recommended in that magazine's pages. My stepmother, whom I visited along with my father for many summers in Providence, Rhode Island, read Mimi Sheraton's reviews in the *New York Times*, so we were aware of goings-on when we visited Manhattan. So, for example, while I dutifully made notes on San Francisco's Fog City Diner for this book in 2010—it's an almost unchanged pioneer of the gourmet diner trend—I had, in fact, eaten there the year it opened, 1985. Still, while undoubtedly influenced by my own rites of restaurant passage, this book is anything but a personal dining-out diary.

Smart Casual is aimed partly at scholars—of American history, design history, food-and-culture studies, the sociology of taste, cultural studies, and visual studies—and partly at the wider world of restaurant producers and consumers. Jargon is minimal. Foodies and those who feed them are the main characters in this story, so I hope they will be its readers.

when fine dining
met casual dining

Did fine dining die? In 2010, critics were wondering. Several spoke of a growing disconnect between the rise of restaurants serving pricey gourmet cuisine and the decline in traditional accompanying formalities, such as tablecloths, suit-wearing servers, and jacket requirements for diners.[1]

It wasn't the first time that writers had pondered fine dining's demise. Craig Claiborne, the authoritative food and restaurant critic who initiated the dining column in the *New York Times* and also that paper's still-practiced star ratings, published an article along those lines in 1959. "Elegance of Cuisine Is on Wane in U.S." claimed that "two time-honored symbols of the good life—great cuisine in the French tradition and elegant table service—are passing from the American scene."[2]

But what Claiborne blamed for fine dining's fall is diametrically opposed to what recent critics think. Claiborne argued that the public who supported restaurants' best work—diners who could distinguish fresh ingredients from frozen, could linger for hours and not rush proper service—was dying out. By contrast, the critics in 2010 pointed to people's greater food sophistication and demand for culinary excellence! It was a question of priorities, they maintained. Fewer people required formal service, luxe surroundings, and dressing up, but what was on their plates mattered more than ever.

Another difference between 2010 and 1959 had to do with the definition of *fine dining* itself. For Claiborne, its meaning was crystalline. It designated specific cuisine style, surroundings, and rituals of service. Contemporary critics were not so sure. They thought new circumstances required a reassessment. By asking whether or not fine dining was obsolete, they partly meant the relevance of the concept *fine dining* upheld by the likes of Claiborne.

That the need for new definitions came up repeatedly in 2010 is not surprising, considering the volatility of preceding years. Between 2005 and 2010, restaurant appraisals underwent paradigm-shaking upsets. The accolades heaped on the hypercasual Momofukus were part of a pattern: surprising honors were going to places with the most informal styles imaginable.

In late 2005, when standard-bearer *Michelin* released its first restaurant guide to New York City (for 2006), Florence Fabricant of the *New York Times* reported on one of its much-anticipated verdicts in shock: "The Spotted Pig, a no-frills Greenwich Village pub with an idiosyncratic menu, got a star, putting it up with restaurants like Babbo and Gramercy Tavern, while respected restaurants like Chanterelle, Felidia, The Four Seasons and Union Square Café got no stars."[3]

Fabricant had seen nothing yet. The 2011 *Michelin* guide, compiled in 2010, awarded two out of a possible three stars to a restaurant set in the prep kitchen of a Brooklyn grocery store. This made it, according to *Michelin*, one of the three hundred best restaurants in the world. The 2012 guide topped that, giving it three stars. At the time of ratings, the Chef's Table at Brooklyn Fare's chef, César Ramirez, was personally serving a twenty-course tasting menu over a placemat-bedecked stainless-steel table. It took up most of the middle of the kitchen, which accommodated just eighteen guests on utilitarian metal stools. Meanwhile, the historically high-ranking Manhattan establishment Bouley, the eponymous venue of Ramirez's superstar chef-mentor, David Bouley, a restaurant with an actual dining room and battery of servers, received only one star in the same guides.[4]

Unprecedented rankings were coming from other quarters as well.

The one most astonishing to me came in the July 2010 "Best New Chefs" issue of *Food & Wine*. In it, Roy Choi was named one of the ten most "fantastically skilled, creative, and driven" young chefs in America.[5] After sampling Choi's cuisine, I don't disagree. The judgment was surprising because it represented the first time that *Food & Wine* so honored a chef for opening a taco truck. Granted, the Kogi BBQ truck Choi launched in Los Angeles in 2008 was no ordinary case. It introduced the ethnic-fusion dish known as the Korean taco. It also jump-started a nationwide traffic jam of gourmet food trucks of every conceivable theme—from vegan-only to artisanal ice cream to, yes, even French *haute cuisine*! They multiplied at such a pace that the Food Network on cable TV wasted no time making them the focus of a reality competition show. Celebrity chef Tyler Florence began hosting *The Great Food Truck Race* in the summer of 2010. That same year and for the first time, the annual National Restaurant Association conference devoted an entire section of its floor show to food trucks so that conferees could learn how to start their own.[6] So, yes, the *Food & Wine* honor went to Choi for a very special taco truck. But, still—a taco truck?!

These upsets were legitimate reasons to question the definition of *fine dining*. But they shouldn't be mistaken as harbingers of the end of formality. It's just that the gourmet landscape had become complicated.

Consider the trend of increasingly lengthy fixed tasting menus. As restaurants featuring so-called modernist cuisine surfaced in the United States in the 2000s, the service of tasting menus reached new heights of ceremony. The extraordinary number of courses multiplied the occasions of presentation and explanation and made the pacing of courses, some being just one or two bites, a matter of tight choreography. At Moto restaurant in Chicago, I had twenty courses. Alinea, in the same city, served me twenty-six. At minibar, in Washington, DC, I ate thirty.[7] What's more, many offerings arrived to my table with unconventional vessels and utensils unique to the restaurant, requiring me to follow a server's directions to eat. When I opted for wine pairings, the intricacies of service were compounded.

And yet while such formats have raised the level of ceremony, the new formality has been qualitatively different from the old. No longer is the emphasis on inherited rituals—in manners, use of utensils, and so on. Given the vanguard thrust of contemporary gourmet restaurants, the diner shows aplomb by knowing to expect the unexpected. Furthermore, lengthy tasting menus have required of diners something new: a capacity to concentrate on and appreciate, for a sustained period, the chef's—and sometimes also the sommelier's—performance in minutiae.

Also deviating from the old formalities, this new variant of tasting menu has often occurred in ultracasual surroundings. In the case of pop-up (temporary) restaurants, a contrast between complex menu and simple digs has been the norm. Creating the mold for Los Angeles pop-ups in 2007, instigator chef Ludo Lefebvre launched LudoBites on designated dates in the off-hours of a bakery and sandwich shop. I found the height of incongruity in chef Laurent Quenioux's pop-up, LQ@SK. He advertised an eighteen-course, all-white-truffle menu for $350 per person at a quick-lunch café that normally services the downtown-LA office crowd.[8] It's not fancy trappings; it's the uniqueness of the menus and the fact that diners must be in the know to make reservations that give such occasions cachet.

Nor did formality disappear entirely from restaurant dress codes. Its relationship to fine dining, however, had become variable. In 2010, most three-star *Michelin* restaurants in America still required male diners to wear jackets even if they had dispensed with the necktie rule. In October, I checked restaurant profiles for two of the highest-ranking regions on the popular reviews-and-reservations site Opentable.com. The French Laundry, the only three-star place in *Michelin*'s guide to the "San Francisco Bay Area and Wine Country," insisted on jackets. Of the three-starred in New York City—Daniel, Jean Georges, Le Bernardin, Masa, and Per Se—all except Masa required jackets.[9]

The Masa exception signaled changing times. Ironically, as of 2010 Masa was in one sense the most exclusive of them all. Its no-menu *omakase* meal, including some of the finest and rarest sea creatures as well as other luxe ingredients such as truffles, caviar, and *foie gras*, was the most expensive *prix-fixe* menu in America. Including one relatively modest bottle of sake, my solo dinner there in August 2010 came to a before-tip reckoning of $726.85. And yet on its website (masanyc.com), Masa described a dress code of "casual and comfortable." So, even at the *Michelin* pinnacle a range of formality had come to pass. Relatively speaking, formal dress persisted. But gourmets no longer saw the link between it and the finest, most costly dining out as axiomatic.

Apart from the very top tier, the general trend was toward dress codes relaxing. In 2005, among white-tablecloth restaurants this had advanced to a point worthy of special comment by the *Zagat* survey. Its *America's Top Restaurants* guide stated in the introductory assessment of new trends, "Just a few years ago, jacket and tie were *de rigueur* at fine restaurants . . . today, they're *de rigor mortis*—'jacket suggested' is the most formal requirement that all but a few *America's Tops* places make."[10] White-tablecloth places were increasingly specifying diner attire by *business casual, smart casual,* or some other qualified-casual code.[11]

Compared with the exacting *jackets required,* the terms *business casual* and *smart casual* are vexingly ambiguous. They leave wide room for interpretation. They also seem ambivalent. Their approval of casualness is hedging. I see the ambiguity and ambivalence as a middle-sector parallel to the categorical confusion caused by value compression on both ends of the gourmet spectrum. Despite the enormous range in establishments' level of elegance—the gap between the French Laundry and the Kogi BBQ truck is, undeniably, huge—the gourmet credibility and influence of places at both extremes had become equivalent.

The decoupling of the traditionally fancy and the gourmet did not, however, happen suddenly after the year 2000. In fact, all the foundations of a new, omnivorous approach to restaurant style were laid between 1975 and 1985. During that time, a new generation of restaurateurs broke with the chandeliered precedent of American fine-dining establishments. Inspired by the settings and cuisines of modest neighborhood restaurants and bars, they produced novel mixtures of fine and casual dining.

groundbreaking restaurant settings

Pioneers of more casual gourmet environments emerged in parts of California and in New York City. They influenced gourmet restaurants across the country through their high critical regard and by the strength of their own lineages of chef-protégés and restaurants.

Chez Panisse (Berkeley, CA), 1975

In California, Chez Panisse, which Alice Waters opened in 1971, was the earliest example. Its mix of fine dining and informal setting was sufficiently evolved, and it became broadly influential. The restaurant took on national importance in October 1975, when Caroline Bates reviewed it in the prestigious *Gourmet*.[12] Its novel combination of perfectionism and informality gained further traction by her emphatic and empathic account of it.

On the one hand, Bates was impressed by Chez Panisse's culinary originality and virtuosity. She praised chef Jeremiah Tower, whose menu, she declared, showed deep knowledge of French cuisine while departing from the "monotonous regularity" she found at most other French restaurants of the time. She also lauded the staff's constant pursuit of the freshest and best ingredients, evident to her by their habitual "blind tastings of butters, creams, and olive oils."[13]

And yet Bates was also charmed by Chez Panisse's lack of pretense. She interpreted the service—in which, she noted, the staff had little experience—as endearingly sincere. The surroundings also radiated a gratifyingly homey quality. Under their spell, Bates wrote, "the two-story home looks lived in and loved. It is warm with the honesty of natural wood." She was also taken by the restaurant's simplicity:

> The dining areas downstairs are furnished simply with a few old-fashioned fixtures, unmatching straight-backed chairs, and tables covered with napery and nosegays. Just inside the main dining room a still-life table arrangement of flowers, unblemished fresh fruit and glistening fruit tarts suggests that this is a restaurant more interested in art than artifice.[14]

The décor that Bates appreciated was an amalgamation of several informal sources. One was the country farmhouse restaurant. Thomas McNamee, in *Alice Waters and Chez Panisse*, explains that Waters visited many local restaurants in 1970 in a determined search for ideas for her own place. A farmhouse restaurant in small-town Bolinas struck a special chord. Indeed, McNamee's description of Gibson House parallels Bates's account of Chez Panisse in 1975: "It was a converted Victorian farmhouse, surrounded with flowers. . . . There were flowers everywhere and inside as well, and patchwork quilts on the walls, and mismatched china and flatware."[15] That Waters furnished Chez Panisse with nonmatching flea market finds of Victorian vintage, and insisted on abundant but rustic displays of flowers, reveals the aesthetic imprint of Gibson House.[16] It must have reminded her of her first exhilarating experience of a country-house restaurant in Brittany in 1965, during her initial, and life-changing, trip to Europe as a student.[17]

Other inspirations were the everyday cafés and bistros of Paris, where Waters first fell in love with French food. Aspects of the interior Bates remarked on, such as bare wood floors and straight-backed chairs, were frequent sights at these modest but proud establishments. In addition, the "handwritten menus on the bistro chalkboards" and the daily changing fare that McNamee says so impressed Waters in Paris made their mark on Chez Panisse's daily fluctuating dishes and often cursive-scripted menus. I found many in a six-volume compilation from the restaurant's first eight years.[18]

Of Chez Panisse's various models, those of bistros and cafés had the most widespread and lasting impact on gourmet restaurants in America. The Chez Panisse kitchen was famous for incubating future star chefs who carried the torch of casual style into their own places. They, too, appropriated everyday genres, whether bistros and cafés or some other informal types—brasseries, trattorias, bar-and-grills, and so on. Chez Panisse alum Mark Miller opened Berkeley's Fourth Street Grill in 1979 and Santa Fe Bar & Grill in 1981. Jeremiah Tower modeled his renowned San Francisco restaurant, Stars, which opened in 1984, on brasseries in Montparnasse.[19]

Michael's (Santa Monica, CA), 1979

A further force for informality in California was Michael McCarty's restaurant, Michael's. By the time Bates raved about it in the May 1980 *Gourmet*, the restaurant had already garnered a stellar reputation as far reaching as New York and Paris for its combination of a "revelatory" menu and a "casually sophisticated" design.[20]

McCarty had aimed to create what he called a "modern American restaurant."[21] He went about this by setting it in a 1930s modernist home, whose unadorned walls he used to emulate the style of a mid-twentieth-century American modern-art gallery. Bates described the interior as "painted art-gallery neutral." The point of this, she continued, was "to set off Michael's private collection, which leans to the works of Richard Diebenkorn, Jasper Johns, and David Hockney." Michael's was indeed a novel mixture of restaurant and gallery. The minimalism of the gallery style extended to the furnishings. In the dining rooms at Michael's, Bates observed "sleek chairs and large sofas with pale pink upholstery."[22]

The gallery aesthetic cleanly broke with American restaurants' prior association of formality with ornamentation. But it was not by itself informalizing. Like temples of gastronomy, art galleries can connote reverence and hushed decorum. And yet, in combination with the servers' attire, McCarty's vision of a "modern American restaurant" came to life as a stylish statement of informality. The sofas' pale-pink upholstery appeared as an organic extension of the servers' pale-pink shirts.

Reading histories of the California gourmet scene, I was fascinated by occasional mentions of McCarty's adoption of preppy, pink, Polo-insignia shirts instead of the expected tuxes or dark suits for his wait staff. But these statements were unsatisfactorily brief. I arranged to speak with Andrew Turner, Michael's knowledgeable general manager and sommelier, over dinner at the restaurant. He graciously filled me in. When preparing to open in 1979, McCarty wanted a look for his staff that wasn't stiff. Tuxedoes were out of the question. Even suits were too uptight. He asked a friend of his in the apparel industry to recommend a designer, specifying that he wanted one both "up-and-coming" and American. The friend suggested Ralph Lauren. With very few and brief exceptions over the years since, the servers at Michael's, male and female, have been wearing the current cut of pale-pink, long-sleeved, collared Polo shirts and Ralph Lauren ties.[23] They were wearing them when I visited in the summer of 2010.

Immediately after Michael's, other ambitious gourmet restaurants adopted similarly informal server attire. An early photograph of the young chef Wolfgang Puck and his wait staff at Spago, which opened in Los Angeles in 1982, bears witness (fig. 2). It features male and female staff wearing long-sleeved button-down-collared shirts in an array of

2. Wolfgang Puck and staff at Spago, West Hollywood, circa 1982.

pale pastels.[24] In 1985, critics were already noticing the emergence of jacketless servers at their most praiseworthy new places in New York City. When Bryan Miller gave restaurateur Drew Nieporent's Montrachet three out of four stars in a *New York Times* review that year—a rare honor for a restaurant seven weeks old and with a then little-known chef, David Bouley, at the helm—he couldn't help but also note the novelty of the staff's jacketless costume: "[Drew Nieporent's] waiters scurry around the room in black shirts, pants and ties looking like a team of cat burglars."[25] Since then, countless top restaurants have followed suit(less), creating aesthetically coordinated, stylish looks for servers without the dressiness of jackets. From my visits to restaurants for this book (see the appendix), I noticed that jacketless and Oxford-shirted, with dark slacks and a waist-down apron, was by far the most pervasive look for servers.

The increasing informality of servers' dress tended to go hand in hand with the evolution of a more relaxed style of service. In her review of Michael's in 1980, Bates admired the ebullience of the staff.

Theirs was nothing like the slick, aloof treatment she had come to expect at fine restaurants. Per Bates: "The waiters (all innocent of the world-weary cynicism of the professional) wax eloquent about the evening's dishes, describing the minutest cooking detail. One learns that the garlic in a dressing has been blanched twice for a salad composed of duck legs, *foie gras*, lobster, and blueberries; or that the peppercorns in another sauce are the romantically mysterious *baies roses* . . . grown on an island 'somewhere off New Guinea.'"[26]

Not surprisingly in retrospect, Bates's account of the service at Michael's mirrored her impression of Chez Panisse's from five years earlier. At both restaurants, she was witnessing the first hatchlings of a new kind of service. It paired culinary erudition with an inviting and easygoing manner. Along with the California pioneers, leading gourmet restaurants in New York City, such as Montrachet, became associated with this new style.[27]

In 1999, *New York Times* food critic William Grimes acknowledged the new service style's sweeping impact. His article, "Easygoing, Not French and Formal," also summarized the chief characteristics of what he called "the new American service." One was interactivity with guests, a "conversational, rather than presentational" approach. The new service was also more helpful than the former so-called French style. New-style servers walked their customers halfway to the restroom when asked its location; they didn't just point. In addition, Grimes claimed that this relaxed manner belied a rigorous study of the cuisine. It was common, he wrote, for servers to know the menu top to bottom and the ingredients in each dish.[28]

Chez Panisse Café, 1980

On April 1, 1980, Alice Waters made new stylistic inroads by incorporating elements of informal cafés and pizzerias. She unveiled a thorough redesign of Chez Panisse's kitchen in its upstairs dining room, calling it the Chez Panisse Café (fig. 3). The new kitchen featured, among other things, an oak-burning brick oven, and it was open to the dining room. The remodel was hugely consequential for Chez Panisse and the restaurant world as a whole. Previously, the upstairs at Chez Panisse had been nondescript. Waters (literally) carved out a new niche.[29]

3. Alice Waters in the downstairs dining room of Chez Panisse, Berkeley, CA, with staff assembled in the open kitchen, 1985. © Roger Ressmeyer / CORBIS.

When Bates got around to reviewing the café in *Gourmet* in June 1982, it was too late to cover it as something new. She had to define it as the instigator of a "café restaurant" trend. In fact, her review was of three such places, all with *café* in their name.[30] By her wholehearted approval of its mix of quality with informality, Bates was not only a witness to a trend but a coconspirator. About this one, she beamed, "cafés have become synonymous with the best places to eat." More praise: "These cafés are the most interesting development on the local restaurant scene in years."

Bates furthered Waters's own elevation of common genres by asserting that the trend was sophisticated: "The new style café is . . . the product of a well educated, well traveled generation that has absorbed European food traditions and is interpreting them with an American perspective and the materials at hand. It is honest, serious, and sometimes original." Also like Chez Panisse Café itself, Bates linked the traits of integrity and sophistication with those of casualness: "What the cafés have in common are an informal, unpretentious atmosphere, inexpensive prices, and, most importantly, a menu that changes daily and emphasizes fresh, seasonal foods."

Bates credited Chez Panisse Café not only with instigating the café-restaurant craze. She also revealed that it was the first gourmet restaurant to feature a wood-burning oven in the décor. About this, too, Bates, like Waters, gave gourmet credibility to a plebeian form. She loved that Waters had modeled her oven after the one at Tomasso's pizzeria in San Francisco's North Beach, which Bates called "venerable" and "the only genuine old-world pizza oven in the Bay Area." Moreover, she claimed, "The installation of a pizza oven in the upstairs café . . . gave respectability to a food cheapened by American franchise operations."[31]

That the Chez Panisse Café had launched a trend of gourmet pizzerias, not just café-restaurants, was also already evident to Bates in 1982. "Now pizza, the bread of peasants, has become chic," she announced, "and high-class pizzerias with special ovens, wood-burning and otherwise, have cropped up in San Francisco, clustering in the Union Street area, and as far south as Los Angeles."[32]

Little did Bates know at the time how incessantly, in the following decades, restaurants across the nation would copy open kitchens and wood-burning ovens. Wolfgang Puck's Spago in Los Angeles made a central feature out of both when it opened to great acclaim in January 1982. After a fire at the restaurant, Chez Panisse itself reproduced the format in its downstairs dining room, which reopened in April 1982 with an open kitchen, as in the upstairs, also containing a wood-burning oven.[33]

A number of chefs who worked at Chez Panisse installed open kitchens when they established their own restaurants. In 1984, Jeremiah Tower opened Stars with one; Joyce Goldstein started Square One in San Francisco with one; and Jonathan Waxman, formerly chef at Michael's and Chez Panisse, took the feature cross country, for unveiling at Jams in New York City.

Aside from the Chez Panisse alumni, there was Puck himself, who with Spago's success opened additional restaurants throughout the 1980s, 1990s, and the first decade of the 2000s that nearly all presented open kitchens. Spago's many chefs, including its first, Mark Peel, also furthered the trend. On and on it went. Open kitchens—once common only in casual places such as diners, where the sight of manual labor and the smells and sounds of food prep had been better accepted— became ubiquitous at high-status gourmet restaurants.

Mustards Grill (Yountville, CA), 1983

Chef Cindy Pawlcyn and her business partner, Bill Higgins, were also stylistic pioneers. In their earliest ventures, they boldly combined elements of fine dining with roadside Americana. Their first such place was Mustards Grill, which they opened in the Wine Country town of Yountville, California, in 1983. As a type, the American roadhouse is a come-as-you-are bar serving food and offering a brief respite for truckers and travelers. With its rural location; big, beckoning sign by the road; spacious front parking lot; and plain, wood-slatted exterior, Mustards Grill emulated that no-nonsense genre. Yet, as Pawlcyn herself summed it up in conversation with me, she envisioned her place as both a truck stop and a fine-dining destination. From the beginning, great care and creativity went into the combinations and choice of ingredients, many grown on site in the garden, and the food was prepared with the trend savvy and finesse of a skilled and worldly chef. She made a point of telling me that unlike a traditional roadhouse, the restaurant maintained white tablecloths, fine glassware, and an extensive wine list. Nonetheless, diners could get in and out fast if they wanted. But they could also linger over a four-course lunch. In the summer, Pawlcyn added, one could arrive in shorts but sit at an elegantly dressed table, order a hamburger but also a three-hundred-dollar bottle of wine.[34]

The earliest outpost of stylistically omnivorous dining in the Napa Valley, Mustards played an important role in establishing the area's reputation for laid-back sophistication, its blend of farmer style and urbane food-and-wine connoisseurship. It was so immediately successful that already in 1986, *Gourmet* reported that Pawlcyn and Higgins, who incorporated as Real Restaurants, had opened several more places in the Napa Valley and San Francisco.[35]

Fog City Diner (San Francisco), 1985

One of those early restaurants was arguably more influential than Mustards in its mixture of fine dining with casual Americana. Fog City Diner, which opened in San Francisco in 1985, was the first diner headed by a rising-star gourmet chef. Architecturally, it was the theatrical production of designer Pat Kuleto. As Kuleto told me, he fashioned the at-once archetypal and yet uncommonly swank thirties-forties diner out of an old garage on the site. His design bore classic elements: a streamlined bullet shape, ribbed stainless-steel wraparound trim, deco-scripted sign, neon outlines, black-and-white checked tile, and the traditional oversized clock with punchy saying—in this case, "Don't Worry."

But, as Stanley Dry noted in his 1986 review for *Food & Wine*, this was no ordinary diner. What ordinarily would have been a dining counter was instead a cocktail bar crafted from marble. At one end of the open kitchen stood a ravishing display of shellfish on ice, and throughout the place, he wrote, there was mahogany, carpeting, spacious booths, and shiny black tables.[36] Dry didn't mention it, but I remember that Fog City's glamorous effects were also a function of brilliant lighting design. Deviating from the bright and even cast of a typical diner, Fog City was generally dark and lit selectively and dramatically. It summoned forth the electrifying nightlife side of deco. Surfaces glistened from a combination of backlighting; stunning behind-the-bar shelves stacked with twinkling bottles; profile lighting of customers by boothside wall sconces; and overhead sources of varied light, soft and diffuse from covered lamps and sharp and pointed from bare, narrow cans.[37]

The Fog City Diner was a sudden success and powerful influence. Other sophisticated diners quickly appeared, proffering serious wine lists, elegant dishes, and adult atmospheres. Atlanta's Buckhead Diner and Los Angeles's Kate Mantilini followed Fog City in 1987. At this writing, all three are still open; and one finds an abundance of other diners with a certain gourmet twist, if not necessarily posh surroundings. Enough have opened over the years to keep the Food Network's host Guy Fieri full of material for his *Diners Drive-Ins and Dives* program since its debut in 2007. The show's sole focus is the places across the United

States that have somehow transcended the typical diner, drive-in, or dive. They feature house-made preparations, use top-quality ingredients, or come up with original, worldly, and on-trend dishes.

Odeon (New York, NY), 1980

New York had its own forgers of omnivorous style. Odeon, which opened in 1980 in the barely gentrified Tribeca area of Manhattan, was the first acclaimed place to put together fine dining and downtown funk. Reviewing Odeon in 1981, both Mimi Sheraton of the *New York Times* and Jay Jacobs of *Gourmet* were impressed by American chef Patrick Clark's *nouvelle cuisine* and his exceptional training in France under the world-famous chef Michel Guérard. On the basis of Clark's choice of ingredients, Jacobs even went so far as to compare Odeon to one of the most revered restaurants in New York at the time: "To the best of my knowledge, Odeon is the only New York City restaurant aside from Le Cirque, where the fresh product is available in season."[38]

Both reviews also dwelled on what seemed to them rather dissonant décor for a place of such high culinary standard. Odeon duplicated the atmosphere of a nightclub or singles bar. Without saying so explicitly, Sheraton recalled such places when she described it as "a swinging scene" and pointed out the kitchen's late hours and hipster crowd: "From dinnertime to 2:30 in the morning, the cast of patrons arrives at this Art Deco restaurant . . . in everything from punk to black-tie, from urban cowgirl and thrift shop rag-bag to plain clothed uptowners." Further likening Odeon to a nightclub, Sheraton highlighted the prominent role that the restaurant's bar and music played in setting the tone: "At the Odeon, the bar scene makes guests feel as though they're at a party, and the 1930's and 40's background music is not too objectionable as a result."[39]

Odeon wasn't the first restaurant to attempt to meld fine dining with the singles bar. To lure the first generation of "swinging singles," impressario Warner LeRoy opened Maxwell's Plum in 1966.[40] LeRoy, however, had molded his place as an elegant alternative to the competition of the time: New York's first singles bar, T.G.I. Friday's, which opened in 1965. LeRoy thus gave Maxwell's Plum a style of over-the-top art nouveau opulence. He refined it further by hiring a renowned

French chef and installing a fancy *belle-epoque*-esque dining room in the back.[41]

While Odeon also had a French-trained chef, its furnishings were mostly lowbrow quotations. When reviewing the venue, Jacobs put greater emphasis on these chicly raffish elements. He took stock of Odeon's salvaged vintage furnishings, which co-owner and designer Keith McNally had picked out from particularly "plebeian" sources: "a wall clock rimmed in garish neon, and, in the vestibule, a Takacheck queue-ticket dispenser [to which the designers] added a marvelously kitschy Art Deco bar (salvaged from a Long Island City warehouse), a period mural scrounged from an old luncheonette, a mismatched collection of used bent-metal chairs, some trim banquettes, and plain geometric wall sconces." Accentuating the discord, he added, "Odeon may be the only *nouvelle cuisine* showcase in the world where glasses of toothpicks are included among the furnishings."[42]

Jacobs quoted McNally, who claimed that the ultimate goal of this pastiche was comfort. To Jacobs, it seemed like a success: "All sorts of people *do* seem to relax at this restaurant, where the patronage ranges from Scarsdale matronage to purple-haired punkhood."[43] How right he was. Odeon launched the careers of brothers Keith and Brian Mc-Nally, who have been known ever since for their production of some of New York's most highly anticipated gourmet restaurants. Their success, moreover, derives from a combination of recruiting top gourmet kitchen staff and designing dramatic, spot-on stylish interiors whose themes—from the simulation of an archetypal French brasserie (Balthazar, 1997–) to the recreation of a neighborhood pizza place (Pulino's, 2010–)—consistently follow the tendency to borrow from everyday aesthetics.

Union Square Café (New York, NY), 1985

Odeon may have been among the first to merge fine dining with the atmosphere of a nightclub or bar. Yet the literal, physical merger of fine dining and bar would have to wait till 1985, when restaurateur Danny Meyer opened Union Square Café. Stylistically, Meyer was aiming for a modern American interpretation of a Roman trattoria. In his memoir, *Setting the Table* (2006), he recalls wanting to fuse "the best of European fine dining with the ease and comfort of American style." The inspirations he named were a mix of *haute* and homey: "I imagined Union Square Café as a combination of three very different kinds of restaurants one encountered in the late 1970s: first, the earthy, seasonal, local, food-loving places in Berkeley and San Francisco; second, the refined gastronomic temples of Paris; and third, the mama-and-papa trattorias of Rome."[44]

Meyer's attempt to fuse genres resulted in a significant innovation for gourmet restaurants: the use of the bar as a dining space. Andy Birsh praised Meyer in his *Gourmet* review of 1986 for thus accommodating the single visitor: "One of the matters that Mr. Meyer has turned his attention to is the care of the solitary diner. The bar is built with the lone customer in mind. It has no raised edge on which drinkers can lean, and so it accommodates complete place settings. A chalkboard above the bar spells out the oysters . . . in season and in the house."[45] He restated the point in another review from 1991: "From the outset [Meyer] encouraged customers to eat sitting at the long and surprisingly comfortable bar, and they still do now." According to Birsh, bar dining had the effect of making the fine-dining setting less formal: "Folks in their best attire continue to sit comfortably next to others who have sauntered in wearing jeans and sweaters."[46]

In *Setting the Table*, Meyer didn't give credit explicitly, but his institution of bar dining was likely inspired in part by a popular trend in Spanish restaurants. The American rage for tapas exploded before Union Square Café's opening on October 21, 1985. Tapas are the myriad house-made appetizer-sized snacks typically served in Spanish bars during the hours between meals. A full-blown tapas-bar trend in the United States began making headlines as early as May of 1985.[47] Considering its importance at the time, the tapas bar remains surprisingly in the background of Meyer's story. He does mention patronizing a popular tapas bar that had opened in 1984, but only in an aside and not as an influence on his own restaurant. He says only that when planning Union Square Café, he had "scribbled" notes for it "on tapas napkins at El Internaçional."[48] Could one of them have referred to El Internaçional's bar? It was, as it turns out, used for dining. *New York Times* critic Bryan Miller distinctly pointed out this feature at El Internaçional in 1984. He described it as the "comfortable long marble bar in the front room," where, as in two other dining areas, one could order "a full range of intriguing tapas."[49]

Meyer's use of the bar as a dining space may also have been the upshot of a trend in communal tables—another casual form catering to mixed parties, including singles—that surfaced on the New York dining scene before the Union Square Café opening. In a *Food & Wine* article of February 1986 entitled "The Good News about Dining Alone: The Communal Table Has Arrived," Stanley Dry called the communal table, a form with centuries-old roots in European roadhouses, "a nascent trend in restaurants." He singled out Sandro's, a Roman-style restaurant that had opened in Manhattan months before Union Square Café: "The best contemporary example I've seen of a restaurant that offers the option of a private table or a communal one is Sandro's . . . an inviting restaurant that opened last March. In the center of the room is *il tavolo degli amici*, or 'table of friends,' where single diners can eat with others. The table itself, which seats 12, is a copy of a 15th-century monk's table."[50]

As at tapas bars and places with communal tables, bar dining at Union Square Café encouraged looser forms of sociability—lone dining and gregariousness among strangers—than had ever prevailed at American fine-dining restaurants. The drop-in-for-a-bite leniency of bar dining also promoted "grazing," a customized approach to meal sequencing that spread the habit of building a meal ad hoc from multiple appetizers instead of following the more rigid app-main-dessert structure.

*   *   *

Over the decades since Odeon and Union Square Café opened, the merger of bars and restaurants in leading gourmet establishments has steadily progressed. Frank Bruni's "When Is a Bar Not a Bar?" in the *New York Times* in 2008 and Michael Bauer's "Is It a Bar or a Restaurant?" in 2010 for his column "Inside Scoop SF" both registered the continued strength of the trend from opposite ends of the country.[51] As further evidence of its persistence, a local paper reported that the 2010 *Michelin* guide to the San Francisco Bay Area and Wine Country "added three new categories that reflect cutting-edge dining trends: restaurants notable for their small-plates menus, cocktail programs and sake lists."[52] Such menu formats wouldn't have evolved if not for the blurring of boundaries between bars and restaurants.

By that point, the avalanche of bar-restaurant mergers had gathered more momentum from a related tendency born of the mid-1990s: formal dining rooms offering adjacent, more casual dining spaces anchored by bars. Here, Danny Meyer also led the way when he opened Gramercy Tavern in New York City in 1994. The entire front room of the restaurant was (and still is) a distinct dining room set against a bar, with a colorful mural running along one side of the room and a partially open kitchen on a portion of the other. There, customers order from a separate "Tavern Menu" and dine without the curtained-off back room's tablecloths and relative quiet.

In 1998, *Food & Wine* journalist Mary Alice Kellogg was already calling Gramercy Tavern just one among the many places across the United States offering adjacent barrooms with menus.[53] By the early 2000s, this format could be found in the most exclusive places. In New York City, the Daniel Lounge opened next to Daniel. Only a curtain separated Nougatine at Jean Georges from Jean Georges. A few paces from Masa, a diner could duck into Bar Masa. In 2006, Bruni acknowledged this trend in "Let's Hear It for the Lounge Act." He described it as a way of "trying out top restaurants without the usual fuss."[54]

In trendsetting gourmet restaurants, the communal table, too, became a favored form. Its shining moment, however, wasn't until the 2000s, when it appeared in notable places across the country, including the venerated Momofuku Noodle Bar in Manhattan, chef Paul Kahan's the Publican in Chicago, and chef Roy Choi's A-frame in Los Angeles.

Notwithstanding the many recent ripples of early trendsetters, the tendency of restaurants to incorporate casual-dining formats was clear to critics as early as 1985. In August, *Food & Wine* published a feature about it. John Mariani's "Eating Out Loosens Up" surveyed a nationwide trend toward gourmet restaurants borrowing from casual genres. Of innovators such as Chez Panisse, Spago, and others, he wrote, "These places and the new generation of restaurants quickly growing up about them are a winning combination of French bistro, Italian trattoria, German rathskeller, Spanish tapas bar and American bar & grill all in one."[55]

I don't want to blow the point out of proportion. Although increasing informality does distinguish most new approaches to gourmet restaurant settings since the mid-1970s, it isn't the whole omnivore story. Restaurants featuring swank, hushed environments continued to emerge and stake their claim to gourmet greatness. In the mid-1980s, Manhattan's sparkling Quilted Giraffe (1979–92) was as revered and relevant as Union Square Café. San Franciscans boasted of the sumptuous Masa (1983–) as well as the likes of Stars and Square One. After the 1980s, gourmets continued to uphold both ends of the style spectrum. In New York City, for example, gourmets of the 1990s admired the elegant Aureole (1988–2009) while raving about Gramercy Tavern; foodies of the 2000s paid as much attention to the splendid Per Se (2004–) as to Momofuku Ko.

turning points in restaurant cuisine

Cuisine underwent a parallel development over the same period. Leading American fine-dining chefs began fashioning menus that mixed refined and plebeian dishes or offered dishes that finessed or creatively reinterpreted everyday favorites. Some of these innovations appeared in restaurants of the sort I've just discussed. However, in keeping with the rise of omnivorous taste, others were served in more formal dining rooms.

Beginning in the mid-1970s, up-and-coming chefs deviated from the repertoire of classic dishes drawn from *la grande cuisine*. In spite of a culinary revolution in France known as *nouvelle cuisine* in the 1960s, *la grande cuisine* had been reproduced with little variation at so many American fine-dining restaurants since Manhattan's Le Pavillon. It was codified in its modern form by Ritz hotel chef George Auguste Escoffier (1846–1935) in his *Le Guide Culinaire* (1903) and through generations of professional-cook "brigades" who reproduced his methods in the most urbane and elite institutions.

The aesthetics of *la grande cuisine* depend on high degrees of transformation in the form and texture of raw ingredients. Such refinement, which is both literal and figurative, relies on multistepped, labor-intensive processes that, through techniques such as sauce making and straining, tend to remove coarseness—literally, the unrefined nature of raw ingredients. The basis of *la grande cuisine* is a series of refinements known as "mother sauces." By combining these with other ingredients, chefs can generate the myriad other sauces necessary for *haute cuisine*'s many applications.

The sauce making of *la grande cuisine* epitomizes *haute cuisine*'s logic of refinement. It's also emblematic of its professionalism. The cultivation of "mother sauces" is one means of standardizing a kitchen's output, ensuring the consistency necessary to maintain renown in the fine restaurant's demanding commercial world.

Even so, and despite their own high standards and market pressures, new-style chefs found sources of inspiration that were quite the opposite of *haute cuisine*'s refinement and professionalism. Among them was the rusticity and relative simplicity of home cooking.

When it came to French cuisine, what piqued chefs' interest was the so-called *cuisine bourgeoise*—the everyday fare that, unlike the *haute cuisine* that was traditionally the province of men, was often made by women. One might sample it at a countryside inn or in the family-run, urban-*quartier* bistros and cafés. In the early and mid-1970s, these venues were among the many inspirations for the innovative and influential menus that Alice Waters and Jeremiah Tower drew up at Chez Panisse. Bates commented on it in that all-important *Gourmet* review of 1975, where she described Tower's cooking as a departure from the *haute-cuisine* routine: "Like many creative young chefs in France today who have turned away from the pretentiousness of *la grande cuisine*, he strives for the simplicity and directness that characterize French provincial food with its emphasis on fresh ingredients and the integrity of each taste."[56]

Both Waters and Tower had idolized several early advocates of culinary "simplicity" and home-cooking traditions. One was Maurice Edmond Saillard (1872–1956), the French culinary writer with the *nom de plume* Curnonsky, who upheld simple over complicated cuisine. In her *Gourmet* review, Bates made special mention of a pen-and-ink poster of Curnonsky that had a place of pride on a wall at Chez Panisse. It wasn't an empty gesture. The restaurant's menus from the week of February 11–March 1, 1975, initiated "Three Weeks of the Cuisine of Curnonsky," which entailed presenting dishes inspired by him.[57]

Waters and Tower also followed Elizabeth David, an Englishwoman living in France. In her introduction to *A Book of Mediterranean Food* (1950), she seemed to agree with Curnonsky when she said of her subject, "It is honest cooking, too; none of the sham Grande Cuisine of the International Palace Hotel."[58] When Waters put out an ad for a chef for Chez Panisse in 1973 and, with it, managed to recruit Tower, her solicitation explicitly named Elizabeth David as one of the reference points for the style she wanted.[59]

Richard Olney, an American gastronome and writer who had lived in France since the 1950s, was another ideal.[60] Like Curnonsky and David, Olney stressed simplicity, a quality highlighted in the title of one of his books, *Simple French Food* (1974). This and his *The French Menu Cookbook* (1970) guided Waters and Tower in the early years of planning menus and developing their own styles. In *Simple French Food*, Olney celebrated the sensuousness of "regional cooking" and romanticized it by conjuring colorful backdrops: "crowded out-of-door markets" with "banks of fruits and vegetables, freshly picked" and "crates full of live snails and crabs, both of which constantly escape and wander in wide circles around the vendor's stand."[61] When he had a book signing at the specialty cookware store Williams-Sonoma in 1975, Waters and Tower made sure to be there to introduce themselves. (Tower later became romantically involved with Olney, and helped him develop The Good Cook series for Time-Life Books.)[62] Both during and after Tower's work at Chez Panisse, the restaurant's menus made frequent homage to Olney. In Linda Guenzel's compilation of Chez Panisse menus from its first eight years, there are examples of dinners that were explicit tributes to Olney from 1975, 1976, and 1979.[63]

Fine-dining chefs in America were also increasingly drawn to Italian cuisine for its rusticity and its origins in regional folk traditions outside the transnational realm of *haute cuisine*. This influence first became apparent in restaurants that were not strictly Italian. In the late 1970s, even before the installation of its wood-burning oven, Chez Panisse made pizza—what Bates had called the "bread of peasants," referring to the dish's Neapolitan origins. Pizzas appeared multiple times on the regular menu in 1979, for example.[64] In December 1982, Bates declared the elevation of pizza in gourmet restaurants a bonafide trend among California chefs: "According to reports drifting in from the other coast, pizza, no less, has become pivotal to what out-of-state journalists like to call 'California cuisine.'" Further: "With two of the state's most influential chefs—Alice Waters in the north and Wolfgang Puck in the south—devoting part of their considerable talents to the perfection of pizza, California has been pizzafied at the highest levels, and that must mean something."[65]

Chefs also introduced pasta to otherwise non-Italian menus. In 1977, Craig Claiborne reported in the *New York Times* that restaurateur Sirio Maccioni had added "Pasta Primavera" to the mostly *haute* Francophile menu at his original Le Cirque (1974–97). This exemplar of Italianate simplicity is an easy assemblage of pasta, fresh spring vegetables, and a light cream sauce. When Claiborne published the recipe in all its beautiful brevity, Le Cirque's break with precedent catapulted both the dish and the restaurant, one of New York's most formal and fabulous, to nationwide notoriety.[66] Subsequently, it became more common for non-Italian fine-dining restaurants to offer pasta dishes. Spago's menus from the early and mid-1980s had sections devoted to pastas and pizzas.[67]

But by the fall of 1983, the gourmet press was also hailing a new breed of Italian restaurant. It promoted the same aesthetic as the French *cuisine bourgeoise*—rustic and elemental. Critics applauded the style's authenticity. Stephanie Curtis's article in *Food & Wine*, "The Italian Restaurant Circa 1983," trumpeted the new incarnation and highlighted examples from coast to coast.[68] Among the standouts were Manhattan's Il Nido, which opened in 1979, and Felidia, which opened in 1981, as well as Valentino in Los Angeles, which had undergone a transformation since its start in 1972. In the early 1980s, critics took note of all of them for their relatively unmediated presentation of regional ingredients.

Regarding Il Nido, in 1980 Jay Jacobs didn't mention any elaborate or refined preparations. But he wrote effusively of the presence of exceptional and authentic ingredients. He adored the porcini mushrooms and *rugola*. He savored his first experience of a white Piedmont truffle.[69]

Caroline Bates likewise emphasized the purity of ingredients at Valentino. The restaurant, she explained, had evolved since its early days of trying to please an unknowing American palate. Whereas in 1974,

she recalled, Valentino "looked like a suburban steak house and the Ve-
netian chef cooked 'scaloppine of veal your way,'" the place had become
a model of *cucina*: "By 1980, Valentino was importing white truffles
and *mozzarella di buffala*."[70] In 1987, Bates credited Valentino with being
among the first to import Italian ingredients such as radicchio and the
first to bring white truffles and porcini mushrooms to Los Angeles.[71]

Felidia offered its own version of rusticity. The restaurant took pride
in, among other things, dishes with modest ingredients such as organ
meats. They got star billing on the menu in a section of their own entitled "Piatti Gastronomici." In 1981, Mimi Sheraton spotlighted this
portion of Felidia's menu and explained that the glorifying title was
"the menu's polite way of saying innards."[72] Felidia's daring to high-
light offal on the menu—including the tripe, kidneys, and calf's liver
that Sheraton detailed—and to position it as the most gourmet of its
options elevated what had long been in the larders of poor people.
From deprivation, they had mastered the art of coaxing flavor from
parts of animals that, with few exceptions, American *haute-cuisine* establishments had rarely put on the menu. Fine-dining critics in the
1980s, however, were receptive. In 1985, Jay Jacobs lovingly called Felidia's exaltation of Italian *povera* "earthy" and "hearty and robust."[73]

The valuation of rusticity and home-cooking traditions was also
one aspect of "New American" cuisine. The novelty of this trend
crested in the summer of 1985, when Mimi Sheraton wrote a feature
entitled "The Fun of American Food: Eat American!" Its publication
in the high-profile pages of *Time* magazine signaled the trend's full
bloom by that time.[74]

What was New American cuisine? According to Sheraton, who had
interviewed chefs across the country in preparing her article, answers
varied, but there were common themes: it was inspired by indigenous
recipes; it was eclectic, owing to the influence of diverse immigrants;
it used fresh ingredients grown in the United States, with geographic
origins often cited on menus; and, increasingly, it involved cooking by
American chefs in restaurants staffed by Americans. (This last was a
break with the dominance of Europeans in top US kitchens.) Among
the leading practitioners of New American cuisine were Alice Waters
in Berkeley; Jeremiah Tower in San Francisco; Paul Prudhomme in New
Orleans; Larry Forgione, Barry and Susan Wine, and Anne Rosenzweig

in New York; Richard Irving and Wolfgang Puck in Los Angeles; and Lydia Shire in Boston. Sheraton sprinkled many other names throughout the article.

Those attracted to the homey side of American cookery drew on hordes of regional recipes handed down and compiled by generations of home cooks. In doing so, many were inspired by James Beard (1903–85). The most influential post–World War II advocate of this strain of American cooking, Beard had been a cookbook author, TV cooking-show host, restaurant consultant, and mentor to many young chefs.

As a hired consultant at the innovative corporate fine-dining group Restaurant Associates, Beard had a profound early influence on the service of American cuisine in top American fine-dining restaurants. In 1958, he and other experts, including Mimi Sheraton, worked with chef Albert Stöckli to shape a menu with a strong American accent for the opening of RA's newest Manhattan creation, the Four Seasons (1959–). The restaurant's menu drew not just from Continental fare but also from the history of American cookery, and listed its dishes in English at a time when pricey establishments (the Four Seasons dared to be the most expensive restaurant in New York) unerringly served and spoke French. Designed in a stark modernist idiom by Philip Johnson inside Mies van der Rohe's equally minimalistic steel-and-glass Seagram Building, the Four Seasons also declared its alliance with America—the birthplace of the skyscraper—in architectural terms. While it did offer European classics, from *coq au vin* to beef stroganoff, and demurred to the sentimental popularity of dishes *flambé*, from the beginning its menus strongly recalled historic American foods: "Amish ham steak with hot rhubarb," "larded pigeon with candied figs," "chocolate velvet cake." That Craig Claiborne championed the Four Seasons in the *New York Times* the year it opened as "perhaps the most exciting restaurant to open in New York within the last two decades" gave it its first boost. His praise also helped solidify Beard's guru status for chefs of the New American generation.[75]

Beard imprinted New American cuisine also through his extraordinary and hefty *James Beard's American Cookery* (1972). A culmination of decades of studying American culinary heritage, it gave lay cooks and professional chefs alike access to Beard's extensive expertise and his treasure trove of US regional recipes. In the process of cataloguing hundreds of these recipes, he explained the origins and mutations of particular dishes and foodways. While a few in the book's collection derived from fine restaurants or required elaborate preparations for which the assistance of a houseful of servants would have been handy, the vast majority were manageable feats for homemakers.[76]

Some of the recipes were quite old, predating ovens and their predictable temperatures. But Beard adapted them for modern equipment, giving them new life. At the same time, the temporal distance of many recipes occasionally made New American dishes inspired by them—such as Jeremiah Tower's "Virginia ham with fresh figs" on a Chez Panisse menu from 1976—remote from contemporary diners' everyday experience and, therefore, not especially informalizing except where the plating was home style.[77]

Nevertheless, in the introduction to *James Beard's American Cookery*, Beard impressed readers with the humble origins of many of the book's recipes. He described them as the products of "small communities" where "excellent natural cooks began to blossom, whom all the local ladies tried to emulate." He went on to describe the evolution of recipes in a way that emphasized their homespun nature: "These gastronomic voices of the hinterland are evident when one peruses collections of recipes compiled by the Ladies Aid societies, missionary societies, hospital volunteer groups, neighborhood houses, and women's exchanges all through the country."[78]

Beard was influential not only because he sustained the traditions of home cooks through his own work, but because he nurtured similar efforts in others. As one of the earliest American gourmet celebrities—he began publishing cookbooks in the 1940s—many leading chefs after 1975 sought out and received his counsel. Throughout his memoir *California Dish* (2003), Jeremiah Tower emphasizes Beard's consistent influence on his own cooking and that of his peers. Beard's taste was directly applied in the case of Chez Panisse alum Judy Rodgers. With the 1982 opening of the Union Hotel in San Francisco, where Rodgers would be chef, Caroline Bates explained that Beard's longtime assistant, Marion Cunningham, a cookbook author and keeper of American heritage in her own right, played an advisory role:

The owners, deciding they wanted an authentic American dining room, hired as menu consultant Marion Cunningham, a well-known authority on American cooking who modernized the twelfth edition of *The Fannie Farmer Cookbook* (1979). She, in turn, persuaded Judy Rodgers, an alumna of the celebrated Chez Panisse, to become the chef. The result of this inspired and intelligent collaboration is one of the most authentically American restaurants anywhere, serving forth the likes of panfried chicken with spoon bread, Pennsylvania Dutch eggs with pickled beets, homemade Philadelphia scrapple, New England corned beef hash, and rich cream biscuits."[79]

The predilection for regional, homespun cooking was not the New American cuisine's only omnivorous legacy, however. New American chefs also embraced the opposite, appropriating food icons of mass culture. Examples of this practice were in evidence before the 1980s. A 1973 review of Maxwell's Plum snickered at the incongruous possibility of spending $175 to chase a foot-long hotdog with a Cheval-Blanc '47 on chef Jean Vergnes's otherwise *haute* menu.[80] A 1974 review of Le Cirque, where Chef Vergnes reappeared, mentions a chicken potpie among other "rustic peasant dishes," including risotto and *choucroute garnie*, to show that *haute cuisine* was not all that the restaurant served.[81] Yet it wasn't until the early 1980s that one could speak of a trend.[82]

Leading gourmet chefs were crafting their own versions of foods indelibly identified with mass media and big business. They took up symbolically loaded hotdogs, hamburgers, tacos, pizzas, and other fast-food-franchise staples. Despite such foods' ultimate origins in related immigrant recipes, their mass marketing and mass-market transformations allowed them to transcend ethnic specificity and become meaningful as emblems of American mass culture. Chefs came up with new takes on mass-produced and widespread supermarket convenience foods, such as mac-and-cheese and Fluffernutters. Less frequently, they created twists on items, such as iceberg-lettuce salads, that contemporary gourmets, in thrall to the likes of arugula, associated with unsophisticated tastes of the 1950s and 1960s.

Such foods quickly became pop icons. Their emergence as the symbolic playthings of leading gourmet chefs marks the rise of a distinctly new fine-dining sensibility. Yet chefs typically couched the dishes within menu offerings that were more rarified in their ingredients or conception and thus distinguishable as gourmet. Also, there was no mistaking these chefs' versions—house-made with quality ingredients and distinct from the original recipe—for their pop inspirations. West Beach Café, considered a trendsetting restaurant in Los Angeles during the early 1980s, put a new spin on a pop item with its "duck tacos."[83]

Tower was among the first celebrated chefs to serve gourmet hamburgers. A 1983 review of his café-style Balboa Cafe the year it opened in San Francisco described its burger as elevated by Tower's use of quality ingredients and caring preparation methods—"twice-ground chuck, hand-shaped, but handled as little as possible," and placed not on a generic fast-food bun but "on a toasted sourdough baguette." Unconventional condiments also distinguished Balboa's burger. Among the various dressing options were "mango chutney" and "*salsa cruda*."[84] Tower offered similarly lauded versions of a hotdog and a hamburger on the menu at Stars alongside more experimental gourmet fare, such as "hollowed-out Brioche with Marrow, Lobster Sauce, Poached Garlic, and Chervil" and "Blanquette of Veal with Summer Vegetables and Crayfish Sauce."[85]

The menu at the Fog City Diner, already based on an Americana theme, was *haute* pop through and through. According to Bates in 1986, "[Chef Pawlcyn] has transformed [the chili dog] from the scroungy cur of roadside drive-ins into a Vienna red hot show dog smothered in a beany chili made with pork tenderloin, lamb, and sirloin steak." Moreover, speaking of Pawlcyn's restoration of integrity to foods bastardized by fast-food outfits, "She makes her own horseradish pickles and ketchup." In the same breath, Bates recounted unique dishes with adventuresome ingredient combinations totally devoid of pop-cultural associations, including a "timbale of creamy garlic custard . . . surrounded by *shitake* mushrooms and walnuts," "a sautéed veal scallop with raisins, parsley, and pine nuts in a tart lemon dressing," and a "grilled blue-fin tuna with a lemon and green chili salsa."[86]

In the trendsetting kitchens of New York City, the same was happening. At Jams, Jonathan Waxman served a "mesquite grilled [chicken]" with what critic Ron Rosenbaum described in 1985 as "a veritable mountain of shoestring-fried potatoes." Thus, a relatively proletarian pile of fries shared the menu with such precious things as artful compositions of "baby vegetables," as well as dishes, such as "Rabbit with Potato Cakes and Pommery Mustard Sauce," reminiscent of New American food's rustic side. Referring to a restaurant simply called America, Rosenbaum pointed out this tendency to mix the rarified and the pop on the same menu:

> Alongside such New American Cuisine entrees as Salad of Roasted Fresh Root Vegetables with N.Y. State Goat Cheese and Balsamic Vinaigrette, you can find a 1950's relic described as Heart of Iceberg with Thousand Islands Dressing. You can get something as sophisticated as Corn flour Vermicelli Tossed with Duck Sausage, or you can go for the primitive entrees like truck-stop Meatloaf. You can get a faddish dessert such as the White Chocolate Macadamia Mousse. And you can get a classic Fluffernutter Sandwich—white bread slathered with gooey Marshmallow Fluff and peanut butter.[87]

In his article, which surveyed leading New American restaurants, Rosenbaum called the *haute*-pop subtrend "Serious-Fun" food. This phrase acknowledged the cuisine's humorous, even camp, aspect.

Rosenbaum saw the generational aspect of *haute*-pop cuisine. He explained it as "a generational revolution that has made such totems from the childhood of the baby-boom generation as fruit popsicles, Heath bars and Marshmallow Fluff the symbol signature dishes in a number of the new American restaurants that have captured the affluent yuppie crowd."[88] However, he couldn't have known then that the tendency he was describing in 1985 would continue to delight decades of diners, not only boomers. Since its ascendance in the early 1980s, the tendency to gourmandize pop food icons has strengthened. Indeed, all the culinary trends I've discussed have evolved further.

Even so, as with restaurant settings, the recent history of gourmet culinary style and taste has been multifaceted. In the late 1970s, at the same moment that some New American chefs were gaining acclaim for relatively rusticated presentations, the opposing precious stylings of chefs influenced by French *nouvelle cuisine* were enjoying a belated phase of chic. *Nouvelle* chefs had made the dining experience more mannered. It was they who introduced the format of fixed multi-course tasting menus. They became famous as well for their virtuosic yet minimalistic compositions of foods set off against unusually large white plates.[89]

In the 1980s, even as New American was enjoying a surge and *nouvelle* was on the wane, highly composed culinary styles continued to emerge.[90] When he became head chef of Manhattan's Gotham Bar and Grill in 1985, Alfred Portale initiated a trend in structured vertical arrangements, a quasi-architectural layering of foods.[91]

The more recent trend in lengthy tasting menus represents a resurgence and dramatic extension of *nouvelle*. Some esteemed chefs have even chosen to revive *nouvelle*'s original source of inspiration for the meal as a multicourse, highly ritualized progression of small courses—Japanese *kaiseki*.[92] In Manhattan in 2007, chef David Bouley collaborated with the Tsuji Culinary Institute of Osaka, Japan, to open a restaurant, Brushstrokes, devoted to this fine art.[93]

I am fascinated by the question, what fueled the powerful ascent of omnivorous restaurant style and taste over the formative decades? I turn next to examining the various emergent cultural and economic factors, within and beyond the American restaurant industry, that most contributed to the change in gourmet dining out.

new shapers of trends and taste

The formalities that prevailed at the finest restaurants before the mid-1970s declined as their social advantages were lost. For gourmet restaurateurs and diners, a mix of the refined and the commonplace grew more gratifying. But why did the interests of both parties change? How did their preferences become omnivorous? My answer looks to long-range changes in the compositions, special interests, and cultural outlooks of the two groups.

a growing gourmet public

At least until the 1960s, the most reputable fine-dining restaurants in America were answerable, above all, to high society.[1] This elite social stratum was limited to members of the nation's most prominent and wealthy families and to political leaders and corporate moguls, usually of those families. Rarely, it included celebrities such as movie stars. Yet—as in politics, business, and the arts—this small world was a big force in fine dining. Without loyal patronage by the upper class, the reputation of an ambitious establishment wilted. It behooved restaurateurs to cater to it.

Certain formalities served this elite group's interest in social distinction. Luxe décor, tradition-bound rituals of service, and codes of dress and decorum recalled the aristocracy on which high society modeled itself. Along with the *maitre d*'s art for snubbing outsiders and providing preferential seating, restaurants' time-honored fancy and fussy trappings reinforced social hierarchies and gave the clientele a stage for expressing their status with sartorial finery and "civilized" manners.

Despite earlier challenges to the influence of elite tastes on public dining in American history, until the end of the 1950s this upper stratum still set the style of the "best" restaurants.[2] What there was of restaurant reviewing did little to unseat its authority. Reviews were more often promotional than critical. The food experts capable of discrimination, such as James Beard on assignment for *Gourmet*, mainly wrote about the places and foods they loved, not what they found wanting. Writers with less culinary expertise also kept a positive tone about their main subjects. In the musings of the top-hatted Lucius Beebe, the promotional style of reviewing restaurants reached its peak. Beebe had earned his stripes as a chronicler of upper-class leisure—yesteryear's version of a society gossip columnist. He became relevant to gourmet history as a regular writer for *Gourmet* from its launch in 1941 through the 1950s. His "Along the Boulevards" column introduced readers to the haunts favored by the upper crust—as well as by Beebe himself, of course—and offered a glimpse into their ambiences, fashions, and menus. Beebe was simply too cozy in those clubby enclaves of San Francisco and Manhattan to be counted on for frank appraisals.

In the late 1950s, a critical style emerged. Craig Claiborne's appointment in 1957 as the first *New York Times* food critic was pivotal. He approached his job like any other *Times* journalist—in service of the public's right to know. In Claiborne's memoir, *A Feast Made for Laughter* (1982), he recalls avoiding taking "gifts" from restaurateurs to maintain his integrity, and wanting to distinguish his work from the fluffier food writing of the time. As he so witheringly put it: "The only much-read and much-quoted critic in town was Clementine Paddleford [of the New York *Herald Tribune*], a well-meaning soul, whose prose was so lush it could have been harvested like hay and baled. . . . The truth of the matter was, however, that Clementine Paddleford would not have been able to distinguish skillfully scrambled eggs from a third-rate omelet."[3]

Thus, Claiborne believed, it was his duty to point out faults, if they existed, even at restaurants presumed to be unassailable. With no place beyond the critic's reproach, the media became an independent influence on the elite restaurant.

Claiborne made it even more influential in 1963, when he began ranking restaurants by numbers of stars. At the time, only the prestigious *Michelin* guide used a star system, and there were no *Michelin* guides for American cities at the time. By adopting a star system of their own, *Times* reviews gained a comparable air of authority.[4] Furthermore, star counts were unambiguous and facilitated comparison among restaurants. The addition or subtraction of a star drew immediate attention, and gave the critic the power to make or ruin a place. Restaurants became more interested in the newspaper's approval. High society's sway over fine dining receded.

The *Times* may have initiated the change in food journalism, but it soon belonged to a trend. An industry report from 1971 entitled "Influence of New Breed of Restaurant Critic" announced a tendency toward independence and rigor. Critics were being "extraordinarily candid" about food and ambience, dining anonymously, and not allowing restaurant owners to pay for their meals. "For each food-review column in *New York* magazine," the report elaborated, "Gael Greene spends an average of $250, which may represent four visits to the same restaurant."[5]

Claiborne's successors at the *Times* continued in this vein, while some advanced the public's interest in new ways. Mimi Sheraton, the paper's food critic from 1976 to 1983, occasionally devoted full articles to critiques of restaurant habits she viewed as exclusionary. Her 1981 "Taking the Obfuscation Out of Restaurant Menus" railed against the menus' continued use of French and "wild flights of literary fancy" for describing dishes that she found "ridiculous and pretentious" as well.[6] To best represent the experience of the average diner, Sheraton insisted on anonymity. She knew that restaurateurs would try to influence a critic with special treatment, so she made a point of dining in disguises.

When Ruth Reichl took over the post from 1993 to 1999, the once-scorned general public gained another spirited (and costume-clad) ally. Among her first bold moves at the *Times* was to review the renowned and famously cliquish Le Cirque as a tale of "two contrasting experiences": one, before anyone knew who she was, characterized by neglectful and then rude service; the other, once she was recognized as the *Times* critic, marked by a practically royal reception.[7] By outing Le Cirque's undemocratic ways, she struck a victory blow for hordes of potentially ill-treated readers.

Dining critics thus effectively lobbied the restaurant industry on the greater public's behalf. Already by the early 1980s, however, that public was asserting itself more directly. The earliest and most important vehicle for this diner-centric development was the *Zagat Survey*, whose restaurant scores were based entirely on tabulating thousands of questionnaires mailed in by anonymous diners. Starting their survey in 1979 as a small community newsletter for restaurant ratings, the founders, Tim and Nina Zagat, had published their first for-profit edition by the end of 1982 and were able to quit their law jobs by 1990.[8] By 2010, the Zagats were publishing guides for over one hundred countries and had expanded into surveying a host of other leisure activities, from shopping to golf.[9] Their restaurant survey's awesome success made the dining-out masses impossible to ignore.

Since the turn of the twenty-first century, any diner with Internet access has had the potential to make an impact on taste with even less mediation. Pioneers of culinary dialogue on the web, such as eGullet .com, which became eGullet.org, are still thriving. Yet the field has grown vast around them—to the point where, today, it's not farfetched to assume that every other restaurant diner is to some degree a published critic.[10] Sites such as Yelp.com, Opentable.com, and Urbanspoon .com post user reviews and ratings.

They've gained considerable industry influence. At a panel discussion I attended at the Getty Center in April 2010, veteran restaurateur and KCRW radio host of *Good Food*, Evan Kleiman, brought up, unprompted, the near-tyrannical power of Yelp.com over restaurants' fortunes. Her statement wasn't surprising, considering what websites of that kind have offered their users. Unlike printed guides, they've been free, have allowed interaction, and have had no space limitations. Some have even helped diners make reservations.[11]

Amateurs have become important arbiters of taste through blogs as well. In the 2000s, blogs became so popular that to remain relevant, magazines and newspapers had to start their own—*New York Times* food critic Frank Bruni began one (nytimes.com/dinersjournal) in 2006.[12] Amateur blogs also became vital sources of content for the traditional, professional food media. A case in point is ex-chef, writer, and TV personality Anthony Bourdain's *No Reservations* show on the Travel Channel. In a Q&A session after Bourdain's live program, which I saw at UCLA (June 16, 2010), an audience member asked him how he gets ideas for restaurants to visit for his television show. Bourdain admitted that blogs were crucial. He said something like, if you want to know which *pho* stands to go to in Vietnam, there's probably a guy who's spent the last six years visiting every single one, writing about it, and posting pictures of everything he ate. No professional food critic could be that thorough.

Blogs joined America's gourmet establishment conclusively, I'd say, the day they were tacitly accepted by the establishment's inner sanctum. Beginning in 2010, the James Beard Foundation ceased to distinguish between online and print for its annual restaurant-reviewing award. This opened the door for bloggers of any background to compete for one of the highest honors in food journalism.[13]

Thus, in recent decades, the gourmet public has gained an increasingly powerful voice. Still, its ever-greater representation in the food press is just half the story of its growing influence. It never would have achieved so much influence unless its members, as a base of potential consumers, had phenomenally expanded in number.

The ranks of American gourmets swelled significantly for the first time in the wake of World War II. Postwar prosperity, the increased use of credit by the middle class, and especially the advent of the Boeing 707 transatlantic flight (the first was made in 1958) meant that more Americans than ever before were traveling abroad and becoming exposed to world cuisines. The French government particularly encouraged US tourism as a way to revive its nation's postwar economy.[14]

In the 1960s, interest in matters gourmet soared. When the glamorous Kennedys broke precedent in 1961 and hired a French chef to run the White House kitchen, French cuisine gained nationwide cachet. Two years later, the public-television debut of Julia Child's *The French Chef* made French cooking more accessible than ever. Child's down-to-earth persona and increasingly nationalized TV reach during the 1960s inspired previously untapped audiences.

In her history of American cooking shows, Kathleen Collins divulges a pattern of growing public interest in line with French cuisine's heightened exposure. Between 1958 and 1969, the number of articles about French cooking in American magazines jumped 60 percent above that figure for the 1945–58 period. Between 1959 and 1969, Americans bought 68 percent more French cookbooks than they did over 1940–58.[15] Child's own cookbook, *Mastering the Art of French Cooking* (1961), was a trend leader. A *Time* magazine cover story on Child in 1966 declared her book a best seller in the field.[16] Such coverage in a widely circulated magazine was also sign that gourmandise was growing in the United States.

Throughout the 1960s and 1970s, evidence of this growth mounted. Between 1967 and 1971, *Gourmet's* circulation doubled.[17] Even nonculinary media jumped on the gourmet bandwagon. Over the 1960s, *Playboy* regularly gave tips for the kitchen as well as the bedroom. To position itself as a font of know-how about sophisticated living in addition to a publisher of centerfolds, the magazine published in-depth monthly articles on gourmet food and drink.[18] In 1970, ABC News became the first news outlet to air a regular culinary segment. For *Eyewitness Gourmet*, a reporter would visit a restaurant and feature the preparation of a house specialty.[19] By the mid-1970s, it was possible to report on surging sales of specialized cookware, from Cuisinarts to mortars and pestles; the rising interest in gourmet ingredients, such as *escargots* and specialty cheeses; further jumps in cookbook sales; and a recession-defying restaurant business. *Newsweek* magazine documented all these trends in 1975. A cover story conveyed their overall gist with the bold title "Food: The New Wave."[20]

One sure sign that something has gained widespread currency in a short time is when it becomes a target of parody. Dan Aykroyd's *Saturday Night Live* impression of a clumsily knife-wielding and consequently bloodied Julia Child, blithely continuing to prepare a holiday feast, wouldn't have worked for *SNL*'s general audience in 1978 without a mass familiarity with Child's endearing ungainliness.[21] The same could be said about the 1984 publication of *The Official Foodie Handbook*. This satirical guide to all matters gourmet wouldn't have been viable without a broad public exposure to the subject.[22]

All kidding about them aside, the number of foodies continued to multiply during the 1980s. More and more chefs, their idols, were being dubbed celebrities by the media, and food-magazine circulations continued to rise.[23] Were it not for the steady growth of a gourmet public throughout the 1980s, the instigators of cable TV's Food Network wouldn't have been able to justify its launch in 1993.

Over the 1990s and early 2000s, the Food Network was itself a tremendous spur to audience expansion. Beginning with just 6.5 million cable subscribers, by 2005 the channel was reaching 87 million out of a total 109 million households—a saturation comparable to CNN's.[24] In 2007, the Food Network had double the viewership of CNN for the totality of time slots and even more in prime time.[25] Between 2008 and 2010, TVFN's ratings jumped again, as much as 40 percent.[26] By 2010, the Food Network's cup had so run over that its parent company, Scripps, launched the Cooking Channel, a new cable outlet to catch the excess advertiser demand.[27]

TVFN's success echoed throughout the cable universe. Between 2005 and 2010, the number of food-program hours on TV more than tripled.[28] Up sprang a cottage industry of reality-TV programs with cooking, eating, and running restaurants as their central themes. It wasn't that surprising that a slew of food-related shows cropped up on TVFN's sister networks, such as Travel Channel, Discovery Home, Home & Garden Television, and the now-defunct Fine Living Channel (which became the home of the Cooking Channel). But the investment made by stations with no necessary connection to food—NBC (first with *The Restaurant*, launched in 2003), Fox (beginning with *Hell's Kitchen*'s first season in 2005), the Learning Channel (starting with *Take Home Chef*, debuting in 2005), Bravo (entering the field with *Top Chef* in 2006), and, more recently, Syfy (getting into the act with *Marcel's Quantum Kitchen* in 2011)—indicates a much greater foodie resonance.

Just how big did the gourmet audience become? Using winter 2007–8 data compiled by the Simmons Market Research Bureau from

twenty-five thousand adult survey respondents, Packaged Facts concluded that as many as 14 percent of American adults could be described as "foodies"—a relatively devout contingent of "food aficiona-
dos" who "use food to define who they are in greater society."[29] Even
if Packaged Facts overestimated the population by several percentage
points, it would still amount to massive.

So what is it about the rise of the new, and much bigger, public that
encouraged increasing informality in gourmet restaurants? A growing
enthusiasm for gourmet cuisine can't explain it completely. One decisive factor, I suggest, is increasing time constraints.

Marketing reports from the 1990s and early 2000s suggest that
gourmets have come disproportionately from dual-income and single-
person households. Since its launch in 1993, the Food Network has
consistently attracted a core audience of adults in dual-income households.[30] The Packaged Facts study of American foodies found that the
subgroup it calls "restaurant foodies"—9 percent of US adults—were
14 percent more likely than other American adults to live in dual-
income households. The study also revealed that restaurant foodies
tended to delay marriage, staying single longer to focus on careers and
partake of culturally enriching experiences such as exploring the restaurant scene. They are thus also part of the broader American trend
of increasing numbers of single-person households. According to Eric
Klinenberg's *Going Solo* (2012), the percentage of adults living alone
jumped from 22 in 1950 to 50 in 2008, and most single-dwellers today
are middle-aged.[31]

Both dual-income and single-person households are historically associated with time pressures. Their time crunch began in the 1950s,
when the presence of women in the labor force—especially from
middle-income families, where women working outside the home had
been rare—started to escalate dramatically. The number of working
wives doubled and working mothers quadrupled between 1950 and
1960.[32] Between 1960 and 2000, the employment of all women doubled, from one-third to two-thirds.[33] The population of working mothers reached as high as 78 percent.

Not only were more women, historically the homemakers, working.
Women were working more. Although in 1965 half the mothers had
employment that was distributed throughout the year, in 2000 over

three-quarters did. The average number of weeks they worked rose, too, from thirty-eight to forty-seven.[34]

Women's increasing employment took its toll on home cooking specifically. From diary-based "time use" studies spanning 1975 to 2000, the authors of *Changing Rhythms of American Family Life* (2006) discovered that the hours per week married mothers spent on housework, including food preparation and cleanup, declined by an average of fifteen. This finding brought married mothers in line with their historically time-pressed single counterparts. The authors further concluded that while working mothers exercised some autonomy in their allocation of nonworking hours, their total discretionary time got squeezed. They were sleeping fewer hours per week.[35]

Although childless single workers wouldn't have felt their temporal pinch from child rearing, they would have had other historically new sources of time constraint. The trend of men and women staying single longer meant that the time-consuming activity of socializing with other singles—including over meals out—had increased and become an important part of life for more people. Also, since foodie singles have tended to delay marriage to focus on careers, their commitment to work advancement would have further diminished their time for housework, including everyday cooking.

Unsurprisingly, consumer expenditure studies from the early 2000s show that the biggest purchasers of food away from home are dual-income and single-person households.[36] In 1985, an article in *American Demographics* indicated that this trend was manifesting itself on the restaurant scene already by the early 1980s. It declared, "The increasing number of women working outside the home has been among the most important trends in the restaurant industry in the past several years." What's more, the article reported, the "2 groups behind the rise in dining out" were "young adults and working women."[37]

These trends make dual-income and single-person households—and, by extension, gourmets—the leaders of a broader trend in declining home cooking. (Specifically, I refer to home cooking of the everyday kind. Hobbyist home cooking, by contrast, surged over the same period—a phenomenon I address in chapter 3.) The National Restaurant Association reports that restaurants' share of Americans' food dollar grew from 25 percent in 1955 to 48 percent in 2009.[38] The growing infrequency of home cooking looks worse still if we account for the percentage of at-home meals made from scratch, which dipped from 72 to 59 percent between 1980 and 2010; or if we consider the expansion, especially since the 1990s, of the market for prepared or semiprepared meals is considered.[39] In 1996, half of American adults were buying take-out food from either restaurants or markets at least once per week, a 43-percent increase from 1989.[40]

It's reasonable to think that as the population of gourmets grew to include more workers with time-taxing lifestyles, their demand for more casual gourmet-dining options would have escalated. Casual outlets would have satisfied their gourmet palates while accommodating their time-pressed everyday lives. In the context of busy routines, the fuss and fanciness of traditional fine dining are too burdensome.

This explanation allows for formality's continued existence—on a special-occasion basis or, for hardcore foodies, as a substitute for other leisure activities—as well as the fact that even those occasions have become more relaxed. Dropping tie requirements for men, for instance, is a likely adaptation to restaurant clientele's acclimation to informality elsewhere.

star chefs

The proliferation of casual gourmet forms is also a product of chefs becoming restaurant-industry tycoons and media stars. The *haute*-casual approach to restaurant design advanced the specific occupational and branding interests of this newly empowered group.

Before the mid-1970s, most chefs in the United States had little social status. Those with any reputation tended to be European, but even they were largely eclipsed in managerial power and public face time by *maitre d*'s.

The high public standing of *maitre d*'s likely derived from their pre-eminence at every site—on the telephone, at the front door, and in the dining room—where their dominant clientele demanded social exclusion. *Maitre d*'s performed the all-important work of literally policing the gates. They decided whom to let in with fanfare and seat prominently, whom to slight. They were also directly responsible for the service, décor, and dining-room conditions through which their customers expressed social hierarchy. Seating was an important means of social distinction. Tellingly, the tables deemed the best were in the front, near the gatekeeper himself; the worst were in the back, near the chef.

The cuisine in the finest places was certainly excellent, but these restaurants' general adherence to a repertoire of Continental classics caused their chef's individual vision to be not the greatest point of differentiation among them. That the *maitre d'* played a prominent role as chief personality and authority is why we find Henri Soulé as the main character in histories of Manhattan's Le Pavillon—from Joseph Wechsberg's 1962 *Dining at the Pavillon* to Patric Kuh's 2001 account in *The Last Days of Haute Cuisine*. It's why, in 1959, Craig Claiborne marked Gene Cavallero's nearly forty years as *maitre d'* of New York's the Colony with a profile in the *New York Times*.[41]

Sirio Maccioni has always been the biggest name associated with Le Cirque—even in the early years between 1974 and 1978, when Maccioni co-owned the restaurant with the chef, Jean Vergnes.[42] But Le Cirque's *maitre d'*-centrism hasn't been the norm since the mid-1970s. The *maitre d'* retreated as the chef stepped into the limelight.

Manhattan's Lutèce was an early example of the transition. It was the first American fine-dining institution in the twentieth century to be primarily identified with its chef. It was unlikely for the chef to be full owner, and therefore in total control, when chef André Soltner became sole owner of Lutèce in 1973. Yet he had already garnered sufficient accolades to be able to command a marquee value rare for chefs in America a few years prior. In 1968, Soltner had been awarded the medal and title of Meilleur Ouvrier de France from the French government—an achievement doubly amazing for a French chef working in New York. A 1970 article in *Gourmet* went into detail about Soltner's award for craftsmanship. It gave him recognition before most chefs in the United States could even be called professionals.[43] Not until 1976 did the American Culinary Federation succeed in lobbying the US Department of Labor to reclassify chefs from the category of service workers in its *Dictionary of Occupational Titles*.[44]

Meanwhile, a group of French *nouvelle cuisine* chefs had been bringing a more glamorous model of their occupation to light. For its "Food:

The New Wave" cover story of 1975, *Newsweek* featured a grinning *nouvelle cuisinier*, Paul Bocuse, on its cover—arms folded and clad in brilliant chef whites—and an article insert that portrayed the chef's occupation as anything but the kitchen grind it had long been, even in chef-loving France. The work had typically involved a painfully slow rise in the ranks, culminating, with luck, in the command of a single restaurant. By then, the suffering of slow ascendance was replaced with pain in the joints and feet, a cruel reminder that kitchen toil was meant for the young.

Bocuse may have endured his share of aches and pains, but he had managed to escape the drudgery of his profession. The forty-nine-year-old featured in *Newsweek* was a publicity-savvy, globe-trotting superstar and multiple-holdings CEO. According to *Newsweek*, he "choreograph[ed] the in-flight cuisine on Air France, along with his three [chef] buddies Roger Vergé . . . Michel Guérard . . . and Gaston LeNôtre"; he started a "Beaujolais wine label, distributed by D. Sokolin Co. in the U.S."; and, in Japan, "he [taught] a three-week cooking course at Sezo Suji's Hotel School in Osaka."[45] *Time* magazine ran a similarly aggrandizing feature on Bocuse and his colleague Guérard in 1976. Their careers were quite a departure from even the acclaimed Soltner, who remained at the helm of one restaurant until the end of his career.[46]

Bocuse and his peers weren't forces on the American restaurant scene. Yet the publicity about them gave chefs based in this country something to aspire to. Over time, they surpassed their idols.

The plucky, Austria-born yet California-launched Wolfgang Puck set the gold standard for what historians call the "super chef" or "branded chef."[47] In the 1980s alone, he published cookbooks (1981, 1987) and opened multiple gourmet restaurants. As soon as he saw that he would be opening more than one restaurant, he incorporated (as Wolfgang Puck Food Company, in 1983). He also attained a regular spot on television (for the culinary segment of ABC's *Good Morning America*, in 1986), and entered the frozen-food business (partnering with ConAgra on a line of frozen pizzas in 1988).

In the 1990s, Puck branched out at an accelerated rate. He entered the quick-service sector (with the grab-and-go Wolfgang Puck Express, in 1991), was the first star chef to turn a fine-dining restaurant (Spago) into a multiunit concept (they're all over the world), and was the celebrity-chef pioneer of the Las Vegas restaurant scene (with Spago, 1992). Vegas since then has gone from culinary wasteland to a star-chef wonderland that rivals New York. Puck forged on with a line of cookware (under the Wolfgang Puck Products Company in 1995), which he sold on TV (via QVC and the Home Shopping Network). He even started a catering company (Wolfgang Puck Catering & Events, in 1998).

When, in 1999, Puck became the first chef to make the Forbes Celebrity 100 list, *Forbes* still hadn't seen all the chef would do. In 2001, he launched yet another company (Wolfgang Puck Worldwide, Inc.) just to handle his twenty-first-century franchising and licensing.[48] As I write this, the chef continues opening new gourmet restaurant concepts.

While few chefs have covered as much ground as Puck, some have overtaken him in specific areas or ventured into new territory. Some turned out to be bigger television stars. Emeril Lagasse is often credited with singlehandedly bringing the Food Network to life in 1997 with his live-audience cooking show, *Emeril Live*. Tom Colicchio has a growing fleet of restaurants, but may be best known as head judge on Bravo's chef-competition program, *Top Chef*. Cat Cora attained the coveted title and role of Iron Chef on TVFN's star-chef cooking-duel extravaganza, *Iron Chef America*, before opening a single restaurant of her own.

Some—including Jacques Pépin, Anthony Bourdain, Emeril Lagasse, and Eric Ripert—have exploited the lucrative business of live appearances. Chefs performing solely as entertainment, like rock stars, is a 2000s trend distinct from the charity fundraising that the first crop of star chefs in the United States, including Puck, initiated. By the end of the first decade of the 2000s, a few were commanding fees of between $35,000 and $50,000 per appearance. Bourdain has claimed that he's made more from live tours than from his books or *No Reservations* show.[49]

Another frontier for celebrity chefs in the 2000s has been the gourmet store. In Yountville, California, Thomas Keller opened the first of many Bouchon Bakeries. For four years, David Bouley experimented with a Bouley Bakery & Market concept in New York City. Chris Cosentino founded a San Francisco *salumeria*, a shop for cured meats, named

Boccalone. The largest-scale project to date has been Eataly. This fifty-thousand-square-foot, gourmet Italian-food bazaar houses several restaurants amid the shelves of olive oils and fresh mozzarella. Mario Battali and Lidia and Joseph Bastianich partnered with an Italian market of the same name to bring Eataly to Manhattan's Flatiron district. At this writing, the team is contemplating other locations across the country.

Star chefs' economic footprint has grown huge. To manage their deals, publicity, and appearance logistics, they've hired agents, lawyers, publicists, and managers. To handle their food operations, they've employed thousands of restaurant workers and suppliers.[50]

The media stardom of some has made chefs the restaurant industry's leading tastemakers. They've become such important models of good taste that the few standout success stories of fine-dining restaurant companies *not* overseen by chefs—such as Danny Meyer's Union Square Hospitality Group, Keith McNally, Drew Nieporent's Myriad Restaurant Group, and Pat Kuleto Restaurant Development & Management Company—have made their good names in part by working with noted chefs.

Significantly, once in the position to dictate their own terms, chefs increasingly chose to showcase their work in relaxed settings. Barry and Susan Wine launched Manhattan's the Casual Quilted Giraffe after establishing their high-style bona fides at the Quilted Giraffe. Once Gray Kunz had developed his reputation at New York City's splendorous Lespinasse, he opened the casual-dining Café Gray. Having gained global respect for innovative and impeccable fine dining at the French Laundry, Thomas Keller went on a casual tear—first with Bouchon, a bistro now in multiple locations, and then with Ad Hoc, a chipper, no-tablecloth place in the Napa Valley serving family style. Likewise, in Chicago, Paul Kahan opened the bar-seating Avec, followed by the even more down-to-earth gastro beer hall the Publican, after making his mark in fine dining with Blackbird.

In the 2000s, many top fine-dining chefs went hypercasual. A slew of them opened burger joints—as did Hubert Keller by opening Burger Bar; Laurent Tourondel, BLT Burger; Bobby Flay, Bobby's Burger Palace; Charlie Palmer, DG Burger; and Nancy Silverton and Amy Pressman, Short Order. All these examples are part of a pattern in chef careers in the United States since the 1980s, when star chefs began opening multiple restaurants.

The recent trend in pop-up restaurants is yet another case of chefs choosing informal spaces. A growing number of established chefs have developed special tasting menus for limited runs during the closed hours of cafés, bakeries, and similarly modest venues owned and operated by others.

Fine-dining chefs benefit from casual formats. Wherever the food is more luxurious and artful than the décor would suggest, it is the chef, not any *maitre d'*, who has star billing. Wherever the kitchen has become a dining-room stage, open to full view, the literal, architectural transfer of star power from the so-called front of the house to the formerly hidden back of the house is evident. There, it's the chef's labor, the chef's creativity, that's onstage. In the case of pop-ups, chefs benefit from the freedom to experiment without worrying about whether or not their dishes will suit the style or theme of a more permanent venue.

The long New York City career of Daniel Boulud—the epitome of chefs who have opened progressively more casual restaurants—offers further insight into how such an evolution can be advantageous to a fine-dining chef. A French émigré, Boulud spent his first years in American restaurants paying his professional dues. He developed his craft and emerged as a head chef to watch while at Le Régence at the Plaza Athenée from 1984 to 1986, and then at Le Cirque from 1986 to 1992.[51] At Le Cirque, Boulud got noticed for the first time for the kind of originality that celebrity chefs are made of—an ability to create new dishes, not just master classic ones.[52] Looking to distinguish himself further and get out from Sirio Maccioni's shadow, Boulud opened his own place in 1993. The eponymous restaurant, Daniel, allowed him to become a culinary star on a stage of his own.

Having shored up *haute-cuisine* kudos from Daniel, Boulud began to indulge what had grown into a pent-up longing for creative freedom. Daniel's intricate dishes fit the restaurant's ensemble of sparkling décor and elaborate service, and had been necessary to move Boulud into four-star territory. But as his sole creative outlet, it had become something of a risk-averse straitjacket. Boulud himself said as much in a 2010 video interview on Savorycities.com. He openly described the cozier dining room and the less structured, yet still original and artful dishes of his next restaurant, Café Boulud (1998), as a welcome relief from Daniel.[53]

That Boulud opened a series of even more casual places after that, over the first decade of the 2000s, reveals his continued satisfaction with casual formats. Literally and figuratively, he progressed from uptown to downtown with his opening of restaurants in New York. At present, his operations at both ends of town represent the two extremes of Manhattan's fancy-to-casual gourmet-dining spectrum.

Fittingly, Boulud's most formal restaurant, Daniel, sits on the stately Upper East Side. It has been in the neighborhood in elegant digs since 1993. Yet after relocating to the Mayfair Hotel in 1999, Daniel changed to an even grander, ballroom-scale setting. Gazing through neoclassical arches while sitting at a balcony table overlooking the sunken central dining room, I was able to take in the interior's magnificence along with the full floor show of its dark-suited, exacting servers. The six-course tasting menu—with each dish appearing tightly structured, complex, and labor-intensive—suited the extravagant scene.

DBGB Kitchen & Bar (2009–), one of Boulud's most casual restaurants, is, by contrast, located in the Bowery—a few doors down, in fact, from the now-defunct but legendary punk nightclub CBGB. In the spirit of that location, DBGB is a no-tablecloth, concrete-floored, clamorous open-kitchen environment with stacks of plates, shelves of copper pots donated by chef friends, and jars of the punk rocker Marky Ramone's namesake brand of pasta sauce on view. On glass walls through which light pours into the restaurant's front room from the fully visible street are ceiling-to-floor quotations from notables spanning Escoffier and Ben Franklin. When I visited this gregarious space, easygoing servers in tweed vests carried out rustic plates of hamburgers and sausages and campy mountains of baked Alaska and ice cream sundaes.[54]

Boulud's embrace of casual forms is a story of creative liberation and self-fulfillment. Once he had enough professional clout to do what he pleased, he indulged his desire to further experiment with ideas, techniques, and formats under less strict and more hip circumstances. I would argue as well that casual surrounds and service gave Boulud and chefs following a similar path a better chance to exceed diners' increasingly jaded expectations of four-star places. DBGB upholds the core sources of pride and passion that have always undergirded Boulud's work—ingredients of the best quality, artisanal production, precise cooking, and the creation of new dishes—without Daniel's stylistic rigidities and crushing pressures. While Boulud now deigns to serve hamburgers and sausages—oh, what hamburgers! What sausages!

A recurring theme of Anthony Bourdain's many books and TV shows about professional-kitchen culture is that fine-dining chefs prefer to eat food in the style of DBGB rather than that of Daniel. He should know. As a former chef and current food-media star, he's been palling around with the best in the business for years. And if he's right, chefs' opening more casual places further implies that they've been asserting their personal tastes.

Going informal has not only been creatively freeing and possibly personally indulging for chefs. It has also helped them make the transition from critically acclaimed artists to larger-scale business entities—gourmet brands. Formal fine-dining restaurants, where they have traditionally fine-tuned their craft, have notoriously low profit margins. In order for chefs to make the business gains that allow them to become brands, they must enter the restaurant industry's more lucrative casual side.

Casual dining's higher profits follow from a host of design features entailing less overhead and speedier dining. Avoiding table linens, carpets, intricate place settings, expensive silver and crystal, and opulent, fresh floral displays saves on maintenance costs. Hard chairs and close table placement, as well as harsher lighting and acoustics, keep diners from lingering. Simple linen-less table settings also facilitate table turnover by being easy to clean and reset. The reduced time commitment for diners encourages repeat visits by more people. Greater sales volume with less overhead equals more profit. The cost-effectiveness of casual design explains its appeal not only to chefs who want to scale up their business but also to the many nonchefs who regularly invest in star-chef ventures.

It's little wonder, then, that at the 2007 annual Aspen Food & Wine event, the hot topic of conversation among branded chefs and power-restaurateurs was an emergent restaurant category called "fine fast." It combines the high-quality ingredients and creative combinations of gourmet fare with the efficiencies of a fast-food operation. The idea had materialized the year before, when Atlanta restaurateurs Pierre Panos and Jesse Gideon, a chef, launched the Fresh To Order chain, also known as f2O. One reporter described it as "fine-dining American fusion food in under 10 minutes for under $10." As a sit-down restaurant with beer and wine and such items as a "Bourbon Filet with Balsamic Cabernet Reduction and Garlic Jack Grit Cake," f2O departed from gourmet-style takeout concepts such as the Wolfgang Puck Express, launched in 1991, or chef Tom Colicchio's sandwich outlet, Wichcraft, begun in 2003. The category continued to buzz among restaurateurs after Aspen, as the details of designing for high-volume restaurants with gourmet integrity were again the focus of a business seminar held at the annual StarChefs.com International Chefs Congress in 2010.[55]

Top-chef branding is incomplete, however, if advanced by casual formats alone. Success demands an omnivorous approach. Notice how, even as reputed chefs opened more casual places, they kept cultivating their *haute-cuisine* associations. After launching the bistro concept Bouchon, Thomas Keller not only maintained the French Laundry but opened Per Se in Manhattan—the equivalent in every way, including numbers of *Michelin* stars, of the French Laundry in Manhattan. Boulud didn't close Daniel once he opened DBGB. For chefs of Keller's and Boulud's stature, the turn toward informality wasn't so much a repudiation of fine dining as the development of a diverse portfolio.

To be successful, brands must maintain the source of their credibility. Gourmet chefs must uphold what earned them acclaim in the first place: a combination of technical chops, tastefulness, artistic originality, and use of best-quality ingredients. These marks of chef excellence culminate in *haute cuisine*. For this reason, fine-dining chefs can't entirely forsake it.

A parallel exists in the way fashion designers span high and low turf to create mass luxury brands. Like *haute-cuisine* chefs, *haute-couturiers* such as Gucci, Prada, and Louis Vuitton maintain their high-fashion profiles and, in doing so, keep credibility as star designers. On *couture* runways, designers can fully show off, as chefs can in *haute-cuisine* restaurants, their technical virtuosity, tastefulness, imagination, and use of the finest materials. But, as for chefs, the big money for designers— and the key to their brands becoming mass status symbols—lies in more affordable, large-market products. Whereas chefs can launch fine-fast concepts, designers can sell handbags and perfume.[56]

It's true that some of the more recent star chefs—such as April Bloomfield and Roy Choi—managed to skip the formerly necessary step of starting *haute-cuisine* restaurants of their own before they opened places featuring riffs on pub food and rice bowls. However, they've compensated for the missing link. Their made-for-press biographies have made it known that they worked in the *haute-cuisine* kitchens of other renowned chefs while coming up through the ranks. In addition, they've distinguished themselves by applying a fine-dining approach to casual fare. Their versions of commonplace dishes aren't run-of-the-mill. They represent original ingredient combinations, careful house making of even the humblest components in a dish, and top-quality ingredients.

nonconformity as a dominant professional ethos

The adoption of casual genres may have been rewarding for chefs. But for the trend to progress as it did, it couldn't have been so *only* for chefs. Why, then, did gourmet diners also embrace it so? Yes, informality appealed to their need for convenience. But time constraints alone can't explain foodies' enthusiasm for the entire phenomenon, witnessed by the surge in gourmet audiences and the persistence of casual trends. To understand their zeal, we must acknowledge overarching cultural changes affecting diners and chefs alike.

Circumstances leading to the industry empowerment of chefs— the change from the traditionalist, self-effacing occupation that the forerunners of André Soltner knew to one in which young chefs such as Bobby Flay can achieve wealth and celebrity on the basis of signature styles—weren't limited to chefs. All sorts of professions turned to embrace rule breaking and uniqueness. Nonconformity became the dominant ethos of professionals.

As a professional ethos, nonconformity fosters the appreciation of omnivorous taste. By definition, resistance to convention favors less rigid forms—in settings, dress, behavior, and the styles of things. Yet the competitive nature of occupations provides an opposing impetus for admiring professional virtuosity. In the context of gourmet restaurants, this means that chefs and diners can value relaxed and refined styles—say, DBGB and Daniel—simultaneously.

The cultural change underlying omnivorous style and taste has gone by various names: "the condition of postmodernity," "the rise of the creative class." They describe the same shift. In advanced economies, the demands for labor and sources of wealth moved away from the realm of goods manufacturing and toward the production—in every field, from fashion to finance, media to medicine—of new ideas.[57]

In *The Rise of the Creative Class* (2002), *Cities and the Creative Class* (2005), and *The Flight of the Creative Class* (2005), economist Richard Florida documents the decline of the manufacturing labor force and the increase in workers charged with innovating or problem solving, who he calls "the creative class." According to his analysis of government labor statistics, the manufacturing sector peaked at 40 percent of workers between 1920 and 1950, then declined to 25 percent by the early 2000s. By contrast, the creative class grew dramatically. From less than 15 percent in 1950, it rose to 20 percent in 1980, and then jumped to as high as 30 percent of the workforce—surpassing the manufacturing sector—by the early 2000s.[58]

Although, by then, service workers were the most populous of all—approximately 45 percent of the labor pool—Florida explains that the creative class has been culturally dominant. Its leading role in decision making and, therefore, wealth creation, has made it the designator of cultural norms.[59]

Florida's story of the rise of the creative class is consistent with the boom in higher education and with education's growing economic value. Due to favorable conditions, such as postwar prosperity and the 1965 Higher Education Act, which subsidized universities and student tuition, the number of college students tripled between 1965 and 1975. Institutions of higher education also proliferated as never before, from 2,000 in 1960 to 3,200 in 1980. The financial rewards of a college education also surged. In 1980, college graduates earned 35 percent more than high-school graduates. By the mid-1990s, they were earning 70 percent more; those with a graduate degree, 90 percent more. The deindustrializing economy was rewarding producers of ideas the most.[60]

According to Florida, members of the creative class differ from the previous generation of American elites in their ethos of creativity, individuality, and openness to cultural diversity. As he points out, these characteristics have been vital to their function as idea generators within a fast-paced economy of ideas. His characterization of creative-class values follows also from analysis of US census data from the 1990s, which indicates that producers of new ideas tended to cluster in or around places, usually urban, where the most diverse cultural expressions and lifestyles thrive. He argues that companies should locate in such areas in order to lure top talent.[61]

The validity of Florida's argument isn't limited to the 1990s. In *The Big Sort* (2008), which concerns Americans' increasing demographic and ideological self-segregation, Bill Bishop and Robert Cushing find that the tendency of those with higher incomes and education—in other words, Florida's creative class—to flock to urban areas began in the 1970s. The cities that grew fastest and richest were those where the more educated congregated. Over the 1990s, concentrations of wealth and education became self-reinforcing, and income disparities grew ever wider. As a consequence, geographic polarization by education and affluence was exacerbated.[62]

By then, as Thomas Frank argues in *The Conquest of Cool* (1997), the assertion of nonconformist "hipness" had become the lucrative norm of business—what the counterculture of the 1960s had considered the "technocratic" antithesis of creativity—in the fields of fashion and advertising.[63] Yet the phenomenon wasn't isolated to artistic fields. Forecasters of businesses of all kinds were forcefully promoting this value. In *Generation Ageless* (2007), J. Walker Smith and Ann Clurman reveal that as those who birthed the counterculture reached their peak in professional status and earnings, a slew of best-selling guides to business success baldly promoted nonconformity. Remarkably, this one theme resounds in one title after another that the authors list: *Breaking the Rules: Removing the Obstacles to Effortless High Performance* (1998); *First, Break All the Rules: What the World's Greatest Managers Do Differently* (1999); *How to Think Like Einstein: Simple Ways to Break the Rules and Discover Your Hidden Genius* (2000); *The Internet Entrepreneurs: Business Rules Are Good; Break Them* (2000); *Break the Rules and Get a Great Job* (2001); *Extreme Success: The 7-Part Program That Shows You How to Break the Rules and Succeed without Struggle* (2002); *10 Golden Rules of Freelance Writing and How I Broke Them to Make It as a Magazine Writer* (2003); *Who Cares What You're Supposed to Do: Breaking the Rules to Get What You Want in Love, Life and Work* (2004); *Breaking the Rules of Project Management* (2005); and *Breaking Robert's Rules: The New Way to Run Your Meeting, Build Consensus, and Get Results* (2006).[64]

These, however, are late symptoms of the transformation of non-conformity into a mainstream professional ethos. This paradoxical change had begun manifesting itself at least a decade before these publications appeared. One form, of special interest here, was infor-mal dress. A page had turned in the late 1980s, when IBM, a corpora-tion famous for its strict dress code—it required of men not only a necktie but also a shirt of no other kind than white—instituted "busi-ness casual" attire, and not just on Fridays. In this trend, IBM was a leader. According to Sherry Maysonave's book on casual work wear, *Ca-sual Power* (1999), media about dressing down at work first appeared in the early 1990s.[65]

Both Maysonave and Florida, who devotes a chapter of *The Rise of the Creative Class* to the "no-collar workplace," point to similar origins of business casual: the rise of a management paradigm that respects individuality. Maysonave identifies the new ideology with Top Quality Management, an approach that emphasizes giving workers flexibility on many fronts—in work schedule, work location, and dress—in order to enhance morale and productivity. This approach stemmed from the presumption that professionals require the same loose structures—personal comfort, self-expression, and work time-and-place flexibil-ity—that other "creative" people, such as artists, have traditionally insisted on.[66]

Dressing down at the white-tablecloth restaurant directly followed sartorial slackening in the white-collar workplace. Between 1994 and 1998, articles appeared in *Forbes* and the *New York Times*, as well as more specialized trade journals, *Restaurant Hospitality* and the *Nation's Res-taurant News*, to comment on a flurry of formal restaurants loosening their dress codes. Even stalwarts of stodginess such as Manhattan's the Four Seasons, Le Cirque, and the '21' Club began bending long-held rules about ties in the dining room. Articles cited the advent of business-casual work attire as the chief catalyst for this change.[67]

The direct influence of white-collar workplace on white-tablecloth restaurant makes demographic sense. Contemporary gourmets match the profile of Florida's creative class. Evidence extending from the early 1970s through the end of the first decade of the 2000s suggests that they've been relatively affluent, educated, urban, and in managerial or professional occupations.

Some of the evidence comes from reports on gourmet-media audiences. An *American Demographics* article from 1999 quoted a marketing representative of Cuisinart on the point that the company had advertised in *Gourmet* since 1972 in order to reach its affluent market.[68] Studies of *Gourmet* and *Food & Wine* audiences from 1983 to 2009 characterized them as upscale. Since its launch in 1993, the Food Network's core audience has been college-educated, relatively affluent, urban adults.[69]

Consumer Expenditure Surveys of the US Bureau of Labor Statistics reveal that the biggest spenders on food away from home fit this income-education profile. Although survey contents have varied, data on income and education were comparable and consistent over the years—1984, 1988, 1995, 2001, 2003, 2007, and 2009—that I consulted. Surveys from 1988, 1995, and 2001 also correlate those traits with managerial or professional occupations.[70]

desire for a shared frame of reference

If the merger of contrasting values, nonconformity and professionalism, can explain gourmets' appreciation of relaxed and refined styles, what can account for their equally omnivorous taste for *haute*-pop cuisine? Recall that before the 1980s, serious gourmets generally shunned mass-produced, commercialized foods.

In *Foodies* (2010), Josée Johnston and Shyon Baumann find that contemporary gourmets have had a similar prejudice. They've spurned "big-box" supermarket and restaurant chains. That, of course, doesn't explain why certain mass-cult foods have become the themes of *haute*-pop cuisine.

Something culturally changed. An earlier generation of American gourmets could disassociate gourmet from mass-cultural foods entirely, because *haute cuisine* had a dominant and distinct definition. It was French.

In contrast, by the 1980s, when *haute*-pop food emerged as a noteworthy trend, contemporary American gourmets were experiencing a more pluralistic scene. Starting in the mid-1970s, *haute cuisine* morphed into a field of variant personality cuisines based on the unique, ethnically eclectic styles of individual chefs.

Over the same period, American culture became more fragmented in other ways. Belief in the existence of a common popular culture, for instance, had reached its zenith in the 1950s. At that time, the growing omnipresence of mass media—the increased circulations of magazines such as *Life* and the *Saturday Evening Post* and the spread of television—coincided with broadly shared consumption of those media. TV had just a few channels, and the heyday of the general-interest magazine was in full swing. Also, marketers believed in appealing to the largest audience possible. This common experience of media meant that at least the myth of a shared "American" culture—whether one liked it or not, and to whatever extent it concealed painful differences—was universally recognized.[71]

Yet growing geographic self-segregation, the segmentation of media audiences into sources for special-interest news and entertainment, and the displacement of mass marketing by increasingly niche- and individual-targeting strategies encouraged a pluralistic conscious-ness.[72] So did the rise of nonconformity as a mainstream value.

Against this backdrop of cultural pluralism, contemporary gour-mets may have valued the culinary reference to mass culture as a means of reclaiming a common frame of reference lost from gourmet cuisine itself—albeit one that required an ironic distancing. While other forces worked to break up American culture further, pop-cultural foods stand out for their persistence over the decades as a symbolic bonding agent. It's no accident that *haute*-pop's most frequent mass-cultural themes—hamburgers, mac-and-cheese, milk shakes, and so on—are those that have remained national, even international, sym-bols of American culture.

That role has taken decades to solidify. As Harvey Levenstein details in *Paradox of Plenty* (2003), from the 1920s to the 1960s, powerful indus-try influences forged this shared conception of "American" food. De-spite the background continuation of diverse and regional foodways—which culinary historians such as Beard later tried to recoup—the rise of industrial food processors, food preservation methods, nationwide transportation and warehousing systems, industrial aesthetic design,

and the proliferation of mass media together created a common concept of "American" food that was neither diverse nor regional.

On the home-cooking front in the 1920s and 1930s, mass-circulation
magazines such as *Better Homes and Gardens, Good Housekeeping,
Women's Home Companion, Ladies' Home Journal,* and *Woman's Day* promoted their advertisers' canned and processed foods. They published
recipes utilizing advertisers' brand-name ingredients.

Because marketers realized that the demographic middle of America was in the Midwest, and sought to appeal to the largest cross section of Americans, the Midwest farmer's hearty but bland diet—heavy
on beef, pork, grains, and dairy products—became the generic culinary
ideal of popular women's magazines and cookbooks. *American Cooking,
Better Homes and Gardens, Good Housekeeping Cookbook,* and *The Fannie
Farmer Cookbook* propagated it as quintessentially "American."[73]

Few other ethnic influences entered this melting pot. Of those that
did, such as the Italian American, their popularization, too, owed a lot
to the efforts of large food corporations. Chef Boyardee began selling
a canned version of spaghetti with tomato sauce in 1928. Kraft came
up with a related, and now equally iconic, Kraft Macaroni Dinner
in 1937.[74]

After World War II, the spread of large supermarket chains—which
by 1956 accounted for 62 percent of the nation's grocery sales—helped
homogenize American food culture further. Their market advantage
over independent grocers had, after all, derived from inherently standardizing processes: the chains' vast distribution networks and the
food-processing conglomerates' ability to produce and market their
products on an industrial scale. The food corporations' capacity to
spend vast sums on marketing their products—via package design and
advertising—also spurred their territorial expansion.[75]

By the late 1950s, a limited notion of "American" food became
so shared that it crossed class lines. From his study of recipe books
compiled at the time by people of differing social classes, Levenstein
concludes:

The weekday dinner table at a corporate lawyer's household in upper-
middle-class Flossmoor, Illinois, looked little different from an insur-
ance company clerk's in Levittown, New York: Campbell's canned or
Lipton's dried soup, broiled meat, frozen French fries, and a frozen

green vegetable, with supermarket ice cream or a Jell-O concoction for dessert—an all-American "square meal."

Such commonality, he asserts, derived in part from the fact that marketers aimed their advertising toward an American majority. At the time, this meant middle-class families with annual household incomes of $3,000 to $10,000. They comprised an unprecedented 63 percent of the population, and 72 percent of consumer sales.[76]

The spread of fast-food restaurant chains also had a homogenizing influence. In *Fast Food: Roadside Restaurants in the Automobile Age* (1999), John A. Jakle and Keith A. Sculle attribute this process in part to "place-product-packaging." The earliest fast-food-chain success stories, White Castle (1921) and Howard Johnson's (1931), pioneered this strategy of designing and repeating a distinctive, instantly recognizable architecture and menu. A complementary strategy the authors name is "corporate territoriality"—the plan to expand geographically.

Expansion shifted into high gear in the 1960s as the assembly-line production of limited menus using fast-cooking methods made operations more efficient, franchising became more common, and big-budget food conglomerates with advertising muscle got into the act. Jakle and Sculle's list of 1960s corporate launches and takeovers is filled with brands that continue to be the most iconic:

General Foods bought Burger Chef, Pillsbury bought both Burger King and Steak and Ale, Heublein bought Kentucky Fried Chicken, United Brands bought A&W, and Quaker Oats bought Magic Pan. PepsiCo developed both Pizza Hut and Taco Bell. Royal Crown launched Arby's. Pet, Inc. purchased both Stuckey's and Hardee's. Ralston Purina took over Jack in the Box. General Mills developed the Red Lobster and Olive Garden chains. Hershey Foods bought the Friendly Ice Cream chain.

In accordance with these developments, the number of fast-food places tripled between 1963 and 1983. They then accounted for 40 percent of all dining-out dollars. By the late 1990s, chain restaurants dominated America's restaurant landscape, outnumbering independent restaurants.[77]

I shouldn't overstate the case for homogeneity. As Richard Pillsbury points out in his history of American restaurants, *From Boarding House* to *Bistro* (1990), fast-food chains expanded in somewhat regionally biased patterns. Still, it's hard to ignore the impact of the fast-food giants' aggressive nationwide advertising and their overall pattern of geographic expansion. To cite a famous statistic: already by 1970, 96 percent of American children could recognize Ronald McDonald.[78]

Since the 1970s, fast-food franchises continued to saturate the American landscape, and the market for supermarket convenience foods also escalated. Large-market brands such as Kraft and McDonald's have persisted in transcending niche boundaries, and have been joined by many newer brands in doing so.

By producing or consuming novel variations on such widespread food memes, gourmet chefs and diners have asserted their distinctive taste. In contrast to earlier gourmet culture, contemporary distinctions between high and low cuisine have taken place, literally, on the same menu or plate.

Still—how to explain the positive valuation, however partial, of the pop-cultural icons conjured on those menus and plates? Unlike the avant-garde art world, in which audience discomfort and distaste is sometimes considered a sign of great work, even the most avant-garde chefs wouldn't stay in business if they created unappealing food. If it's on the plate, it must offer some reassurance of existing taste.

Pluralistic society has distinctive tensions. As the identity politics of newly empowered ethnic and gender groups has shown, the culture of diversity comes with fractiousness as well as liberation. Amid the tensions of diversity, it's possible that mass-cultural references have offered welcome affirmations of a common bond. For gourmet chefs and diners of our more splintered age, there may be something gratifying in the persistence of a shared frame of reference. Hence the often affectionate use of the term *comfort food* in gourmet media to describe such TV-dinner standards as chicken potpie and mac-and-cheese. While these foods are undoubtedly comforting to the senses—warm, bulky, and palate coating—they're also comforting culturally, covering over differences.

* * *

In essence, every restaurant trend incorporating casual forms advances the creative-class interests of chefs and diners. Also, each one encompasses contradictory values of that class. The question remaining is, how have trends in design, the material forms of omnivorous style, organized those oppositions? Design, by definition, subsumes potentially disparate parts under a unifying order. That order is never simply physical. It reinforces cultural priorities.

To decipher that cultural logic—in particular, the bases of a new conception of sophisticated taste—the details of restaurant design must now come into sharper focus. The next two chapters look closely at the design trends that have been the most pervasive, enduring, and profoundly upending of past distinctions between fine and casual restaurants. In each chapter, I identify and interpret the stylistic and thematic patterns of a trend. I also reflect on why certain variations of the trend have been the most celebrated.

Chapter 3 takes up the rise and spread of exhibition kitchens in gourmet restaurants. Proliferating and persisting on the gourmet scene irrespective of restaurant genre, and in numerous forms, display kitchens have been the single most influential feature in the transformation of gourmet restaurant style. I ask why they became such prized features of gourmet restaurants.

Chapter 4 addresses the most pervasive omnivorous trend in cuisine: chefs creating gourmet versions of commonplace dishes. Moving beyond my summary of the phenomenon's first decade in chapter 1 and my gloss over the trend's cultural motives here, chapter 4 explores in depth the trend's remarkable polarities—the embrace of stylistic and symbolic opposites in the sources of common foods and in their idioms of gourmet transformation.

exhibition kitchens
and the theater of
manual labor

Since the 2003 opening of minibar, the intimate gastronomic restaurant by chef José Andres, reservations
have been hard to come by.[1] Not just because Andres
is one of the world's most vaunted chefs have gourmets vied to get in. The other reason is that minibar
offers the foodie equivalent of a front-row seat and
a backstage pass at a sold-out show. At this writing,
the restaurant's "dining room," on the top floor of another Andres restaurant in Washington, DC, is little
more than six bar chairs facing a slim copper counter (fig. 4).[2] Guests' main focus is the tiny but well-
illuminated kitchen. From a workspace no wider or
deeper than the counter, for two seatings a night, for
almost two hours at each seating, three chefs take
diners on a full ride of personal service and dialogue.
Along the way to thirty unique and ambitious courses,
they juggle clockwork timing and synchronous presentations with jovial Q&A.

Had a time-traveling American gourmet from the
1960s dropped into this scenario, she'd have found it
laughable, a sure sign that her yardstick for measur-
ing social status had landed upside down. Who would
compete and pay top dollar to watch and talk to cooks?
In her time, just sitting near a closed kitchen door in a

4. minibar, Washington, DC; view of dining counter, 2010. Photo by author.

reputable restaurant was synonymous with the worst seat in the house.

After all, in the United States until the 1980s, exposed kitchens were largely confined to inexpensive, commonplace eateries. And lending prestige to a place wasn't one of their functions.

In some places, open cooking was for advertising food. Passersby on a New York City street in the 1920s, for instance, were to be lured by a cook making pancakes in the storefront window of a Child's cafeteria-style lunchroom.[3]

In others, exposed kitchens simply made the most of cramped quarters. Cooks manning ranges behind communal counters were common sights nationwide in pre–World War II diners. With minimal travel for servers between cook and customer, hot food reached its destination posthaste.

Open kitchens might also have been used to energize a space. Hence their appearance in the splashy "Googie" coffee shops that spread from Southern California across the country between the late 1950s and mid-1960s. In keeping with animated exterior features—sky-skewering signs, steep glass walls, and zigzag rooflines—the sight and sound of kitchen action between walls enlivened many of the coffee shops' sprawling interiors.

The most common purpose of kitchen display in everyday eateries, however, was to gain public trust. Exposed kitchens reassured custom-ers of honesty and hygiene in the historically suspect lowbrow sector of the restaurant business. Since their spread in the 1920s, fast-food places revealed their kitchens for this reason above all.

Apart from everyday contexts, cooking occasionally appeared in high-concept restaurants as part of themed entertainment. "Dinner houses" that emerged in the 1920s on the edges of cities instigated the steakhouse style of open charcoal flame broiling. The scene of the hearth was part of a meat-themed act, which began with the tableside presentation of a choice of raw cuts.[4]

In the postwar era, cooking might be displayed in restaurants with an ethnic theme. San Francisco restaurateur Johnny Kan reportedly opened Kan's in 1953 with an open kitchen to keep his kitchen staff on their toes concerning hygiene and to educate diners about the prepa-ration of Chinese food.[5] In the 1960s, some places made cooking part of a greater spectacle. Launched appropriately in Manhattan's theater district, Benihana of Tokyo (1964–) featured large, communal tables fitted with grills, at which *teppanyaki* masters prepared food while performing knife juggling and chopping stunts. New York City's Latin American restaurant La Fonda del Sol (in original form, 1960–70) of-fered an equivalent sensory riot. Graphics with the names of foods— "mole poblano," "seviche," "tamales," and so on—in varying fonts, sizes, and colors covered the wall around a doorway fronted by a butchering station and pig parts hanging from hooks.[6]

In 1972, San Franciscans saw the opening of the likewise dramatic Fournou's Ovens. Caroline Bates captured my own memory of it best in a 1977 review in which she called the restaurant a meat-grilling "am-phitheater." Tiers of tables descended toward a "great oven." Props ro-mantically evoking Mediterranean culture framed it—a tapestry, old brass fixtures, and pewter plates; bay-leaf, garlic, and red-chile gar-lands; and sage-stuffed urns.[7]

As glamorous as cooking could look in theme restaurants, it wasn't on show for its own sake. Display cooking served other cultural narratives.

The earliest gourmet restaurant that I am certain displayed its kitchen solely to show routine operations was the Depuy Canal House in High Falls, New York.[8] Following a four-star review by Craig Claiborne in the *New York Times* in 1970, chef John N. Novi became so overrun with customers that he undertook a major renovation to enlarge the inn's 1797 premises.[9] By the summer of 1974, he had not only increased the size of the eight-by-ten-foot kitchen but also made it visible to guests. Novi recently told me what drove him to open the kitchen: "I wanted to meet my guests face to face, but since I was chef, I could not take the time out to visit the table. Many people wanted to meet the *New York Times* four-star character." Novi removed the kitchen ceiling, added a second-floor loft, and installed tables there that gave guests a balcony view over the kitchen (fig. 5).[10]

5. Depuy Canal House, High Falls, NY; view of kitchen and chef's table from second-floor loft, 2011. Photo by Jamie McGlothlin.

6. Depuy Canal House, High Falls, NY; view of chef's table inside kitchen, 2012. Photo by John Novi.

At the same time and for the same reason, Novi unveiled a subtype of the open kitchen now commonly called a chef's table (fig. 6). In the newly renovated space, he began using a ten-foot-long table inside the kitchen itself as special seating for parties of two to eight diners. The guests there could ask the chef questions and would receive extra tasting plates.

Perhaps due to unfortunate timing, Depuy Canal House didn't spark an open-kitchen trend. Novi's first significant recognition, from Claiborne, preceded the renovations. The chef's subsequent accolades focused on his New American culinary innovations, this coming after a gourmet display-kitchen trend was already under way.[11]

As I indicated in chapter 1, the true tipping point for the gourmet open kitchen was the early 1980s in California. In 1982, Alice Waters's Chez Panisse Café in Berkeley and Wolfgang Puck's Spago in Hollywood gained national attention for making their wood-burning ovens, grills, and ranges a component of gourmet-dining-room décor.

The following year, Puck's ethnic-fusion restaurant, Chinois on Main, in Santa Monica, introduced a new format for the gourmet open kitchen. Guests were treated to a close-up view of the cooking at a communal dining counter right at the kitchen's edge. This setup borrowed from the downscale pre–World War II diner and the newly upscale Japanese sushi bar. The former was the obvious precedent for dining counters facing cooks working over heat. The latter made sense in light of Puck's Japanese culinary influences. Even some of the cooks he initially hired for Chinois were Japanese.[12]

The California scene of the early 1980s was poised to ignite a nationwide trend. The chefs involved shared a social network. Puck's visit to Chez Panisse was one of the inspirations for his open kitchen at Spago. Waters even referred Puck to the same wood-burning-oven builder she'd used. In addition, over the first half of the decade, California reached a critical mass of highly reputed restaurants with exhibition kitchens. Several chefs who'd worked at Chez Panisse—such as Jeremiah Tower, Joyce Goldstein, and Judy Rodgers—and even some who hadn't, such as Cindy Pawlcyn, installed open kitchens in their own local restaurants. Furthermore, the press drew attention to the California kitchens because their typical features, wood-burning ovens and grills, were integral to critics' definition at the time of an ascendant "California cuisine."[13]

After this watershed, variations on the exhibition kitchen spread to acclaimed restaurants beyond California. Notable milestones include Jams in New York City in 1984, where California-scene veteran Jonathan Waxman installed an open kitchen, and Charlie Trotter's in Chicago, which instituted a chef's table in 1987, the year it opened. The book *Charlie Trotter's* (2000) cites French precedents rather than Novi's restaurant for what Trotter called his "kitchen table." Still, Trotter's setup was basically the same as Novi's and typical of many chef's tables since: a specially reserved table in the kitchen itself where guests enjoy a customized menu and direct attention from the *chef de cuisine*.[14] To the best of my knowledge, the kitchen-counter variant that pioneered at Chinois on Main next surfaced in New Orleans in 1990 as the immensely popular "food bar" at chef Emeril Lagasse's flagship, Emeril's (1990–).[15]

By that point, however, exposed kitchens in gourmet establishments were becoming ubiquitous. A sign of their normalization came in the 1989 edition of Regina S. Baraban and Joseph F. Durocher's guide for would-be restaurateurs. *Successful Restaurant Design*, which highlighted many gourmet examples, devoted a section to advice on designing several varieties of "display kitchen." The 2001 and 2010 editions of the book continued this practice. Meanwhile, articles since the early 1990s in industry journals such as *Restaurant Business*, *Lodging Hospitality*, and *Nation's Restaurant News* have called exhibition kitchens "widespread" and prophesied that they'd persist. A report from 2008 claimed, "Display kitchens are a trend that is here to stay."[16]

Since the late 1990s, chef's tables in particular have received special attention in press directed to business, traveler, and foodie audiences. Articles touting their virtues and popularity have appeared in *Forbes*, *Fortune*, *Black Enterprise*, *Crain's New Business*, *Celebrated Living*, *Gourmet*, and the *New York Times*.[17]

That business journals began recommending a chef's table to impress clients shows that a wider swath of elites beyond gourmets started to see it as a status symbol. At the forefront of this trend, Charlie Trotter's opened a "studio kitchen" in 1994 in addition to the chef's table, expressly to accommodate large corporate parties in chef's-table style. According to *Charlie Trotter's*: "A chef, two waiters, and a sommelier are assigned to the studio kitchen, and several of the dishes are prepared right there. Two overhead TV monitors in the 20-seat dining room allow the guests to watch their other dishes being prepared in the main kitchen."[18]

By the time of my visit to the exalted minibar in August 2010, exhibition kitchens had become such a chic feature of gourmet restaurants that casual-dining chains wanting an upgrade had begun redesigning units to include them. Mostly in the first decade of the 2000s, industry writers reported on many instances of brands—from Houlihan's to Rubio's to Kona Grill—defining their makeovers as "upscale" moves.[19] The irony—this appropriation of what was once a downscale feature— testifies to the open kitchen's steep surge in prestige.

Why the reversal in value?

adaptation to necessity or organic expression?

It's tempting to assume purely cultural drivers of the change. But what if open kitchens have proliferated out of necessity? If they've been a response to economic constraints, we would have to conclude that their rise in prestige was a secondary effect, a grafting of cultural values onto necessary circumstances, and not a more organic outgrowth of cultural motives.

Have display kitchens been cost cutting? To find out, I combed the decades of industry literature on open kitchens and questioned several longtime restaurant producers—three chef owners and three nonchef restaurant developers who collectively span over thirty-five years in the industry and have experience with open-kitchen design across the United States.

I found a consensus that open kitchens generally don't save money. In fact, they normally add cost. Certain reasons for the extra expense came up repeatedly, and regardless of whether experts were referring to the early 1980s or the turn of the millennium. The HVAC (heating, ventilation, and air-conditioning) systems are more complicated and expensive for front-of-the-house (FOH) than for back-of-the-house (BOH) kitchens. For FOH kitchens, the system must handle the additional job of preventing the dining room from sharing in the unpleasant, yet typical, conditions of smoke and heat in the kitchen. Also, more attractive materials and finishes tend to go into display kitchens. These add significant cost—up to 30 percent of a kitchen build. Lastly, since open kitchens are part of the décor, they sometimes subtract square footage from spots where paying tables could go.[20]

Some experts noted minor exceptions to the rule of open kitchens' extra cost. If FOH kitchens allow for a smaller overall footprint by, say, eliminating the space servers must walk between kitchen and dining room, there can be some savings in that. In addition, chef's tables can be considerable moneymakers. As long as a restaurant can fit a table inside its kitchen without adding extra space and can charge diners hundreds more for eating there than in the dining room, a common practice, chef's tables are a clear financial winner. That is, of course, if the extra revenue is sufficient to justify the expense of dedicating some staff solely to the service of chef's-table guests.[21]

But since, for the most part, open kitchens haven't been cost-effective, and since the lucrative nature of chef's tables only begs the question of preexisting demand, economic necessity alone can't explain the remarkable spread of either. The fashion for gourmet open kitchens must be the product of cultural forces. A first step toward uncovering these influences is to identify for whose satisfaction open kitchens have existed.

gratified parties

Who's found open kitchens personally fulfilling? Examine the case of restaurant producers. From my interviews and the industry literature, I found that the advantages of such kitchens declared by chefs differ qualitatively from those noted by other restaurant producers.

Nonchefs—including owners, designers, and food-service consultants—mentioned many benefits that are consistent with exposed kitchens' historical functions in everyday and theme restaurants. With reference to cases spanning the entire trend of gourmet open kitchens, nonchef restaurant producers most often cited giving the impression of freshness and cleanliness, lending sensual appeal, and providing excitement and entertainment as the chief benefits.[22] A few experts mentioned further reasons. Referring to Spago in 1992, designer Barbara Lazaroff suggested that diners want to feel like they're gathered around a big eat-in home kitchen. Food-service consultant Ron Kooser, speaking generally in 2010, said that guests want to feel connected to the preparation of their food. In conversation with me, Pat Kuleto, founder and CEO of Pat Kuleto Restaurant Development and Management Company, and Rob Wilder, CEO of ThinkFoodGroup, both mentioned diners' desire to be close to the chef.[23]

The nonchefs' reasons are varied, but all represent benefits to customers. Their own reward for open kitchens, having a successful business, is an indirect result of satisfying others.

By contrast, chefs commonly expressed personal benefits. The pattern is clear in the industry literature and my own interviews from statements made by chefs of acclaimed restaurants in all major regions of the United States. The examples I gathered are from New York, Virginia, Massachusetts, New Orleans, North Carolina, Illinois, and California.

Only a minority of chefs mentioned advantages of open kitchens that other restaurant producers had given. Referring to the Chez Panisse Café, Waters noted the sensuality of kitchen sights, sounds, and

7. View of open kitchen at Spago, West Hollywood, as it looked after opening in 1982. Photo by Michael Montfort.

smells. On the subject of Spago (fig. 7), Puck noted the display kitchen's entertainment value.[24]

But the bulk of chefs' remarks cited a range of psychological and professional gains for them. In a 1992 interview regarding his restaurants to date, all of which had open kitchens, Puck stated that cooking in front of diners offered him and his staff the morale boost of being recognized, the satisfaction of seeing happy guests, and the opportunity to get to know customers. In 2003, Gale Gand, chef and co-owner of Tru in Chicago, likened her chef's table to a creative "sketchpad." The immediate feedback from guests sitting close by, she said, spurred her improvisation process. Speaking with me in 2010, Wylie Dufresne, chef and co-owner of Manhattan's WD-50, conveyed great pride in his kitchen and a desire to show diners the source of their food. David Chang put his satisfaction in more vengeful terms. Explaining in *Momofuku* why he made Ko in New York City counter-only, with chefs serving diners directly, he claimed exasperation with the restaurant tradition of servers pocketing all the tips![25]

Chefs also noted the professional bonus of staff discipline. In discussion with me, both Pawlcyn, who has featured open kitchens in several of her restaurants, beginning in 1983 with Mustards Grill, in Yountville, California, and Novi, still heading the Depuy Canal House, noted that kitchen visibility ensures that their cooking staff maintains a professional demeanor. Novi, who regularly hires culinary-school externs, added that the many questions guests ask at his chef's table keep his trainees as well as himself mentally sharp.[26]

What chefs occasionally communicated as perks for customers are also benefits to chefs. In a 1997 interview about the opening of his celebrated Manhattan restaurant Jean Georges, chef and co-owner Jean Georges Vongerichten said he "want[ed] the guests to share some of the enjoyment we have in the kitchen." Lagasse, interviewed in 2000, presumed that his guests wanted to be "connected with the kitchen." About diners finally getting to see the kitchen in the newly renovated Manhattan restaurant Eleven Madison Park, head chef David Humm told a reporter in 2010, "They want to see the room, see the chefs."[27]

Given the personal satisfaction chefs have derived from them, it would seem that display kitchens have been expressions of their interests in particular. In part, the dining concept has been just that. But the capacity of chefs to impose their will through restaurant design has itself depended on the support of a chef-loving public. If the open kitchen hadn't been so appealing to foodies, this costly design feature would never have proliferated and persisted to the extent it has.

favored forms

Any viable investigation into why display kitchens have gained in prestige must pursue their appeal to gourmets. I'll start by distinguishing among variants of open kitchens and noting which types foodies have prized most.

From archival research and personal experience, I've observed that most gourmet display kitchens have taken either one or a combination of four basic forms. Roughly following all three editions of *Successful Restaurant Design*, my own taxonomy of open kitchens below reflects the diner's possible levels of proximity to and interaction with kitchen staff.[28]

Sideshow Glimpses

Restaurants offering "sideshow glimpses" reveal minimal kitchen space and work. Their kitchens may be mostly sequestered behind walls or placed marginally in the dining room. San Francisco's Fog City Diner (1985–) has contained both common features and other barriers to visibility. The dining room's best view of cooks working has been from behind a dining counter through a window-sized wall cutout, which has doubled as an order-pickup pass. But the counter has been confined to one end of the restaurant, and even for people sitting there, the view of the culinary goings-on has been limited. At other times, not only have guests sat back at least a couple of yards from the pickup window, but large, overhanging heat lamps have obscured much of what there is to see from there. Chef Paul Kahan's restaurant, Avec (2003–), in Chicago has presented cooking in the dining room itself, but the kitchen station there has been minimal and peripheral. As small as Avec is—the dining area just a bar for drinking and dining and one row of tables behind it—most diners still can't view the cooking. The small area with a range remains behind the far end of the bar. When I dined at the bar in February 2010, I could hear and smell cooking, but glimpsed it only from the corner of my eye.

Theater Seats

By contrast, everyone in the dining room gets a good floor show when display kitchens are the restaurant's focal point. The original Spago (Hollywood) and subsequent editions, such as the Beverly Hills location I visited (1997–), chef Michel Richard's Michel Richard Citronelle in Washington, DC (after remodeling, 1998–), and chef April Bloomfield's the Breslin in New York City (2009–) are just a few examples from the past three decades where kitchens have been their adjacent dining rooms' visual anchors.[29] Whether a kitchen juts out into a room,

8. View of open kitchen from dining room at the Breslin, New York City, 2010. Photo by author.

as at the original Spago, or cuts a proscenium of bright light along one wall of a dark room, as at Citronelle and the Breslin (fig. 8), guests can watch cooks work their stations as though from seats in a theater.

Front-Row Seats

While such scenarios provide considerably more than a glimpse of cooking, kitchen counters—also commonly called chef's counters—go one better. They offer the theater equivalent of front-row seats. They put diners as close as health regulations permit to the kitchen's edge. At most counters I've been to, cooks have finished plating dishes on a countertop directly in front of my place setting.

Despite their structural commonality, however, kitchen counters can serve up disparate experiences of the kitchen. At the counters of Chinois on Main, Emeril's "food bar," Momofuku Noodle Bar in

Manhattan, and chef Tyler Florence's Wayfare Tavern (2010–) in San Francisco—some examples spanning their history—the diner's privileged proximity to the kitchen hasn't come with special attention from the kitchen staff, such as a customized menu and conversation. For that kind of access, one must reserve what I call a "a meet-the-actors pass."

Meet-the-Actors Passes

At some kitchen counters, access to the kitchen is as good as it gets. For example, at minibar, at Masa in New York City, at Momofuku Ko, and at chef Joshua Skenes's Saison in San Francisco (2010–; fig. 9), counter guests have received a tasting menu predesigned or improvised just for them, and have been able to talk to the kitchen staff. In most cases, chefs have served diners personally.

For the same access advantages, but in a format less amenable to the solitary diner, there are chef's tables. Parties of two or more get

9. View of open kitchen from chef's dining counter at Saison, San Francisco, 2010. Photo by author.

seats inside or directly adjacent to the kitchen. In February 2010, I saw the kitchen table at Charlie Trotter's. The manager was kind enough to give me a tour following my meal in the kitchen-less dining room. Within feet after swinging through the door accessed by a corridor at the back of the dining room, I happened upon a neatly dressed couple at a small table graced with a white tablecloth and basket of flowers. Their oasis of elegance was no more than a few paces from the kitchen's busy staff and equipment: plastic crates of glasses fronting a workstation on one side and the *chef de cuisine* expediting and readying plates for servers on another. If the dining table had inched just a little toward the crates, the staff could have easily tripped over the table. The couple saw the whir of activity around them as something special. The camera on their table said so.

It's no wonder. Over the history of gourmet open kitchens, the closer diners have been to and the more interaction they have had with the kitchen staff, the more enviable the experience.

In molding this impression, restaurant reporters and critics have been powerfully influential. Writing about chef's tables for *Fortune* at the onset of their media buzz in 1996, Ronald B. Liebner claimed that they provided "an experience far superior to that of the dining room."[30] Critics writing afterward elaborated on his message by conveying the various ways that chef's tables and high-access kitchen counters offer unparalleled open-kitchen dining.

One way is monetary. About chef Masa Takayama's counter-only precursor to Masa in New York, Ginza Sushi-ko in Beverly Hills (1993–2004), Caroline Bates remarked on what she considered a steep charge, $499.03 for two people, in 1998.[31] Accounts of Masa by Frank Bruni in 2004 and Anthony Bourdain in 2006 also made a point of the cost—starting at $350 a head the year it opened in 2004.[32] Chef's tables have prompted similar notices. In 2006, Dirk Smillie let his *Forbes* readers know that "in New York City, where dinner at Alain Ducasse costs $230 per person with tax and tip (but not wine), the tab for the chef's table is $500 (including wine)."[33]

Yet writers have also conveyed desirability by stressing how in demand chef's tables and some kitchen counters are. Speaking generally of chef's tables in *Crain's New York Business* in 2007, Lisa Fickenscher prepared her readers: "Some chef's tables are booked seven nights a week. A few have lengthy waiting lists."[34] The difficulty of getting reservations at Momofuku Ko is legendary. "Halfway through dinner at the new Momofuku Ko it hits you," wrote Ruth Reichl in *Gourmet* in 2008. "You will never eat dinner here again."[35] Frank Bruni went into more detail about the trials of making a reservation under Ko's rule prohibiting bookings more than a week ahead:

> Best of luck. Be strong. Be forewarned. You can't fixate on a single night. You can't fixate on a specific hour. You must have patience, an efficient computer, and nimble, fast-moving fingers, because the way to grab one of the 12 coveted seats is to click-submit a reservation request at precisely 10 a.m. precisely six days before you aspire to dine there and then hope against hope and dream against dream and promise the cyberspace gods your firstborn male child if they speed your electronic wish to Ko before all the other electronic wishes get there.[36]

Besides invoking social proof to express the specialness of chef's tables and kitchen counters, food writers have put forth their own glowing testimonials. For the ultimate in gushing, nothing beats Anthony Bourdain's erotically charged take on dining in the care of chef Masa Takayama:

> Imagine if you will: You are one of only thirteen customers sitting at a long, wide, blond hinoki wood counter of such warm inviting loveliness that you want to curl up on it and go to sleep. You want to spend the rest of your life rubbing your cheek—if not your nether regions—against it. The nation's most highly regarded sushi master is standing directly in front of you with a knife, a plane grater, a hunk of fresh wasabi root. On both sides of him are casually deposited heaps of the sexiest looking fish you've ever conjured up in your wildest, soy-spattered dreams of sushi heaven.[37]

It may be obvious from this pattern of valuing access to them that gourmets' desire for communion with restaurant kitchens derives from their reverence for chefs. But saying that doesn't explain the particular appeal of exhibition kitchens, why they've been such an attractive medium through which to admire chefs.

My contention is that they've nurtured a fantasy ideal of the chef's work. Far from being transparent windows onto the professional kitchen, they've been mystifying constructs, marvels of stagecraft in their design and usage.

the theater of manual labor

My earlier use of theater metaphors to describe open-kitchen types wasn't arbitrary. The analogy of the stage is significant.

In a remarkable book from 1959 entitled *The Presentation of Self in Everyday Life*, sociologist Erving Goffman introduced a dramaturgical theory of social interaction and impression management that I find ideal for explaining how and why open kitchens have presented the labor of chefs. According to Goffman, all areas of socially meaningful action and interaction have a performance aspect. As individuals and groups become invested in how social situations are perceived, they present themselves in ways that foster the impression they want to make. They fashion idealizing "fronts"—either solo or in teams collaborating for mutual benefit. These actors may do so knowingly or not.[38]

Unlike actual theater, the presentation of self in everyday life doesn't distinguish between true and false self. The social self is a genuine product of negotiation between selves real and ideal. But like theatrical performance, real-life self-presentations involve the elements—"appearance," "manner," and "setting"—of stage play.[39]

Following Goffman's model, exhibition kitchens haven't outright falsified chefs' work. They've presented it selectively, hiding actions and things inconsistent with fans' ideal. In addition, appearance, manner, and setting have all contributed to the chef front.

Even Goffman's theory of what motivates performances and what makes them successful fits the case of display kitchens. Kitchen workers and consumers alike have sustained exhibition cooking because both parties have been invested in the same ideal. For kitchen workers, that ideal has been a key to social and economic rewards. For diners, it's been a fantasy.

To some extent, the need to manage impressions has always attended exposed restaurant kitchens. In a technical "Restaurant Kitchen" article from 1944, one Harry Blumberg insisted that the equipment used in front of customers for lunch counters and cafeterias look different from that in BOH kitchens. He wrote, "Its appearance, its eye appeal is very important."[40] Yet as exhibition kitchens became vehicles for chef adulation, in the gourmet realm, much more than Blumberg's concern with the beauty of broilers, toasters, and urns came to matter.

Over the decades, a wide range of gourmet-open-kitchen styles has accumulated. No common forms have gone extinct. Yet open kitchens have been consistently unified in their effects. They've downplayed certain aspects of manual kitchen labor and highlighted others. Through a recurring set of devices, they've hidden the more tedious, disgusting, slow-moving, and industrial-scale work. Exhibition kitchens have showcased only the most sensuous, speedy, artistic, and intimate-scale modes of kitchen labor.

The Placement of Work

As a general rule, any undesirable preparation has been situated as far from diners as possible. To this end, most restaurants have maintained entire invisible realms of production. Back or basement kitchens have typically supported display kitchens much like a backstage supports a stage. All three editions of Baraban and Durocher's *Successful Restaurant Design* recommend their adoption: "To be most effective, nearly all of the pre-preparation should be completed away from the display kitchen. Such operations as chopping, slicing, and pounding need to be done out of sight of diners."[41] In a *Restaurant Business* article on open kitchens from 1993, Mary Reinholz stressed the back kitchen's suitability for volume work, such as making bulk sauces.[42] Other design writers, such as Steven Starr (1998) and Gary Bensky (2000), advised keeping not only bulk cooking but also ware washing areas in the BOH.[43]

The type of equipment ordinarily found in backstage versus onstage kitchens is telling. At the original Spago in Hollywood (1982–99), the display kitchen had all the sexy stuff—the two brick wood-burning ovens, a mesquite grill, and various other cook surfaces for dishes' final firing, as well as a front counter near the pickup pass for the frisky foreplay of pizza prep. Meanwhile, a large closed kitchen in another part of the restaurant concealed less exhibitionistic tools—large ovens, a duck cooker, a pasta cooker, walk-in and reach-in refrigerators, dry storage, a smoker, and a station for dishwashing.[44] Café Centro in New York City (1994–)—well publicized when it opened for its display kitchen's size, elaborateness, and extravagance—has kept its three-ring circus of seduction—including charbroilers, cheese melters, and a rotisserie set in a pastoral fantasy of a Tuscan fireplace—on show for diners. Meanwhile, it has sequestered such charmless industrial necessities as a forty-gallon tilt skillet and sixty-gallon kettle.[45]

The size of some prep kitchens is a striking reminder of just how much kitchen work may be withheld from diners. Most guests have never noticed that, at the Zuni Café in San Francisco (after its 1987 renovation) and the Momofuku Noodle Bar, both of which have had prominent open kitchens, additional basement kitchens had taken up their restaurants' entire footprints.

The existence of backstage operations hasn't been a secret. Restaurant staff unhesitatingly told me about them wherever I asked. In rare instances, restaurateurs have even mentioned them unprompted. An e-mail announcement from the team of chef Grant Achatz and Nick Kokonas in 2011, publicizing their upcoming Chicago venture Next, boasted that it would include "not only a state-of-the-art open kitchen, but also a full basement prep kitchen."[46]

Restaurateurs haven't denied the existence of prep kitchens any more than theater producers have denied the existence of a backstage. Nevertheless, hiding the backstage during a performance has always been *de rigueur* in the theater, and so it has been at restaurants.

The Timing of Work

In cases of limited space or atypical architecture, smart planning of time can compensate for the lack of separate space. In restaurants without back or basement kitchens, prep may take place in open kitchens, just not during dining hours. So it's worked at Chez Panisse. Only the food-storage room, or "walk-in," has been separately located, in a building behind the restaurant. In August 2010, a sous-chef explained to me the schedule in place at that time: All prep for the upstairs Café would get done in the downstairs open kitchen before 2:00 p.m. Then, the downstairs team would arrive and do its own prep.

Momofuku Ko and minibar have maintained hybrid operations. When I visited in August 2010, a sous-chef at each restaurant informed me that 90 percent of their prep occurred in the open kitchen during closed hours. The remaining percentage took place in other spaces. At minibar, the surrounding Café Atlantico was receiving and storing its ingredients, washing its wares, and doing some of its food prep. At Momofuku Ko, a downstairs with sinks, a walk-in, and a small workspace has allowed for additional prep and for two junior staffers to prepare items for the open kitchen during service.

Even within onstage kitchen spaces, there are patterns in what's hidden and what's highlighted. The most heart-pumping workstations have been positioned closest to diners. In part, this scheme is functional. The most sensual and dramatic activities—such as sautéing, grilling, broiling, and plating of dishes—also usually represent the last stages of dish preparation. So it makes operational sense to put them nearest the servers in the dining room. Still, it's significant that the placement of workstations has followed the stagecraft logic governing every other aspect of open kitchens.

Multiple design writers have commented on the dramatic advantages of installing fast-moving or sensuous items and activities in the foreground. In the late 1990s, Nicole G. Castagna observed an increased use of rotisseries, Mongolian grills, and wood-fired pizza ovens, and the display of fresh foods near diners.[47] Elaine Martin Petrowski put the theatrics of workstation placement in narrative terms: "Once the food moves to the front line, things get interesting. This is generally the part of the kitchen on view. Here, the cooking is finished and food is plated, garnished, and served; it's also where the crabs are steamed, the chops are grilled, the pizza comes out of the brick oven, and buttery sauces are drizzled over entrées."[48]

The special drama of wood-fired ovens, the use of which Chez Panisse and Spago Hollywood initiated, has become a leitmotif of display kitchens. In some places, such as San Francisco's Zuni Café and A16 (2004–), their sensory impact has reached a maximal intensity. At Zuni, even the multiple tiers of kitchen lines on view have been upstaged by a shed-size, chimney-topped brick edifice—wood piled high along one side as if it's a cabin in the woods—that commands the center of the downstairs dining room (fig. 10). From one of its rus-

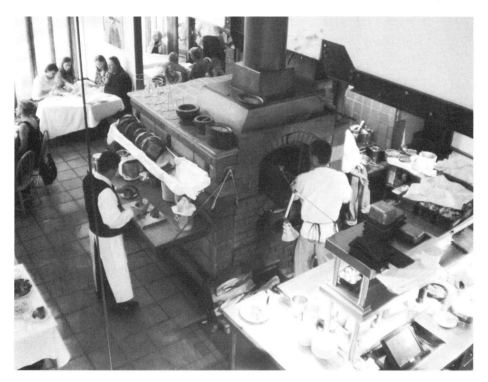

10. View of open kitchen and brick wood-burning oven at Zuni Café, San Francisco, from second-floor balcony, 2010. Photo by author.

ticated nooks: the emanations of a grill. Further "downstage" on the same side: two infernal half moons at which a dedicated cook inserts and retrieves Zuni's glistening trophies, including the signature whole roasted chickens.

For the stimulation of its chef's-counter guests, A16's wood-fired ovens have been arranged side by side with other appealing stations. Diners from left to center along the counter have faced the two wood-burning ovens—one dedicated to pizza, the other to the also mouthwatering roasting of Campagna-inspired entrées and sides. Diners from center to right have been entertained by the final plating of dishes and the colorful mixing of salads. Behind that: hood-covered stovetops for pastas and potions. To the right of the dining counter: the artful composition of cold appetizers and an unmanned tableau of a sculptural slicer and rustic pile of bread.

In places where the display of cooking is more tempered, set farther away from diners, front and back workstations have still been distinguished by their potential for aesthetic and dramatic "heat." At chef Bobby Flay's Manhattan restaurant, Mesa Grill (1991–), where the semiopen kitchen has remained behind a glass wall at the back, the liveliest activities—expediting, plating, sautéing, grilling, and the final preparation of cold and hot apps—have clustered near the window. Behind them, yet still visible: entrée prep. Then, of course, way behind and out of view: the dish- and pot-washing area, and egress to a downstairs prep and pastry kitchen.[49]

Filtering

In spite of manipulation in the order of work places and times, most restaurateurs have still required more devices to limit diners' perception of the noise, dirt, and mess that invariably accumulate in an active restaurant kitchen. Most open kitchens have filtered such unwanted elements via sightline design or decorative obstructions.

Over the 1990s, design writers Carol Lally Metz, Kimberly D. Lowe, Elaine Martin Petrowski, and Pamela Parseghian commented on the frequent use of glass walls to stifle noise and, depending on their position and transparency, to hide food spills on kitchen floors.[50] The practice has continued. The open kitchens of Café Centro, chefs Quinn and Karen Hatfield's restaurant, Hatfield's, in Los Angeles (in current location, 2009–), and chef Vongerichten's ABC Kitchen in Manhattan (2010–) run the gamut of sizes, room positions, and shapes. But all are set behind glass.

To steer diners' attention, designers have also calculated the positions of counters and equipment. Even though the chef's tables at Charlie Trotter's and Citronelle have been set inside the kitchen, solid counters for final plating have occluded most of the diners' view of the workstations and floor. In both restaurants, these guests have dined several feet in front of such a counter.

The design of barriers can be very exacting. Foster Frable Jr. has specified visibility requirements in feet and inches: "There are three critical dimensions in planning a display kitchen: the height of the [ventilation] hood, the width of the aisles and the height of the pass-over [sic] or plating shelves. When possible, try to set the underside of the hood close to 7 feet. Providing an aisle wider than 36 inches to 42 inches between the chef's table and cooking equipment adds many work steps while also exposing more floor area to view." With equal precision, Frable warned against showing too little: "Placing the pass-shelf or counter top higher than 44 inches will block the entire view of the cooking equipment from the dining area, leaving the patrons with a view of the chef's head and the hood."[51] Design expert Dan Bendall hasn't been as quantitative in his remarks on sightline craft, but he has specified wood-burning ovens as something to place just so: "When planning for the oven, always face the mouth of the unit where guests can see inside. This is especially appetizing because . . . you'll see flames inside that light up the interior baking cavity."[52]

One filtering technique I've seen repeatedly is the installation of a lattice of shelves around a display kitchen's perimeter. When I visited chef Michael Mina's XIV in Los Angeles (2008–11) and Daniel Boulud's DBGB in Manhattan (2009–), I noted that the open kitchens occupied a lot of wall space, but that each was surrounded by counter-to-ceiling metal shelving—for clean plates, glasses, and other service items—that reduced kitchen visibility. At the chef's counter at New York City's L'Atelier de Joël Robuchon (2005–12), the same device was used also to create distance. Not only did the tall structure of shelves in front of the kitchen block parts of the kitchen's front line with its still-life arrangements of colorful flowers, fruits, vegetables, and one *jamón ibérico* (Iberian ham). This labyrinth of decoration also cannily put about twenty feet between dining counter and kitchen.

Aestheticizing the Perceptible

The selective showing and hiding of things and actions hasn't been the only means of distorting the realities of restaurant-kitchen labor. In the effort to align scenic components of the kitchen workspace with aesthetic demands of the dining space, what's meant for show has also been manipulated.

Earlier, I noted the use of attractive finishes and materials as well as specially engineered HVAC systems in exhibition kitchens. In aesthetic terms, these devices sync up the environments of kitchen and dining room. In social-symbolic terms, they've done what all the other theatrical devices of open kitchens have done: they've minimized the appearance of a distinction between the modes of work and leisure. Prohibitions against yelling and other BOH behavior that might be unbecoming in the dining room have contributed to the same effect.

Add lighting to this list of mechanisms for matching. Although common in BOH kitchens, experts have warned against using fluorescent lights near diners. Per design writer Steven Starr: "[These lights] tend to make food look green—not exactly the image you want to whet diners' appetites. What to do? The dining room will likely be illuminated with low-level incandescent lights. Carefully position halogen lighting around the expo kitchen so that light is directed away from the dining room."[53] Other experts have recommended using the same lighting for the dining room as for the front line of the display kitchen or installing task lighting at that borderline.

Finally, what performance would be ready without consideration of costume? Kitchen attire has likewise been used to bring kitchen labor in line with dining-room leisure. Starr has advised, "Work with the restaurateur to make sure the staff is dressed to match the expo kitchen."[54] Exhibition kitchens have indeed brought about a new fashion consciousness. In 2009, a *Restaurant Business* editorial attributed the proliferation of new colors, patterns, and fabrics for restaurant-kitchen attire to the popularity of open kitchens. "The result—much of the new kitchen wear is fashionable enough for the street."[55] And, the editorial might have added, for the day off.

supporting scripts

In blurring the line between manual kitchen labor and leisure, exhibition kitchens haven't been the sole factor. Gourmets' other main sources of chef-related consumer culture have come into play as well.

TV cooking shows were probably the original suppliers of display kitchens' leisure-time "script." They'd been collapsing the modes of work and play before gourmet display kitchens existed. According to Kathleen Collins's history of American cooking programs, *Watching What We Eat* (2009), it was 1960s shows such as Julia Child's *The French Chef* and Graham Kerr's *The Galloping Gourmet* that initiated the practice by representing cooking as entertainment, and not simply providing pure instruction.[56] The latter starred a dashing Chef Kerr, who reminisced about inspiring meals abroad, practiced a sort of stand-up comedy routine, pretended to lose track of soufflés in the oven (just kidding!), and, wine glass in hand, slid across a counter to greet his studio audience.

The timing of this transition to cooking as entertainment was significant. As Collins argues, it followed the decline of audiences' everyday home cooking—as more women entered the workforce—along with the rise of gourmandise and, for men and women, cooking as a hobby. Thus, gourmets' association of cooking with the leisure world of elective activity had long been ripe for exploitation. According to Krishnendu Ray, *The French Chef* was successful in the 1960s in part by doing just that. He argues that Julia Child's literal and figurative domestication of professional French cooking could withstand the growing societal challenges to female domesticity of the time precisely by emphasizing pleasure.[57]

In the Food Network era, cooking shows have only intensified the association of cooking with entertainment. Commentators on recent shows have emphasized their voyeuristic, prettifying, and consumption-fostering qualities.

Some authors have even noted the same devices I've identified in restaurant display kitchens. Andrew Chan observed that representations of cooking in shows at the time of his writing in 2003—TVFN's *Two Fat Ladies*, *The Naked Chef*, *Nigella Bites*, *Emeril Live*, and Japan's *Iron Chef*—revolved around "fantasy kitchens."[58] Like display kitchens, they showed no signs of arduous or ugly work, such as stacks of dirty dishes or trash. Also, they represented atypical work environments, more spacious and better ventilated than most professional or home kitchens. Cheri Ketchum drew complementary conclusions. After analyzing the conventions of narrative and imagery in a representative seventy-hour sample of Food Network shows from May to September 2002, she concluded that for shows set in kitchens, a style of fast action and intimate address of viewers prevailed. Some shows of this setting type conjured a "party atmosphere."[59] As I've noted, display kitchens, too, have made thrilling action out of manual kitchen work; they, too, have given their "audiences" the sense of being on intimate terms with chefs.

Recent cooking programs have also portrayed chefs in ways consistent with their open-kitchen fronts. As I have elsewhere argued, they've collectively fashioned an image of the chef as a magical composite of leisure-space and workspace competence and bliss.[60]

In programs such as *Cooking 911* and *Everyday Italian* on TVFN, *Cookin' in Brooklyn* on Discovery Home, *Take Home Chef* on TLC, and *Chuck's Day Off* on the Cooking Channel, chefs have played the role of superlative host. In every episode, they've prepared and served inviting dishes to delighted and fun-filled gatherings of friends and family.

In other programs, chefs have come across as the epitome of professional ambition and achievement. Food Network shows such as *Iron Chef*, its American sequel *Iron Chef America*, and *Chopped* have presented the chef as fearless and driven competitor or seasoned judge. Meanwhile, others—including the Fine Living Channel's *Made to Order*, *Ace of Cakes* on TVFN, *Future Food* on the Green Channel, and *Marcel's Quantum Kitchen* on Syfy—have cast the chef as intense and ingenious perfectionist. For every show, the featured chef has surmounted daunting obstacles in pursuit of some difficult and creative culinary goal.

For more mergers of labor and leisure, we must look to amateur cooking classes. Not surprisingly, enthusiasm for these grew in proportion to their increasing emphasis on entertainment and vacationing.[61]

In the mid-1980s, amid reports of lagging enrollment for courses with a traditional emphasis on recipe transmission, writers for newspapers as geographically far apart as the *New York Times*, the *Philadelphia Inquirer*, and the *Seattle Times* all observed a significant countertrend. Enrollments were actually spiking for courses featuring elements less oriented to manual drudgery and more engaging to the imagination. Writers specifically mentioned the new emphasis on exotic cuisines, discussion of the principles behind cooking, and appearances by celebrity chefs. Such fun-filled options have multiplied dramatically in the years since. According to the Shaw Guides Inc., which began publishing *The Guide to Cooking Schools* in 1989, the number of recreational cooking programs available to Americans jumped from an initial recording of 200 to an amazing 1,206 in 2011.[62]

Reports on the growth of recreational cooking classes have often made the point that amateurs have it easy compared to students in professional culinary programs. Mary Alice Powell, writing in the

Illinois-based *Slate Journal-Register* in 1994, remarked that for non-professionals, "cooking classes serve a good portion of entertainment along with education. Some are so enjoyable that they become vacation destinations themselves. The entertainment is watching a culinary expert demonstrate a few recipes and then being served a sample of each."[63] In the *New York Times* in 1998, William Grimes disabused readers of the notion that amateur classes were all work by declaring that a wide range exists in the proportion of participation to demonstration.[64] In the *Chicago Sun-Times* in 2003, Maura Webber still found this to be true: "The home cook is typically interested in being entertained as well as gaining practical skills."[65]

The tendency has accelerated in recent years, as more and more cooking classes have emerged in connection with vacation travel. Hotels, resorts, and cruise lines have added demonstrations by famous chefs, tastings, and chef-led tours of food markets. In a *USA Today* article from 2010 entitled "Culinary Getaways Are Tasting Success," Kitty Bean Yancey quoted from experts on the growth of culinary vacationing for foodie men, women, and couples: "'Back in 2000, (a kitchen vacation) was a small niche market. Now it's not,' says Olivia Townsend, owner of Epiculinary Distinctive Cooking Journeys."[66]

Among the more luxurious manifestations of manual kitchen work as leisure have been patrons playing chef for a day at reputed gourmet restaurants. A 1995 article by Suzanne Oliver in *Forbes* told the story of fifty-eight-year-old Mr. Jacobson, owner of a landscaping and janitorial services company in Los Angeles, who with a friend paid $1,250 for "A Day in Patina's Kitchen." What Oliver described sounded like a cross between a cooking class and a chef's-table dining experience:

> The course began by inspecting mushrooms at the Grand Central Market at 6:30 a.m., and ended with a five-course dinner for eight. In between, Jacobson watched [the illustrious chef Joachim] Splichal and his helpers prepare food at Patina [in Los Angeles], and was even allowed to roll up bits of rabbit in thinly sliced potatoes that were then inspected closely by the sous-chef and served as a restaurant appetizer.[67]

To raise funds for a culinary scholarship, Charlie Trotter's offered patrons a similar "guest chef for a day" at $500 a head.[68] According to

Urbandaddy.com in 2010, so has RH in Los Angeles. Michelin-decorated chef Sebastian Archimbault has lent his patrons a uniform of chef whites, occupied them with chopping and braising, and then allowed them to take credit while serving their chef's-table party of ten. When publicizing the opportunity, Urbandaddy made sure to clarify that patrons needn't do the dishes afterward.[69]

Foodies' willingness to indulge in a leisure-filled dream of the chef's work devoid of its arduous, gross, and industrial aspects may seem to some a bit ironic. Especially after 2000, many gourmets have known better. Ever since Anthony Bourdain launched a multimedia career from the publication of *Kitchen Confidential: Adventures in the Culinary Underbelly* (2000), gourmets have been feasting on information about the gritty realities of professional restaurant kitchens. In the wake of Bourdain's best seller, an entire cottage industry has sprung up to satisfy the mounting appetite for a kind of virtual open kitchen that's the physical open kitchen's dark twin. The very backstage that restaurant display kitchens have concealed, these stories have thoroughly explored.

Through these sources, gourmets have learned of realities that starkly contradict the portrayal of kitchen labor in exhibition kitchens, cooking shows, and amateur cooking classes. Chief among these is the professional kitchen's industrial, assembly-line division of labor. *Cutting It Fine* (2001) most succinctly conveys the highly specialized nature of a professional kitchen "brigade":

> From the bottom up the ranks run thus: Commis, first (and sometimes second) commis, demi chef de partie, chef de partie, senior chef de partie, the relatively rare chef tournant (the kitchen's jack of all trades, an all-purpose stand in substituting for absent or holidaying chefs, and capable of working on any station, preparing everything from starters to sauce), junior sous chef, sous chef, senior sous chef, head chef and executive head chef. The size of the brigade varies with the size of the kitchen and not every rank is invariably found or required. A small kitchen is unlikely to run a first commis, a junior sous chef or an executive head chef; a large kitchen or a major hotel, where more than one kitchen is running under the same head chef, will have these

and more, with individual senior sous chefs running mini-brigades of their own.[70]

Each position in the brigade has a limited role—not much autonomy. With each increase in rank, it also shifts in emphasis from manual to conceptual labor. The *commis* tends to a multitude of repetitive manual tasks, from chopping vegetables to butchering. The *chef de partie* is head of the food preparation for a specific section of the kitchen. The *demi chef de partie*, another kitchen hand, bridges the roles of *commis* and *chef de partie*. If a kitchen is small, the sous-chef, the head chef's second in charge, is the highest-ranking line cook. If a kitchen is large, the sous-chef becomes the divider between a kitchen's manual and conceptual laborers. He or she won't do as much cooking as paperwork and other office tasks. The head chef generally does even less manual labor and has greater managerial responsibilities, including interfacing with suppliers and managing kitchen staff and operations. The head chef is also the restaurant's creative force, the writer of menus, and so gets credit for the cuisine. This basic kitchen hierarchy, called a "brigade" in tribute to its military inspiration, has been the standard in gourmet restaurants ever since Escoffier instituted it in the late nineteenth century.

No single position in the brigade fits the holistic fantasy of kitchen work as a constantly self-expressive and sensually thrilling handicraft. Most gourmets would find average manual kitchen work too punishing, and typical managerial kitchen work too similar to their own white-collar jobs to be inspirational.

On this point, *Cutting It Fine* and many other books have echoed Gary Alan Fine's groundbreaking sociological study, *Kitchens: The Culture of Restaurant Work* (originally published in 1996). From his observations and interviews with staff at four very different up-market Minnesota restaurants over 1982–83, Fine concluded that the manual labor of most "cooks" and the conceptual labor of most "chefs" both involve undesirable constraints.[71]

Cooks, he noted, typically endure tremendous daily time pressures and hot, dirty, cramped, and dangerous quarters for long hours that include weekends and holidays. In addition, because cooks are generally paid hourly, they have the added anxiety of being sent home, told to not come in to work, or asked to do more in less time should their bosses want to economize.

Chefs, Fine concluded, share the long hours and misanthropic schedules of cooks, but bear different discomfiting pressures. Chief among them is job insecurity. It's chefs whose necks are on the line in the event of budgetary, organizational, or reputational failures; and there are always fewer positions for head chefs than cooks.

Before Bourdain's *Kitchen Confidential*, books for the general reader that countered the leisure-filled fantasy of kitchen work were few and far between. The first one from the contemporary era was probably food critic Jay Jacobs's *New York à la Carte* from 1976. In the course of profiling what he considered the top Manhattan restaurants of various cuisines, he included day-in-the-life accounts of their kitchens. Le Cirque's feature was the most detailed. It gave a minute-by-minute rundown of what happened when and by whom before and during an evening's service. It wasn't until the 1993 publication of Irene Daria's *Lutèce: A Day in the Life of America's Greatest Restaurant*, however, that an entire book chronicled a great gourmet kitchen's daily routine. The next milestone of insight into professional cooking was Michael Ruhlman's *The Making of a Chef: Mastering the Heat at the Culinary Institute of America* (1997). Ruhlman chronicled the challenges he faced as a journalist going through culinary school.[72]

Since Bourdain, many kinds of restaurant-kitchen tell-all have surfaced. One type is a mutation of the cookbook—large format, gorgeously illustrated, filled with recipes—that contains a precise running narrative of a restaurant's daily work schedule. Prime examples are *Chef Daniel Boulud: Cooking in New York City* (2002); Manhattan chef Eric Ripert's chronicle of Le Bernardin, *On the Line: The Stations, the Heat, the Cooks, the Costs, the Chaos, and the Triumphs* (2008); and Ferran Adrià, Juli Soler, and Albert Adrià's *A Day at El Bulli* (2008).[73] These are distinct from the memoirs, which recount the (literal) trials by fire of becoming a chef or maintaining a great restaurant's reputation.[74]

Even the memoirs have sprouted subgenres. Some—such as Jacques Pépin's (2003), Marco Pierre White's (2008), Gabrielle Hamilton's (2011), Grant Achatz's (2011), and Marcus Samuelsson's (2012)—are by chefs. Others—including Leslie Brenner's account of Daniel Boulud's restaurant, Daniel, in *The Fourth Star* (2002) and Lisa Abend's look at El Bulli in *The Sorcerer's Apprentices* (2011)—are journalists' tales of the time they spent as flies on the kitchen walls. Still others, including Bill Buford's *Heat* (2006), are memoirs of journalists who bravely dove into grueling restaurant apprenticeships, crossed the line between amateur and professional, and lived to tell about it. Yet another type has followed Ruhlman in its focus on culinary school.[75]

By parsing a kitchen's schedule into minutes or dramatizing the cuts and burns of professional rites of passage, the many faces of kitchen-confidential literature have collectively portrayed the backstage of restaurants as unforgiving, factorylike settings where only the thick-skinned survive. Since this is the very image that restaurant display kitchens have hidden, how to reconcile foodies' embrace of both scripts?

I see them as not contradictory but complementary. Like exhibition kitchens, agonistic accounts of kitchen life have boosted the image of chefs as accomplished professionals—they even fit the classic hero mold of scarred, then wise—while preserving fans' own distance from their manual-labor trials. They work like war stories on those who weren't there. Because most readers don't personally experience what their storied heroes have braved, and since the narrators recall their time in the trenches from a life stage also removed from the daily manual grind, they can coexist with the leisure script of restaurant display kitchens.

creative-class longing

It's no accident that exhibition kitchens have appealed most to people whose experience of manual kitchen work—indeed, any manual labor—has been mainly elective and, therefore, on their own terms. The fantasy of the chef's work cultivated in these spaces should therefore be understood as motivated not by a desire to actually take up professional kitchen labor but by a longing for work that's both admired and self-determining. Display kitchens have, after all, fostered an impression of the chef's labor as both. They've reinforced the respect for chefs as professionals by giving their prowess a stage, and they've cultivated an illusion of chefs' work that conflates it with the self-directed and self-indulgent realm of leisure.

In chapter 2, I argued that the so-called creative class of conceptual workers, to which gourmets have historically belonged, has shared the often-contradictory values of professional virtuosity and freedom from rigid guidelines. The extent to which display kitchens have provided gourmets with a fantasy about these, however, suggests that for many, this sort of work hasn't been a reality. Many haven't been satisfied by their own work.

In *Shop Class as Soulcraft: An Inquiry into the Value of Work* (2009), Matthew B. Crawford locates a probable main source of dissatisfaction in what he calls "the degradation of white-collar work."[76] Citing studies spanning Barbara Garson's *The Electronic Sweatshop: How Computers Are Transforming the Office of the Future into the Factory of the Past* (1989) and Richard Sennett's *The Culture of the New Capitalism* (2006), Crawford points out what many already know from personal experience: most white-collar work hasn't lived up to creative-class dreams of recognition and self-expression. Instead, it's involved a heavy dose of self-subordination and routine. In argument with Richard Florida's claim that "creative" workers have multiplied to 30 percent of the contemporary workforce, Crawford insists that only a small percentage of this population, by definition, could possibly be empowered enough to play what most would consider a truly creative role.

Crawford's logic is sound, but as I see it, he and Florida don't have an irreconcilable difference. Crawford may be right that Florida overreaches in labeling all those involved in some aspect of idea generation or abstract problem solving "creative." Yet Florida consistently uses the term *creative* less as a judgment about individuals' work than as a description of conceptual workers' shared ethos. In the arguments of both authors, I see plenty of room for agreement over a chasm between these workers' reality and fantasy.

As testament to the pervasiveness of white-collar dissatisfaction, Crawford invokes the popularity of contemporary TV series that offer comic relief from office work. Of special note: the cartoon-based, cubicle-worker parody *Dilbert* (1999–2000) and the mockumentary *The Office* (American version, 2005–). Both have testified, through satire, to the doldrums, superficial camaraderie, and existential pointlessness of many office jobs. To Crawford's list of social mirrors, I would add the film *Office Space* (1999). This story of rebellion by fed-up office drones at "Initech" sends up every recent cliché of phony collegiality and corporate team building.

About team building as a form of individuality suppression, Crawford also has much to say. He traces it from its birth in the corporate culture of the 1970s to its more recent expressions, including Linda Eve Diamond and Harriet Diamond's popular book *Teambuilding That Gets Results: Essential Plans and Activities for Creative and Effective Teams* (2007). Through company-retreat exercises and management techniques, organizations, he argues, have regularly coaxed coworkers into conformity.

The deindividualizing side of white-collar work that Crawford emphasizes suggests a tension within creative-class culture. That culture's exaltation of uniqueness and rule breaking, which I discussed in chapter 2, has all along met with organizations' countervailing stress on esprit de corps. For every leadership guru's rallying cry to "break the rules," there's been a *Teambuilding That Gets Results* to muffle it.

But, what of the super-elites of the creative class? Could their likes have found open-kitchen dining appealing? After all, by contrast to the majority, they've been able to fulfill their dreams of professional innovation and recognition. The Oprah Winfreys and Nathan Myhrvolds—just like the Wolfgang Pucks and José Andreses—have come the closest anyone can to the nirvana of being celebrated for their accomplishments and being able to work on their own terms so that work and play really do become one. I see no reason why they, too, wouldn't have found the ideal of chef's work conjured by exhibition kitchens attractive—albeit from the perspective of having attained its equivalent.

It's beyond my reach here to say whether all people need self-determining work or professional admiration to be happy, or whether that's a myth perpetuated by the creative class. What's relevant here is that few have enjoyed the privilege of professional renown and the "creative lifestyle" suggested by display kitchens. That's why they've made such attractive status symbols.

4 gourmet plays on common food faves

The omnivorous turn in cuisine is a story of puzzling contradictions.

On the one hand, numerous chefs since the 1970s have paid tribute to "slow food." In the spirit of what officially became the Slow Food movement, founded in the late 1980s in protest against the opening of a McDonald's in Rome, these chefs have honored indigenous traditionalism. They've borrowed from the culinary heritage of regional home cooks and the small-business preserves of ethnicity: the likes of French bistros, American diners and bar-and-grills, Italian trattorias, Spanish tapas bars, British pubs, Asian noodle cafés, a global array of street vendors.

Meanwhile, and without controversy, some of the same chefs and many others have saluted the opposition: not "slow food" but "fast food." They've adapted franchise favorites, such as hamburgers and hotdogs, and supermarket standards, from mac-and-cheese to chicken potpie. "Fast foods" aren't simply the products of quick-serve chains. More broadly, I define them as foods that modern technology, mass production, corporate expansion, and mass mediation have allowed to transcend their regional and ethnic roots. They're emblems of modernization and cultural homogenization.

Even some of the foods adapted by chefs have straddled the fast-slow divide. For instance, unlike the hamburger—whose definitive form as a ground-beef patty in a bun took shape primarily in the fast-food industry and remains its preeminent symbol—pizza has come to signify fast or slow food.[1] Which one depends on chefs' inclusion of telltale signs.

For a witty ode to pepperoni pizza served in 2003 at the Evanston, Illinois, restaurant Trio, chef Grant Achatz left the symbolism open. His mix of spice powders and melted mozzarella on a stamp-sized piece of potato-starch paper, presented on the head of a pin as part a tasting menu, evoked the Italian American classic only generically.[2] For Trio diners, the flavors could have brought to mind the "fast" pizza of big business—increasingly likely since the late-1950s advent of pizza chains and frozen brands—or, just as easily, the quaint mom-and-pop pizzeria, a "slow" symbol—perpetuated in film, song, and on many a street corner—of Italian-immigrant culture.[3]

By contrast, chef Wylie Dufresne's "Pizza Pebbles" (fig. 11), on the menu at Manhattan's WD-50 in 2007, clearly referred to fast food. Dufresne has even publicly specified that this dish—a row of crumbly golden spheres nestled in a pepperoni emulsion and garnished with mushroom "chips"—took its cue from the pizza-flavored-pretzel snack trademarked as Pizza Combos.[4]

Still other versions of pizza have recalled the "slow" food of Naples. Gourmet-pizza pioneers, such as Spago in Hollywood, and many more recent representatives, including A16 in San Francisco, have followed the Neapolitan method of blistering single-person pies in a wood-burning brick oven.

And yet, despite openness to fast and slow sources, chefs and, by extension, foodies have all along resisted full identification with either fount of the common. Through the ranking systems of reviewing, awards, and pricing, they've collectively conferred greater status on gourmet cuisine. Moreover, chefs have done a lot to distinguish their dishes and menus from their sources.

Consider the extent of one recent spin on a famous fast food. "BURGER with cheese," launched in 2009 by pastry chef Ben Roche at Chicago's Moto restaurant (2004–), refers specifically to the McDonald's

11. Chef Wylie Dufresne's fully plated dish, "Pizza Pebbles, Pepperoni, Shitake," initiated 2007 at WD-50 restaurant, New York City. Photo by Takahiko Marumoto.

icon (fig. 12). It features a thin patty, a slice of processed cheddar, ketchup, mustard, lettuce, and a sesame-seed bun.

But nothing else matches the McDonald's model, and even the aforementioned parts aren't what they seem. First, as in all Moto dishes, as many ingredients as possible come from local organic farms.[5] Second, the version I had as part of a twenty-course tasting menu in February 2010 was the size of a *petit four* and turned out to be a dessert. The

12. "BURGER with cheese," from Moto restaurant (Chicago) by Ben Roche, former pastry chef and director of research and development. Photo courtesy of www.kevineats.com.

"bun" was peanut macaroon with sesame seed. The "patty" consisted of milk chocolate "ground beef" bound by milk chocolate ganache. The "cheese" derived from roasted-banana puree with lemon juice, water, and the gelling agent carrageenan—heated, cooled, and cut into squares. The "ketchup" was maraschino-cherry puree; the "mustard," thickened pineapple puree. Ironically, for "lettuce," Roche used actual iceberg lettuce.[6]

In my correspondence with Roche about BURGER with cheese, the chef seemed particularly fond of this detail. He told me that the iceberg's natural crunch and nutty flavor works well in a dessert and makes the burger more believable.[7] I couldn't agree more.

Yet, however good the illusion, would anyone really mistake Moto's BURGER with cheese for the fast-food familiar? No more than one would confuse an Andy Warhol silk screen of Campbell's soup cans with Campbell's soup.

Although nothing like Moto in style or cultural inspiration, chef Mario Batali's Babbo (1998–) in New York City's Greenwich Village has been the site of equal poetic license. Throughout *The Babbo Cookbook* (2002), a summation of the restaurant's style and ethos, Batali emphasizes love of invention as well as tradition. His introduction is explicit:

> Many people ask me what type of Italian food we serve at Babbo, and I have no pat answer. While there are certainly a few dishes on the menu that are faithful renditions of beloved regional dishes, like braised short ribs (*brasato al Barolo*), most of them are nothing you would find in an Italian trattoria or home. Yet they feel and taste like dishes you might eat in Italy.[8]

"Mint Love Letters," on Babbo's menu "since day one," is a case in point. The rustic pile of ravioli with a braised-meat *ragù* sticks closely to Italian idiom. Yet the idea to import Moroccan touches of mint and merguez sausage is all Batali.[9]

The composition of Babbo's menu has also been a mix of custom and deviation. Items traditionally separated have been pronounced neighbors. Per Batali:

> What I love about good desserts in Italy is how they are always appropriate to their surroundings. In a fancy ristorante I may be served an exquisite panna cotta scented with a hint of seasonal citrus; a casual trattoria may offer the traditional *sbrisolona*, or crumbly cake, with a glass of local dessert wine. Both are on the menu at Babbo.[10]

This *haute*-casual combination has indeed been a fixture at Babbo. When I dined there in June 2008, my party ordered both desserts, and, checking Babbo's website three years later, I found them still on the menu.

From my photos of the meal I also noticed that Batali had managed to coordinate the otherwise incompatible desserts by dressing up the normally rustic cake. It came to the table tailored, formed in a precise circle, and attended by an elegant *gelato* quenelle. So it looked of a piece with the round mold of *panna cotta* and its *sorbetto* quenelle.

Such discrepancies between common-food inspiration and gourmet interpretation and the gourmet world's embrace of symbolic opposites have made me wonder: How have chefs and foodies mitigated the contradiction of celebrating fast and slow food? What's prompted their omnivorous attitude? Furthermore, what values have chefs transmitted through their gourmet transformations, and how do these values relate to their endorsements of the humble or commonplace?

"comfort food"

Whatever resolution gourmets have sought to the fast-versus-slow conflict has manifested itself in talk of "comfort food." The proliferation of this term in food media, everything from restaurant-review columns to cookbook titles, has generally paralleled the trend of leading chefs adapting common foods. Often, it's been used to describe their dishes.

The term entered gourmet parlance in 1978, with *Bon Appétit's* cover story "Exclusive: M. F. K. Fisher on Comfort Foods."[11] There the esteemed food writer applied the label to foods she considered soothing when dining alone. In 1985, journalists began to use it more frequently. Marian Burros led the way in "Turning to Food for Solace," a *New York Times* column discussing a restaurateur's fondness for the calming foods of his childhood. Through the end of the decade, critics often attached the term to revivals of robust, old-fashioned recipes by trendsetting chefs of the New American persuasion. At An American Place in Manhattan, acclaimed chef Larry Forgione reportedly made a chocolate layer cake from his own grandmother's recipe. In this spirit, critics repeatedly invoked *home* and *mom* along with *comfort food* to suggest reassurance and nostalgia.[12]

After this, the phrase continued to spread, and the meaning stuck.[13] In 1997, the *Oxford English Dictionary* and *Merriam-Webster's Collegiate Dictionary* both added the entry *comfort food* and defined it in terms of solace, traditionalism, familiarity, the familial, and childhood nostalgia. Even comfort-food-trend detractors, such as *New York Times* critic William Grimes, who ranted in 2001 against gourmets' "regressive" embrace of childhood, agreed on the term's definition.[14]

This minority was also helpless to stop it. Incredibly, the first decade of the 2000s witnessed still so much more comfort-food chatter that the 2011 *Encyclopedia of Food & Culture* could legitimately claim, "Comfort food is an increasingly prominent concept in the twenty-first century."[15]

Apart from its escalating use, the most striking feature of *comfort food* has been its elasticity. The term's inclusion in cookbook titles, a consequence of the growing influence of gourmet media, makes this most obvious. Most cookbooks with *comfort food* in the title have been what I consider universalizing. They focus on massified foods—the Americana of fried chicken, meatloaf, mashed potatoes, potpies, burgers, apple pies, and so on.

A classic of this type is Jane and Michael Stern's *Square Meals*—first published in 1985 without *comfort food* in the title and reissued in 2001 as *Square Meals: America's Favorite Comfort Food Cookbook*.[16] It covers every phase of American culinary history that TV has ever enshrined, and represents its greatest hits: classics of the American South, such as pulled pork; the road food of burgers and shakes; and the 1950s' and 1960s' packaged-food cuisine of Jell-O concoctions and eight-can casseroles.

Some titles in the Americana category—including *Comfort Foods: America's Favorite Foods Cooked the Way You like Them* (1996) and *All-American Comfort Food: Recipes for the Great Tasting Food Everyone Loves* (1997)—project certainty that their dishes have universal appeal. Many others invoke grandmas or moms—for instance, *Comfort Food: Home-style Recipes for Feel-Good Foods Like Mom Used to Make* (2008)—as if readers share a family.[17]

The universal mother in question, of course, is pop culture. At least such titles as *The Route 66 Cookbook: Comfort Food from the Mother Road* (2000) and *Mother's Best: Comfort Food That Takes You Home Again: 150 Favorites from Mother's Bistro & Bar* (2009) admit that the mothers they refer to are commercial entities.[18]

Although massified Americana has been the genre's most common theme, comfort-food cookbooks have recently become remarkably wide ranging. Every ethnicity has entered the arena. *Italian Comfort Food* (2002) and *Hip Asian Comfort Food* (2009) have arrived. A sign of the times in 2011, *Saveur* published the all-encompassing *The New Comfort Food: Home Cooking from Around the World*.[19]

Now, no diet has been excluded. Weight watchers and the nutrition minded can consult *The Low-Carb Comfort Food Cookbook* (2003) and *Comfort Foods Made Healthy* (2009). Alternative dieters can open *The Gluten-Free Gourmet Cooks Comfort Foods* (2004) or *Vegan Diner: Classic Comfort Food for the Body & Soul* (2011).[20]

The broader import of this inclusivity becomes clear in light of similar developments, prior and ongoing, in fine dining. Since the 1970s, top chefs in America—some taking up comfort foods, some not—have been variously widening the once culturally narrow space of *haute cuisine*.

New American cuisine is an early example of the tendency. The trend unfolded as a series of ethnic and regional infusions, spanning colonial New England, Creole and Cajun Louisiana, and the birth of a "California cuisine."

Even this already multicultural movement eventually absorbed idioms it had initially overlooked. In a famous case, Texas restaurant consultant Anne Lindsay Greer had been so ruffled by the food media's lack of attention to her state that in 1983 she gathered together several up-and-coming local chefs expressly to define the elements of a sophisticated Tex-Mex style. Henceforth, she and chefs Dean Fearing, Stephan Pyles, Avner Samuel, and Robert Del Grande succeeded in bringing "Southwestern cuisine" into the New American fold.[21]

Similarly, over the past few decades, many world cuisines have stormed the temples of high gastronomy. Some chefs have made their mark as passionate advocates for one specific region, as Lidia Bastianich has been for Italy and Rick Bayless for Mexico. The vast majority, however, have taken an eclectic approach, borrowing from multiple countries or continents.

Wolfgang Puck was a pioneer of fusion cuisine before it was called that. Notoriously, at Spago in 1982, he introduced a pizza topped with smoked salmon, dill cream, and caviar; and as early as 1983, Puck opened the Chinese- and French-inspired Chinois on Main restaurant in Santa Monica, California.[22]

Countless chefs followed suit, turning combinations of world cuisines into personal trademarks. In the late 1980s, Norman Van Aken put the term *fusion* into circulation, and codified his own mix of Latin, Caribbean, Asian, American, and African food as "New World Cuisine."[23] Since then, innumerable East-meets-West amalgams have arisen as the likes of Gray Kunz and Jean-George Vongerichten merged Southeast Asia and France, Ming Tsai developed the Chinese-French connection, and Japanese cuisine bonded with everything imaginable: American ingredients in the hands of Charlie Trotter, Peruvian tradition under Nobu Matsuhisa, Swedish cuisine in the kitchen of Marcus Samuelsson. Eclectic new stars of the twenty-first century, such as David Chang and Roy Choi, have avoided the term *fusion*, a victim of overuse; but they and the many who've since claimed the mantle of "best new chef" have continued to find new frontiers for the same cultural hybridizing.

Likewise, borrowings from vegetarian and vegan cooking have expanded fine dining's horizons. At Saison in San Francisco, on trend when I ate there in September 2010, only one of my eleven courses featured any part of a mammal.

Speaking generally of the concept of *comfort food* in 2000 in "Letter from the Editor: Chewing on the Comfort Question," *Bon Appétit*'s William Garry wisely insisted on its culturally limitless nature. No particular food defines it, he claimed; only associations of reassurance, familiarity, and conviviality.[24]

I would go further. By continually asserting the family resemblance of fast and slow foods, and of common foods from any background, comfort-food parlance has promoted cultural consensus and openness to diversity at the same time. The term's usage has implied that *the melting pot* and *the multiculture,* concepts arguably incommensurable, are compatible. The metacultural appreciation of the familial implied by *comfort food* has blanketed over the difference.

metaculturalism

Why has this metacultural ethos become especially attractive in recent decades? The generic celebration of familial good feeling may have surfaced and sustained itself in part as a palliative against the stress of growing cultural differences.

For instance, ethnic diversity in the United States has increased dramatically in recent times. Although the number of new permanent residents has grown every decade since the 1930s—from an immigration low point of just over half a million to upwards of 10 million in 2010—immigration has surged since the 1980s. By 2004, 53 percent of the foreign-born population in the United States consisted of those who'd arrived since 1990. As of 2009, nearly one-third had immigrated since 2000. Also, recent increases in immigration have accounted for a significant proportion of overall American population growth. In the 1980s, it was already one-third. Furthermore, the ethnic mix has become more varied. During the previous great wave of immigration, in the early twentieth century, 90 percent of newcomers were European. By the 1980s, the tide had shifted to 80 percent Asian and Latin American. In 2009, 53 percent had come from Latin American countries, 28 percent from Asian, and only 13 percent from European.[25]

We could argue that tensions are inherent in the process of ethnic diversification. In *Consumption, Food & Taste* (1997), sociologist Alan Warde proposes that modern society's tendency to uproot people from traditional cultural contexts produces an "ambivalent" desire for the incompatible states of individual freedom and collective security. People become torn between the stimulation and liberation of new experiences, lifestyles, and nationalities and the anxiety of losing the reassurances of their native cultures' constancy and communal reinforcement of preferences. Warde argues that they often attempt to resolve this tension by recreating a sense of shared norms. I'm partial to Warde's theory, because it precisely describes the cultural context and usage of the term *comfort food*.[26]

I would argue as well that the "ambivalence of modernity" Warde delineates is likely to have become accentuated in recent decades, as American society has grown more culturally and politically fractured. I'm referring to the impact of cultural conflicts that arose in the 1950s and 1960s and had by the 1980s hardened into battle lines of institutional identity politics and "culture wars."

Contemporaneous writers acknowledged and weighed in on the growing dissents. Arthur M. Schlesinger Jr.'s *The Disuniting of America* (1998; originally published 1991) and Robert Hughes's *The Culture of Complaint* (1993) are significant not only for the evidence they present of cultural and political division but also for the proof their own impassioned prose gives of its intensity by the early 1990s. Both authors lauded the recent empowerment of formerly silenced minorities and women by civil rights and liberation movements, but found that the extent of cultural balkanization which had since emerged threatened societal cohesion.

Each author lamented the loss of the American ideal of *e pluribus unum* in a different arena. Schlesinger viewed public education as the culture war's frontline. He critiqued what he saw as the extreme ethnocentricity of the various pressure groups that had succeeded in implementing separate Spanish- and English-language education and Afrocentric curricula.[27] Hughes bemoaned the polarization of "politically correct" academics on the Left, for whom ethnocentricity was sacrosanct, and "patriotically correct" politicians on the Right, who viewed America as a Judeo-Christian monoculture. He illustrated the cultural stalemate with stories of fresh battles over sharply divisive issues and sensational symbols, such as the National Endowment for the Arts funding of the work of Andres Serrano, Robert Mapplethorpe, and other controversial contemporary artists.[28]

As conflicts over ethnic and lifestyle differences widened the cultural fault lines, some—like Schlesinger and Hughes, in fact—took a metacultural position, embracing cultural pluralism while also advocating the search for common ground. As a contemporaneous and analogous phenomenon, comfort-food parlance has most likely served a conciliatory purpose.

However, the likelihood of adopting such a metacultural stance in cultural or political matters hasn't been equally distributed. Those who've done so, therefore, have actually been expressing a niche affiliation.

In recent decades, a person's response to cultural diversity has depended on variables of income, education, and geography. According to Bill Bishop and Robert Cushing in their study of divisions in the American polity, *The Big Sort* (2008), the period of the 1950s through the mid-1970s was one of growing demographic evenness throughout the country. But starting in the mid-1970s, the more educated and high-income folks began voluntarily clustering in urban areas with greater cultural diversity, and the clustering trend subsequently compounded itself. Although education levels rose throughout the nation, the percentage differentials among areas widened. By 2000, there were sixty-two municipalities in which less than 17 percent of all adults had finished college and thirty-two in which more than 34 percent had. Variations among twenty-five- to thirty-four-year-olds were even more dramatic.[29]

Those choosing to live in culturally diverse urban areas have also been more likely to espouse tolerance of racial, ethnic, and lifestyle differences. They've tended to vote Democratic, aligning with the political party most linked with this value rhetorically. Demographic trends bear this out. In 1970, the nation's white population was spread evenly throughout areas of varying political affiliation. Over the next thirty years, however, whites concentrated in Republican areas. In 2000, only 18 percent of the nation's white population lived in Democratic landslide counties, whereas 30 percent lived in areas that were majority Republican. At the same time, only 5 percent of the nation's foreign-born resided in overwhelmingly Republican counties, while 21 percent of them lived where Democrats turned out a crushing victory at election time. Even gerrymandered congressional redistricting, a factor in the appearance of increasing political polarization, can't by itself have imposed such a strong and widespread pattern of differentiation.[30]

Data Richard Florida gathered over the 1990s for *The Rise of the Creative Class* (2002) and *Cities and the Creative Class* (2005) confirm and enrich these findings. In one study, Florida found a strong correlation between areas' concentrations of the relatively affluent and educated "creative class"—measured in this case as the ratio of an area's patents per capita in high-tech industries to the nation's—and their cultural diversity in terms of percentages of foreign-born residents, gays, and artists.[31] Although Florida defines the creative class more narrowly in this study than he does elsewhere, when combined with Bishop and Cushing's results, his data support the point that relatively affluent and educated urbanites have disproportionately valued cultural diversity since the 1970s.

As a result, I would claim that the ability to appreciate cultural pluralism has also become a badge of urban-elite status. Since gourmets have tended to fit this demographic profile, their promotion of metacultural culinary values may be seen in part as a display of that status.

Yet through their culinary preferences, chefs and foodies have distinguished themselves further. After all, in spite of welcoming fast and slow, any and all, cultural traditions into the fold of gourmet dining, their commitment to common culture has been only partial. To understand gourmets' idea of sophisticated taste, therefore, it's essential to explore how chefs have altered their sources.

making it deluxe

While in Manhattan for research, I sampled as many relevant restaurants as I could. Ordering a "DB Burger" at chef Daniel Boulud's DB Bistro Moderne (2001–) was on my shortlist. The dish had started what Josh Ozersky, in *The Hamburger: A History* (2008), calls the "Haute Burger Skirmish"—a highly publicized episode of one New York restaurant after another vying to claim the most luxurious hamburger.[32]

The *haute* burger epitomizes what I call the deluxe approach to gourmandizing common foods. Its main feature: the addition of costly ingredients.

For the DB Burger, which Boulud says he invented on a lark as proof that a French chef could outdo Americans at their own hamburger game, he made a tall burger of ground sirloin, stuffed it with red-wine-braised short-rib meat, and stuffed that with *foie gras* and truffles. Extra pomp—perhaps also camp—came with the presentation. Just as I'd imagined from the lurid photos of food blogs, the burger arrived at my table with condiments in ramekins on a separate dish, and stood trophy-like on a plate next to a doily-mounted silver julep cup overflowing with French fries (fig. 13). In 2003, the demand for this $29 burger inspired nearby Old Homestead Steakhouse to introduce a $41 Kobe-beef burger, which led Boulud to counter with the "DB Burger Royale," featuring three layers of Périgord truffles, for $50. On it went as other restaurants joined in.[33]

The burger has been a favorite, but it's far from being the only commonplace food that chefs have made deluxe. An example just as sensationalized as the DB Burger, in fact, but whose heyday in Manhattan I unfortunately missed, was the mac-and-cheese John Delucie put on the Waverly Inn menu soon after becoming head chef in 2006. It remained the restaurant's trademark and a subject of press amazement until Delucie left in 2010. Why the fuss? A heart-stopping heap of shaved white

13. "DB Burger" at DB Bistro Moderne, New York City, 2010. Photo by author.

truffles and the dish's initial base price of $55. Delucie qualifies this figure in his memoir *The Hunger* (2009) as "give or take a hundred for market fluctuations."[34] The ante has certainly been upped since 1988, when at San Francisco's supper club Bix, chef Cindy Pawlcyn, in an early deluxe move, spiked her mac-and-cheese with lobster.[35]

making it pure

Given the stunning price tags sometimes associated with it, it's easy to see why the deluxe approach has gotten the attention it has. Yet it's not the dominant style of gourmandizing humble foods. More pervasive has been a sort of material and ethical purification of them. What I call the pure style has emphasized expressions of unadulterated nature and the chef's true self.

To glorify the naturalness of their ingredients, chefs working in the purist style have made them seem relatively unrefined. They've maintained enough of the original structure of featured plants or animals for ready identification. They've then presented ingredients in loose, uncontrived arrangements. In some cases, they've offered dishes family style, on platters or in cooking vessels—likewise indicating minimal interference in the transfer of earthly bounty from chef to diner. When it comes to cooking methods, purists have emphasized the time-honored—roasting, braising, grilling—thereby stoking primitivistic ideals of hearth and fire.

When I traveled to the Bay Area, I visited the purist Zuni Café in San Francisco, where chef Judy Rodgers has run the kitchen to great acclaim since 1987. By the time it had won the James Beard Foundation award for Restaurant of the Year in 2003, Zuni had become especially famous for one dish that I believe epitomizes the pure style. So I made sure to order the "Chicken for Two Roasted in the Brick Oven; Warm Bread Salad with Scallions, Dried Currants, Red Mustard Greens, and Pine Nuts."

The bird was served almost directly from the wood-burning oven, simply cut into legs, thighs, and breasts and dressed with the leafy bread salad. The rustic toss of bone-in chicken with rough-torn salad on a simple white plate gave the impression that nature and embers had done most of the work.

Pure cuisine often intimates this effect. But the look of straightforwardness can be deceptive. There are hidden reasons why Zuni's roasted chicken may be the tastiest one could ever eat. *The Zuni Café Cookbook* (2002) reveals them. To prepare the dish, one must follow four full unillustrated pages of steps. Not only is the process lengthy; for best results, one needs uncommon tools. And before any actual cooking, one must salt the bird for one to three days; moreover, while Rodgers tries to convince readers they can reproduce the dish in their home ovens, even she has to admit they won't be imparting the distinctive "smoky flavor" contributed by Zuni's singular brick behemoth.[36] Only the appearance of pure cuisine need be simple and spontaneous.

Even so, there's been a range in chefs' expressions of connection to nature. Some have invoked back-to-nature ideals in a dish's service trappings, its situation within a menu, or its environment. I experienced all three while eating the "Chargrilled Lamb Burger with Feta,

Cumin Mayo & Thrice Cooked Chips" at Manhattan chef April Bloom-field's the Breslin. This has been a popular item on the menu since the place opened in 2009.[37]

To set the scene: Bloomfield has been well known for her insistence on ingredients uncorrupted by modern industry. She sources from small farms with freely roaming livestock. Whenever possible, she buys local and seasonal products. A *New Yorker* feature on the chef spent several telling paragraphs following her search for a pig farm to meet her discerning standards.[38] Pat La Frieda, boutique purveyor of top-quality, humanely raised meat to many of New York's best restaurants, was saying a lot to a reporter for *New York* magazine in 2010 when he named Bloomfield his most demanding customer.[39] Bloomfield herself said even more when, for the Breslin's opening, she invited British chef Fergus Henderson to cook alongside her. Henderson is a leader in the "nose-to-tail" trend that's gripped many a purist. His book, *The Whole Beast: Nose to Nail Eating* (2004), is a bible for those who want to restore the preindustrial practice of using all edible parts of an animal.[40]

Who would think midtown Manhattan an ideal place for transport-ing me back to nature? But the chef had managed exactly that by en-veloping my lamb burger in layers of aesthetically effective context. As I ate at the Breslin, I was literally surrounded by nose-to-tail remind-ers. The couple to my left ordered a house specialty of stuffed pig's foot (for two)—a colossus of calf and hoof—and to my right stood the large, oval dining table reserved for whole-suckling-pig dinners. What's more, a section of the menu was devoted to house-made ter-rines, delectable deposits for the sundry parts of an animal.

The presentation of my lamb burger was a form of pastoral poetry. The weighty thing wasn't penned in, on a rimmed plate, but unbound, on a flat carving plank, like the free-roaming animal it came from. The choice of wood was significant. A minimally processed material, it re-tains its link to nature. The "thrice cooked chips" echoed the bucolic theme. They were thick, oak-colored, roughhewn, and piled loosely into a squat, parchment-lined, miniature metal pail. Glistening by the table's lantern, the little bucket conjured visions of old farm tools near wheelbarrows and creeks in Romantic English landscape paintings.

For conveying Romantic naturalism, other chefs have preferred a more reductive aesthetic. This reached its apogee at chef Tom Colic-

chio's Craft (New York City, 2000–). The restaurant's culinary minimalism was sufficiently impressive that in 2002 it received a James
Beard Foundation award for Best New Restaurant. In 2010, after Craft
had multiplied across the country, Colicchio was recognized again by
the JBF with an Outstanding Chef award. Needless to say, on my tour
of pure cuisine, the original Craft was a necessary stop.

Every aspect of a dish's presentation there highlighted the quality
of individual ingredients and suggested artistic restraint. There was
an emphasis on singular cooking methods. The roasted suckling pig,
to share, arrived in a roasting pan to assert its having been roasted.
Beyond that, the animal appeared little handled. Parts had been cut
and separated just enough to distinguish sections of the animal, thus
keeping my focus on nature. The side dishes likewise starred a single
ingredient. The heirloom tomato salad, for instance, consisted of only
tomatoes in a light, colorless vinaigrette. Served on a plain white plate,
the beauty of the dish followed from the extraordinary quality of the
tomatoes and their selection in a range of naturally occurring sizes,
contours, and colors.

Colicchio's insistence that individual ingredients be the focus
was also hardwired into the modularity of Craft's menu. Diners had
to build a meal from ingredients *à la carte*. The menu I kept divided
ingredients by cooking method—"raw," "cured/marinated," "roasted,"
"braised," "sautéed." This preparation can be isolated only if a dish requires only one type, or if the restaurant wants to feature only one to
give the appearance of simplicity. The descriptions of dishes—"Island
Creek oyster," "octopus," "quail," "monkfish," "beef short rib," "swiss
chard"—were similarly brief.

As if to justify the cost of minimal handling, the entire left-hand
column of the menu yielded to the names of twenty-two different
boutique farms from which the ingredients derived. While the kitchen
did little to them, the amount of space used for naming the farms suggested considerable effort went into finding the best.

I found this list of farmers noteworthy also because it exemplifies
one of the pure style's long-standing attributes. Starting in the mid-
1970s, purist chefs revolutionized the language of menus by consistently identifying ingredients and their provenance.

Prior to that, most leading restaurants in America tended to describe dishes by theme. For example, a 1955 menu from Manhattan's the Colony listed the following items under "Poissons": "La Sole Anglaise Bonne Femme," "Les Goujionettes de Flounder Mural," "Homard a l'Americaine," "Les Grenouilles Provençale," "Pompana Sauté Florida," and "Saumon Froid Parisienne [sic]." Theme names were just as pervasive on a menu from New York City's Le Périgord from fourteen years later. Under "Entrées," one reads such titles as "Grenouilles Provençale," "Sole au plat Isabelle," and "Entrecôte Marchand de Vin." Note the similar phrasing on a menu from that city's Le Pavillon a year after that: under "Poissons," for instance, "Grenouille Provençale" and "Sole Anglaise." Even Manhattan's exceptional the Four Seasons, which had an ingredient-based menu language way before its time, caved to custom in the listing of some Continental offerings, as in "Farmhouse Duckling au Poivre" and "Beef Stroganoff."[41]

When not by a theme, a dish might have been described by a cooking method, as in the case of "Broiled Baby Lobster Tails" on a menu of the famous Los Angeles restaurant Romanoff's from the 1960s. Yet even Romanoff's minded the usual terminology for other entries—for example, "Louisiana Frogs Legs Provençale" and "Casserole of Lobster and Shrimps Newburg."[42]

On the rare occasion that a top American restaurant mentioned an ingredient's origins, it was usually to boast of its distant importation. Hence the luxurious connotation of the Romanoff's "Broiled Imported English Sole."[43]

In 1976, however, menu language, like other means of signaling status, underwent a sea change. Jeremiah Tower's "Northern California Regional Dinner" menu of October 7, 1976, at Chez Panisse, Berkeley, California, is widely acknowledged as the turning point.[44] With descriptions such as "Big Sur Garrapata Creek Smoked Trout Steamed over California Bay Leaves" and "Walnuts, Almonds, and Mountain Pears from the San Francisco Farmer's Market," Tower introduced what have since become pervasive features of gourmet menu writing: describing dishes by constituent ingredients, naming ingredients' places of origin, and emphasizing local sources.

Tower had a combination of motives. The emphasis on regional products enabled him to distinguish his cuisine from those of chefs elsewhere—a clue to the growing tendency of chefs to assert individual styles—to advertise his standards of freshness and, to some extent, to signal good stewardship of the earth. Chez Panisse's Northern California Regional Dinner occurred just as farmers' markets were springing up across the nation, and arguably wouldn't have been possible without them. These, in turn, were an outgrowth of a late 1960s and early 1970s anti-industrial, anticorporate, environmentalist counterculture that espoused organic farming and alternative food-distribution systems.[45]

In the mid-1970s, these causes were just emerging as a priority at Chez Panisse, and most of all for Alice Waters. As she grew more committed to environmentalism, the cause increasingly came to define her and Chez Panisse. In parallel, the organic and local-sourcing movements became a growing part of gourmet culture at large. It's mainly in the aesthetics of culinary purism, however, that eco-friendliness has found emphatic expression.

Purist chefs have shown their strengthening commitment to ecological correctness by escalating rhetoric on menus and in other public statements. Already by 1980, the concrete style of menu writing initiated by Tower began to acquire some eco-poetic quirks. Chefs introduced evocative adjectives to describe the special cultivation of their ingredients. The term *free-range* arose to signify livestock allowed to roam pasture unconstrained, eating a varied and natural diet. It set animals apart from the ubiquitous products of modern industrial farms, living in confinement and eating a restricted and processed diet.

David Kamp, in *The United States of Arugula* (2006), traces the expression to chef Larry Forgione, an East Coast trailblazer concurrent with Waters in gourmet local sourcing. In 1980, after searching for a term to do justice to the high-quality, humanely raised birds he got from farmer Paul Kaiser, Forgione finally decided on "free-range chicken."[46]

The phrase caught on right away. I personally remember a "Sauteed Free Range [*sic*] Beef" listed on a menu I saved from a visit to the acclaimed Campton Place in San Francisco while Bradley Ogden was head chef (1983–89). Decades later, I find the phrase pervasive. While in Manhattan in 2010, I noted the "Free-Range Caramelized Quail . . ." at L'Atelier de Joël Robuchon, and the "Pasture Raised Chicken . . ." at Gramercy Tavern. In July 2011 in Los Angeles, I had a "Free-Range

Half Roasted Chicken . . ." at chef David Meyers's modern bistro Comme Ça.[47]

Free-range is one of several phrases to proliferate since 1980 that evoke small-scale, premodern sourcing. *Day-boat*, as in scallops, *line-caught*, as in fish, and *market*, as in vegetables or fruits are some of the others.

In the 1990s and 2000s, new themes of pastoral rhetoric surfaced—if not always on menus, then on websites or other forms of publicity. Restaurants, after all, were taking their intimacy with food sources increasingly seriously. Some distinguished themselves by growing their own food. This wasn't entirely new. Greens at Fort Mason in San Francisco, founded by Chez Panisse alum chef Deborah Madison in 1979, had its own Green Gulch Farm and named it on menus. A "Salad of Green Gulch Lettuces" on a 1980s menu attests to this.[48]

By the end of the 1990s, however, greater numbers of chefs were touting their role as chef-gardeners. An article from 1998 features examples as dispersed as Thomas Keller at the French Laundry in California's Napa Valley—admittedly an area no stranger to gourmet restaurants with gardens since the early 1980s—Craig Shelton at the Ryland Inn in Whitehouse Station, New Jersey, and Greg and Mary Sonnier at Gabrielle in New Orleans.[49]

Other restaurateurs stepped up the communication of farm-to-table connections by hosting special meet-the-farmers dinners. As in so many other trends, Chez Panisse was a leader in this. Waters celebrated the restaurant's twentieth birthday in 1991 with a block party honoring its suppliers.[50] In 2007, the *Nation's Restaurant News* heralded such events as part of a booming national trend.[51]

In the 2000s, various establishments began advertising their nose-to-tail ethics. While April Bloomfield was spreading word of whole-suckling-pig dinners on the Breslin's website, chef Chris Cosentino of San Francisco's Incanto (under Cosentino, 2002–) was telling a *Food & Wine* reporter of his personal involvement in the raising and slaughter of his animals: "My pigs all have names; I've raised some from birth. You need to look your animal in the eye before you put it on the plate."[52] The menu I kept from Incanto in August 2010 reflected his nose-to-tail commitment by offering "Leg of Beast, Ham in Hay, or Whole Pig Dining."[53]

The restaurant's website placed a strong rhetorical frame around these specialties. In a mission statement that voiced Incanto's support of sustainable harvesting and local farmers, its alliance with several environmentalist organizations, and its practice of growing herbs on the roof, the site explained: "Our menu . . . almost always includes one or two dishes featuring 'odd cuts' and offal because serving these parts of the animal honors the whole animal and helps preserve an important, yet increasingly overlooked, part of our culinary heritage."[54]

As full-throated as this rhetoric may sound, it isn't the most extreme I've encountered. That honor goes to Jean-Georges Vongerichten's ABC Kitchen in New York City.[55] Any more elaborate an exegesis of "local," "organic," and "cruelty-free" sourcing on my menu from August 2010 would have been self-parody.

Picture three roughly legal-length pages covered in small print. The two pages of actual menu adhered to the provenance-name-dropping style initiated in 1976. The striking part was the inclusion of a third page—not a menu at all but a sort of manifesto. The sole purpose of its text—tellingly, even more crowded than that on either menu page—was to declare the restaurant's standards and commitments concerning purveyors, and to explain their specific applications. Detailed were not only the ecologically correct origins of the restaurant's food and drink items but also its dinnerware, breadbaskets, candles, cleaning products, building materials, and artwork. The text further allayed any anxiety about the menu itself: "printed on FSC certified 100% post-consumer fiber. no new trees are used. neutral pH and chlorine free."

Still not finished, the same page bore exhaustive lists of every farm and its location for each item category. For the edibles alone, there were separate lists for "fresh produce," "meat, fish, honey, syrup, and dairy," "grains & pretzels," "teas, coffees & spices," and "organic wines, juices, and elixirs." The multiple redundancies these lists engendered may not have shown great design or literary sense, but did succeed in making ABC Kitchen seem more serious about sustainability than any other operation at that time. Judging by the restaurant's JBF award for Best New Restaurant in 2011, the effort was well received.

In context, it's really no wonder. The appreciation of foods uncorrupted by modern industry belongs to a larger pattern of purist enthusiasm for authenticity. Its other face has been an appreciation of the culinary expression of a chef's unique self.

At times, that's come across in signs of a personal touch. The same sorts of menus that have demonstrated eco-friendliness have also noted the in-house fabrication of a dish's individual parts. On the days I visited, Zuni listed on its menu "House-cured Anchovies with Celery, Parmesan, and Coquillo Olives"; ABC Kitchen advertised "Housemade Yogurt with Granola and Market Berries"; Incanto, "House-marinated Olives"; and A16, "House-cured Salumi with Pickles and Grissini." The impression I got from so much artisanal manufacture of the details was a romantic one of small-scale, caring craftsmanship.

When I asked chef Cindy Pawlcyn—a purist *par excellence* from the opening of her garden-adjacent Mustards Grill, Yountville, California, in 1983 to the earthy Brassica Wine Bar & Wood Grill in St. Helena, California, in 2011—what *fine dining* means today, her response was revealing. No longer a matter of formal versus casual, she agreed, it's now a distinction of small-scale versus large-scale mentality and operation. *Fine dining*, for her, has meant running a restaurant from an individual's point of view—in her words, "from the heart."[56]

The conflation of hearth and heart has been so important to the purists that they've tended to stress the personal dimension of their cuisine in all their public relations. Cookbooks by chefs that feature the cuisine of their restaurants are especially comprehensive examples.

In many cases, purists have couched their claim to authenticity in autobiography. The typical narrative follows the chef's discovery of his or her personal culinary idiom through a series of impacting life experiences. An early example of this autobiographical frame is *The Chez Panisse Menu Cookbook* (1982). The introduction by Alice Waters unfolds as a sequence of formative impressions. She recalls savoring applesauce made from the fruit of a certain tree in her childhood; having dinner in France at a restaurant in an old stone house where the daily offerings came from the nearby stream and garden; reading books by Elizabeth David and Richard Olney. These experiences, as Waters puts it, "provided a starting point and inspiration."[57] All along, she portrays herself not as a slavish copier of traditions but as a unique synthesizer of diverse personal encounters and local resources.

Other purist chefs have followed the pattern. In *The Zuni Café Cook-*

book, Judy Rodgers traces her culinary personality from a revelatory "ham sandwich on chewy, day-old pain de campagne" at the restaurant Troisgros in Roanne, France—where she apprenticed as a high-school exchange student in 1973—all the way to her work as a chef at Chez Panisse. Each lesson she learned about technique or attention to seasonal and local foods, she points out, added a new dimension to her own approach.[58] Likewise, in *Sunday Suppers at Lucques* (2005), chef Suzanne Goin of the renowned Lucques in Los Angeles finds the source of her convivial, rustic interpretation of global cuisines and seasonal, local products in a series of affecting memories. Helping her dad make family Sunday dinners as a child, extensive travels abroad, and training at particular restaurants all contributed to Goin's eclectic approach.[59]

Some purist cookbooks relinquish autobiography in favor of characterizing the chefs' work at their restaurants. Yet even those narratives convey the chefs' unique culinary personae by referring to examples of deviations from traditions they nevertheless respect. My reference at the outset of this chapter to Mario Batali's description of Babbo's cuisine is a good example. That statement could have been patterned after Larry Forgione's *An American Place* (1996), where the front flap similarly asserts: "In addition to revitalizing traditional fare, [Forgione] also offers food that won't remind you of anything you've ever tasted before."[60] In comments on recipes throughout *A16: Food + Wine* (2008), A16's founding chef, Nate Appleman, follows both Batali and Forgione. He introduces the recipe for "Budino Tartlets," for example, as an inspired twist on a classic dish of chocolate custard with sea salt and olive oil that moved him on a visit to Italy. The pastry chef's addition of a tart shell for textural contrast qualifies the A16 dish as authentic in the purist sense.[61]

On the basis of other evidence, in *Foodies*, Johnston and Baumann have also argued that contemporary gourmets have placed great value on authenticity. Our studies further share an understanding of what that means. First of all, we don't assume that authenticity is an intrinsic property of things or people, but rather a social construct for classifying them. Second, we recognize that in the modern world, the concept of *artistic authenticity* is inextricable from individualism. It's a reprise of the Romantic notion of being "true" to oneself. For an in-depth study of this phenomenon in another contemporary artistic context, the authors point to Richard Peterson's *Creating Country Music: Fabricating Authenticity* (1997). He found precisely the same dynamic we find in the culinary field: the designation "authentic" accrues to an artist only when she's affiliated herself with a cultural tradition and then idiosyncratically departed from it.[62]

making it surprising

Whereas the purist approach has elevated common foods by highlighting a chef's uncommon pursuit of authenticity, what I call the surprising style has stressed a chef's capacity for technical or conceptual innovation. In their adaptation of common foods, chefs working in this mode have called attention to invention by creating the perception of maximal contrast between the familiarity of a source and the novelty of its transformation. In method, they've leaned in the opposite direction of the purists, favoring extensive manipulation of ingredients and highly composed *dressage*.

An early example of this approach is Jonathan Waxman's *haute*-pop "Heath Bar Cake" at Jams in New York City. In an article from 1985, critic Ron Rosenbaum took the measure of it:

> The whole layered architecture of the commercial candy bar has been translated, transformed, re-expressed with the richest, most buttery pastry base topped with the most exquisite chocolate-caramel mousse. It's better than the Proustian past recaptured. It's more American: it's the past *re-invented*.[63]

What so impressed Rosenbaum was the chef's ability to thoroughly restructure the source while retaining enough of its flavor to trigger the memory of it.

In the 1990s, chef Thomas Keller raised this game of contrast between the recognizable and the unexpected to new heights. Not content to simply refine the material properties of common foods, he introduced a further, conceptual, layer of distance from them by cleverly making dishes allude to other dishes.

From my visit to the French Laundry (under Keller, 1994–) in September 2010, two of the courses I had could be described this way. The first, an *amuse bouche*, was a restaurant signature. The "Cornets" consisted of a mixture of salmon tartare with sweet red onion *crème fraîche* served just like an ice cream cone, scooped inside baked *tuille* cones and wrapped in paper for grasping from a slotted tray. In *The French Laundry Cookbook* (1999), Keller recalls getting the idea from a trip to Baskin-Robbins.[64] By delivering a refined savory starter in the form of an ordinary dessert, the chef toyed with conventions of meal sequence in addition to expectations of flavor and texture.

The other dish, "Coffee and Doughnuts," really was a dessert (fig. 14). Keller's interpretation of the classic duo of American diners and cafés wasn't actually on the menu that evening. I had to specially request it or else miss my chance to sample one more of Keller's famous plays on common foods.

14. "Coffee and Doughnuts" at the French Laundry, Yountville, CA, 2010. Photo by author.

He transformed the source in part by refining it. The delicate cinnamon-and-sugar-dusted mini-doughnut, with its mini-hole balanced on top, rendered the clunky classic in elegant lines and ethereal texture.

At the same time, the chef was up to a semantic ruse. Instead of placing beside the doughnut an actual cup of coffee, Keller filled a demitasse with a cool cappuccino *semifreddo* (semifrozen dessert) and covered it with warm milk foam. My encounter of the differing flavors, textures, and temperatures came as a delightful shock.

It wasn't, however, the most surprising twist on an everyday food that I could have experienced in 2010. The spread of "modernist cuisine" in the United States over the first decade of the 2000s had profoundly raised the bar on surprises.

For something more unexpected, I could have dined at Wylie Dufresne's WD-50 (2003–); José Andres's minibar in Washington, DC (2003–); and, in Los Angeles, the Bazaar by José Andres and its restaurant-within-the-restaurant, Saam (2008–). Andres opened an eight-seat restaurant similar to minibar, é by José Andres, in Las Vegas in December of 2010. A trip to Chicago would have brought me to chef Homaro Cantu's Moto and Grant Achatz's Alinea (2005–).[65]

Modernist chefs mainly in the United States and Europe—where the movement is said to have originated in a series of experiments begun by Catalan chef Ferran Adrià back in 1987—have introduced radically new ways of working that go well beyond my scope here.[66] But it's important to realize that any one of their adaptations of common foods belongs to a broader program of methodological departures from tradition, and has likely been experienced by fans through a media filter in which the chefs and their interpreters have exhaustively publicized them.[67]

Chief among the innovations is a break with *haute cuisine*'s repudiation of the modern convenience-food industry. To develop new food shapes, textures, and temperatures, the modernists have collaborated and consulted with food scientists at industrial food labs. Thus, they've learned to apply and source a variety of chemicals typically used in the mass production of fast foods but previously unheard of in *haute cuisine*. Dufresne told me that his own use of hydrocolloids, gelling or thickening agents, grew out of contacts he'd made over the years with manufacturers.[68] This spectrum of substances, which react differently to hot and cold, have allowed such anomalies as Dufresne's invention of fried mayonnaise.

These culinary futurists have raised the level of surprise in *haute-pop* cuisine also in the process of collaborating with industrial designers. The foods they've created with unusual shapes or textures, after all, have demanded service implements that go beyond the relatively flat world of fork-spoon-knife-plate. When experiments such as the stamp-sized pepperoni pizza made him realize the inadequacy of existing wares, Achatz began developing "service concepts" with industrial designer Martin Kastner.[69] Talking with Kastner in 2010, I learned that their work together since 2003 had resulted in a brisk output of three to five new pieces per year.[70] Among the many I encountered during a twenty-six-course tasting menu at Alinea in December 2008, "CANDY CANE: frozen and chewy" stood out for Kastner's contribution to a novel take on a popular candy. The dish evoked the flavor of candy canes, but the texture and manner of eating cotton candy. To achieve the latter, the dish had to be served on something resembling a stick. A self-supporting vertical skewer Kastner designed and named "the Antenna" literally rose to the occasion (fig. 15). Daring me to bite the puff directly off the end was also a witty way to point to the chef's ultimate goal of challenging and reassuring his diners at the same time.

Other modernists have made references to common foods a centerpiece of their attempt to move beyond the disciplinary mold of gourmet-restaurant chef. Cantu, for example, has considered Moto and iNG, the restaurant he opened in Chicago in 2011, subordinate to his larger enterprise, Cantu Designs, which is dedicated to environmentally sustainable, easily manufactured and distributed solutions to the problem of world hunger. My own dialogue with this Buckminster Fuller of food confirmed that the chef has viewed his gourmet output mainly as a test bench for Cantu Designs.[71]

The gourmet dishes Cantu has conceived of as experimental prototypes have nearly always made reference to pop-cultural foods or symbols. As he explained it to me, offering foods that are comforting in their familiarity is crucial for gaining the acceptance of a larger public. When he insisted, "It has to be comfort food," he meant that only rec-

15. "The Antenna," a "service concept" developed for Alinea, Chicago, by Martin Kastner, founder of Crucial Detail. Photo by Lara Kastner.

ognizable flavors or forms can counteract the potentially off-putting fact of their alien design.[72]

Cantu has called his play on popular foods "transmogrification." A dish is transmogrified when it looks like one food but tastes of another, or looks and tastes like a familiar food but is made from unrelated—in his case, more sustainable—ingredients.[73]

Since the restaurant opened, the first course of a Moto meal has consistently been an example of this. The diner has been asked literally to taste the "tasting menu," an all-organic, edible "paper" Cantu patented that can take on the flavors of all kinds of foods. The first menu I ate in December 2008 tasted like a tortilla chip and came with a dollop of salsa and a margarita-flavored emulsion. My second meal at the restaurant, in February 2010, featured a garlic-bread-flavored menu among other memorable illusions, such as the BURGER with cheese I described at the beginning of this chapter and a witty thing called "RED Bull." This was a soup, tasting exactly of Spanish *paella*. It turned into a multiheaded play on pop culture and Spanish culture as soon as it appeared in the form of an actual sealed can of Red Bull.[74] Canny indeed.

While Cantu has made a specialty of illusions, other modernist chefs have focused on imbuing common foods with novel properties. Take, for instance, the *haute*-pop dish I had at the Bazaar in Los Angeles and again at minibar, entitled, in quotation marks, "Philly Cheesesteak." This was a reengineered miniature of the source, a palm-sized sandwich consisting of strips of Kobe beef draped over a mysterious ovoid of "airbread." The bread was the structural equivalent of one giant air hole inside a normal baguette, which remained fully inflated despite its injection with a cheese sauce. In the case of a dish I had at Saam, "Dragon's Breath Popcorn," the addition of liquid nitrogen to the recipe turned my eating a typical snack food into a bizarre tableside performance in which I exhaled long streams of cold smoke.[75]

Like their predecessors in the game of gourmet surprises, the modernists have used the reference to common foods as a foil for their own inventiveness. Conjuring something familiar has additionally helped them mitigate modernist cuisine's possibly alienating strangeness. Asked if these were the motives behind his allusions to Pizza Combos, bagels, eggs Benedict, *pad thai*, and the many other ubiquitous foods he's taken as points of departure over the years, Dufresne heartily agreed. He also told me that using common points of reference anchors his kitchen's experiments in flavor profiles that are proved to work.[76]

In an interview with *Restaurant Hospitality*'s Bob Krummert in 2005, Achatz made a related point: "If we can successfully place a dish in front of the guest that is visually unfamiliar yet tastes of one of the most comforting flavors known, we have successfully set the tone for the rest of the evening."[77] With this, he encapsulated the one aim common to all chefs working in the surprising style: a tension between the known and the novel that establishes the creativity in the latter.

patterns of inconsistency

The gourmet styles I've just described haven't just produced new forms. They've also implied a variety of hierarchical social distinctions between gourmet and common realms of food production and consumption.

Not all of them are distinctively contemporary. The consumption of rare ingredients—whether pricey, as in the deluxe style, or specially grown or raised, as in the pure—has been a marker of status since the dawn of cuisine. So has the tendency to prize food made and presented with the utmost care and craft.

Anthropologist Sidney W. Mintz's cross-cultural theory of *haute cuisine* and social privilege in *Tasting Food, Tasting Freedom* (1996) names analogous status markers. He concludes, via discussion of a colleague's study of the Sung dynasty in China, that rather than mere quantity, it's the difficulty or expense of procuring ingredients and the care and skill that go into preparing them that has consistently distinguished *haute cuisine* from regular regional cooking.[78]

Admittedly, the purist valuation of local and organic foods, a product of the rising influence of environmentalism, belongs to the contemporary era. Still, its use as a mark of social status is consistent with the historical function of rare foods. In *Foodies*, Johnston and Baumann argue that while nonelites may learn about gourmet foods, including local and organic, those goods remain exclusive. In America, access to foods of even the most basic standard of freshness has been highly segregated by income and geography.[79] I find support for Johnston and Baumann's claim in a 2009 government publication entitled *The Public Health Effects of Food Deserts*. From a series of studies examining data from 1997 through 2007, the authors concluded that "those who live in urban and rural low-income neighborhoods are less likely to have access to supermarkets or grocery stores that provide healthy food choices."[80]

What is, however, new to the dynamics of food-related social distinction is the simultaneous embrace by chefs and diners of the apparently contradictory aesthetics and ethics of what I've called the pure and the surprising styles. Despite their contrary emphases—naturalism versus artifice, heart versus head, primitivism versus futurism—the actual landscape of gourmet practices has encompassed a wide spectrum of stylistic crossbreeds. For instance, although eco-friendliness has been emphasized most in the aesthetics of extreme purists, in fact the use of local, seasonal, and organic ingredients has all along been a universal gourmet ideal.

Furthermore, many leading chefs have adopted a combination of purist and surprising forms. The critic who appreciated Waxman's "Heath Bar Cake" at Jams, for example, singled out the chef's rustic signature dish of shoestring fries piled next to a mesquite-grilled half chicken in the same article. Stylistically, the chicken dish would have fit right in at Mustards Grill or Zuni Café. Moreover, Waxman's were the same "free-range" chickens from Paul Kaiser that Forgione used.[81] More recently, with the international influence of New Nordic cuisine—associated most prominently with Copenhagen chef René Redzepi of Noma, number one on San Pellegrino's list of best restaurants in the world for 2010 through 2012—purist extremes in the use of locally raised ingredients and ancient cooking and preserving techniques have combined with *dressage* so fastidiously composed it makes the art of Japanese flower arrangement look slack.[82]

There have also been leading chefs who, by opening multiple restaurants, have lived parallel stylistic lives. One is Thomas Keller. While maintaining the height of elegance and innovation at the French Laundry—what's made it the only restaurant in all the gourmet-rich San Francisco Bay Area and Napa Valley to consistently receive three Michelin stars—he's also served homey bistro fare at Bouchon (multiple locations, 1998–) and the epitome of purist cuisine in the family-style, free-form presentation of local bounty at Ad Hoc (Yountville, California, 2006–). Likewise, José Andres, whose modernist restaurants have helped define the world's cutting edge of culinary futurism, has concurrently carried on a successful career—through several outposts of his restaurant Jaleo (in multiple cities, 1993–) and his PBS TV show, *Made in Spain* (2008–)—promoting, in purist fashion, the simply composed, ingredient-focused traditions and variations of Spanish tapas.

In a related tendency, gourmets have consistently exalted, in the same breath, gourmet restaurants of opposed aesthetics. When *Food & Wine* issued its first "Best New Chefs" feature in 1988, Rick Bayless was honored for his rustic Mexican cuisine at Frontera Grill (Chicago, 1987–) in the same issue as chef Hubert Keller, who at Fleur de Lys (under Keller, 1986–) set the contemporary standard in San Francisco for refined, intricately styled modern French food. This apples-and-oranges pattern persisted. In the 2010 issue, Roy Choi of the Kogi BBQ food truck, hero of unfussy cuisine, stood next to James Syhabout of Commis (Oakland, 2009–), where the modernism-influenced dishes I tried in September 2010 were composed like jewels.[83]

Food & Wine wasn't an outlier. Best New Restaurant awards from the James Beard Foundation, initiated in 1995, went to exemplars of the rustic—Brasserie Jo (Chicago, 1995–2010), Babbo, and Craft—for 1996, 1999, and 2002, respectively; and to their stylistic opposites Jean Georges (New York City, 1997–), Gary Danko (San Francisco, 1999–), and Alain Ducasse (New York City, 2000–2007) for the alternate years 1998, 2000, and 2001. In 2010, among the JBF semifinalists for Best Chef were the stark-opposite choices of José Andres for minibar and Tom Colicchio for Craft. In 2011, the semifinalists for Best New Restaurant were even more polarized. At one extreme was Roy Choi's A-frame (Los Angeles, 2010–). On the restaurant's website, A-frame has been identified as a "modern picnic." While there, diners are encouraged to eat with their fingers and explore a menu of stoner-fantasy share-fare, including "Cracklin Beer Can Chicken," "Thick Ass Ice Cream Sandwiches," and a creative take on the classic of Mexican *churros* and hot chocolate campily called "Chu-Don't-Know-Mang." At the other end of the spectrum was Benu (San Francisco, 2010–), known for precisely orchestrated tasting menus and dishes so artfully plated that they rival the refinements of the French Laundry, where Benu's chef, Corey Lee, previously ran the kitchen.[84]

Since it began issuing its list of the fifty best restaurants in 1996, *Gourmet* has exhibited the same incongruous valuation standards. In 2000, the top ten in Los Angeles alone included Suzanne Goin's haven of rusticity, Lucques (1998–), and chef Joachim Splichal's sanctum of finesse, Patina (1989–).[85]

How to interpret the apparent contradiction between styles of authenticity and ingenuity, rusticity and refinement, in gourmet taste as a mark of gourmet social distinction? How also to reconcile that with gourmets' similarly omnivorous embrace of the fast and slow poles of common food?

Note first that both polarities are parallel constructs of cultural ambivalence. Both pit primitivism against futurism, folk wisdom against modern science. In this way, extreme culinary purists line up with slow-food cooks, and extreme culinary surprise artists line up with industrial fast-food manufacturers.

The significant difference between the pairs of contraries, however, lies in the way gourmets have reconciled them. As I argued earlier, the metacultural rhetoric of comfort food has resolved gourmets' embrace of contradictory symbols of common foods by subsuming them under a generic appreciation of the familial. Doing so has brought comfort where demographic and ideological tensions have been exacerbated in an increasingly pluralistic society.

At the gourmet level of taste contradiction, however, the resolution has come in quite the opposite guise. Instead of common culture and familial values, what's unified the rhetoric and practices of gourmet chefs has been the promotion of individuality. Whether these chefs have taken a deluxe, pure, or surprising approach in the transformation of common foods, they've distinguished their work in every case from other chefs and practitioners of the traditions they've adapted by asserting their own creativity. Purists have made this distinction by their idiosyncratic synthesis of diverse experiences. Surprise-oriented chefs have done so by highlighting technical or conceptual advances.

As the repetitiousness of menus from highly reputed restaurants I quoted earlier in the chapter demonstrates, individual creativity in the gourmet chef wasn't always so highly prized. But increasing auteurism in the organization of the chef career—in the United States, mainly since the mid-1970s—has changed that. No longer valued largely by their execution of classics, chefs have had to make their good name by asserting a unique repertoire. With the reputation of a chef so dependent on auteurism, it stands to reason that in spite of common culture's comforting allure, it's ultimately individualism that's ruled the gourmet roost.

I would go beyond this and suggest that as contemporary chefs have increasingly drawn on slow- and fast-food traditions for inspiration, the need for auteurist assertions would have grown ever more urgent. For the gourmet chef would have needed to differentiate herself not just from her peers but from the scores of nongourmet chefs from whom she's continually borrowed.

My assumption of a turf war between gourmet and everyday cooks derives from sociologist Andrew Abbott's foundational theory of interprofessional competition, *The System of Professions* (1988). His basic idea is that all representatives of any profession have an interest in consolidating their prestige and access to resources as members of their profession by establishing and controlling access to a distinctive domain of expertise. Such barriers as special skills, standards, and training protect professionals from the takeover of their functions by people in related fields.[86]

I find this explanation entirely applicable. The blurring of the line between two formerly distinct professional realms—fine and casual cookery—could have easily become a threat to the superior status of fine dining had not some new basis for distinction been secured. Questions critics raised about the death of fine dining, which I noted in chapter 1, have indicated that such a concern has been justified. But the gourmet chef's assertion of individuality has ensured the continuity of a distinction between gourmet chefs and those of countless diners, trattorias, bistros, and so on. The latter, for the most part, have remained anonymous.

conclusion

Finally: a reckoning. Having studied restaurant trends individually, I'm compelled to identify markers of sophisticated gourmet status that are overarching, and to ponder their link to broader currents in cultural taste and social rank.

nobrow taste

On every front, from architecture to cuisine, omnivorous style and taste have been a rejection of tradition-bound formalities and categorical exclusions and an embrace of continually evolving displays of a chef's individual freedom, professional virtuosity, originality, or authenticity. The various celebrations of the chef I've revealed at the heart of each restaurant trend have reinforced core values of the "creative class" to which the new leading tastemakers—star chefs and foodies—have largely belonged. Their shared espousal of individuality, creativity, and cultural diversity has, in turn, been founded on the rise of meritocratic ideals. No longer convincing on the basis of patrimony, cultural authority must now derive from exhibitions of individual education and achievement.[1]

In drawing these conclusions, I've been careful not to say that the creative class actually is meritocratic. Neither I nor my sources offer adequate proof for such a claim. I've been referring to an ethos. While meritocratic ideals may in fact be grounded in meritocratic realities, I don't assume a perfect correspondence between ethos and reality. Most people know from experience that nepotism, cronyism, and inherited wealth are still alive and well. The point is that among the creative class, displays of individual merit are what impress. The influence of patrimony didn't cease after the 1960s; it just became more shameful to flaunt.

Except in the details, the sea change in taste and social hierarchy that I've recounted in this book hasn't been limited to restaurants. As I hinted at in my introduction, it mirrors the demise of highbrow-lowbrow distinctions and the rise of a selectively omnivorous taste in all cultural fields. For this reason, established analyses of new taste criteria outside the food world can help bring the case of restaurants into a broader frame.

I find John Seabrook's concept of "nobrow"—which he discussed in regard to publishing, music, art, and fashion in a 2001 book of the same name—especially apt. In nobrow culture, the old distinctions of high and low have been replaced by "cult" and "mainstream." Cult status represents the pinnacle of a pluralistic and commercial hierarchy in which the subculturally authentic and the novel get top honors.[2] Seabrook may as well have been describing the rank of contemporary gourmet chefs and restaurants by signs of individual authenticity and innovation.

Seabrook's time frame for the rise of nobrow encompasses the transformation of gourmet restaurant style. He finds its first stirrings in 1960s pop art and the concurrent rise of a concept of *camp*. These represent to him the intelligentsia's budding efforts to negotiate a selective acceptance of a newly omnipresent, and therefore unavoidable, mass culture. By the 1990s, he argues, nobrow had fully replaced the high-low hierarchy of taste. As evidence of its takeover, Seabrook points to the change in editorial policy at the *New Yorker*. Though the magazine was once a model of highbrow detachment from popular taste, it began taking pop-cultural subjects seriously. Seabrook finds the essence of nobrow's rapacious pursuit of the new in the rise of

MTV. Its instant popularization of obscure subcultural acts vastly accelerated the rate at which cult became mainstream. Only a few years after Seabrook's writing, the popularization of social-networking and user-driven-content websites proved that the buzz could spread "virally," and so even faster.

The changes in restaurant style surfaced about a decade later than nobrow's first emanations, yet otherwise followed its timeline. Its expressions of sophisticated taste also resemble what Seabrook attributes to nobrow. The concept of *camp*, for instance, resonates especially in connection with chefs' and foodies' ironic approach to common foods.[3] Daniel Boulud's hamburger that shuns the norms of the hamburger, Thomas Keller's proxy for an ice cream cone that doesn't hold ice cream, and the "Philly Cheesesteak" by José Andres whose name needs quotation marks all represent playful negations of the commonness of the common foods that chefs have nevertheless shown affection for.

Certainly, not all noted aspects of camp apply to the gourmet context. Camp's frequently theorized associations with a particularly homosexual or otherwise marginalized cultural perspective aren't relevant here. But as a concept, it has always been a big tent. Indeed, some facets of a campy manner of interpreting things that Susan Sontag first pointed out in her popular, if inconsistent, 1964 essay "Notes on Camp" do match the spirit by which chefs have interpreted their common sources and diners have consumed the results.[4]

In "deluxe" renditions of common foods, I recognize Sontag's description of camp as a way of seeing "everything in quotation marks," and of "dethron[ing] the serious" to celebrate playfulness, excess, artifice, and vulgarity. "Surprising" transformations of common foods indulge less in the comedy of excess and vulgarity, but conform to Sontag's broader speculation that camp reflects a cultural ambivalence—a genuine enjoyment of the culture that presumably naïve people consume along with an opposing desire to show that one knows better. In cuisine, this means admitting our attachment to a common food while altering it, or appreciating its alteration.

The competitive pursuit of the new that characterizes nobrow taste likewise serves as a point of distinction for gourmets. In *Snobbery: The American Version* (2002), a reflection on cultural taste and social hier-

archy congruent with Seabrook's, Joseph Epstein gives this marker of
sophistication the catchy name "with-it-ry."[5] An individual's ability
to stay ahead of most people's knowledge of the latest cultural hap-
penings—to be with-it—shows the meritocratic leanings of the new
elites, and follows from these people's contemporary market context
of accelerated cultural-fashion obsolescence. The quickening turnover
of fads since the mid-twentieth century—a "postmodern" product, in
part, of the expanded role of mass media—has only made the identification of new and worthy ideas—in any cultural field—that much
more a test of individual work ethic and expertise acquisition.

Competitive and *perpetually in motion* describe not only the behavior
of top chefs, as I outlined it in chapter 4, but also that of their fans.
By being the first to scoop The Next Big Thing, foodies have distinguished themselves from one another and other consumers.

Since they first surfaced, portraits of foodies have consistently identified competitive novelty-seeking as one of their core traits. According to Ann Barr and Paul Levy's *The Official Foodie Handbook* of 1984,
a foodie has tried to be "a setter not a follower of trends," and in this
pursuit has been restless:

> Foodies are typically an aspiring professional couple to whom food
> is a fashion. *A* fashion? *The* fashion. . . . Foodism being fashion, you
> don't live with the same menu for years—you discover, embrace, ex-
> plore minutely, get bored, and move on tomorrow to fresh meals and
> pastas new.[6]

The same notes sound again in books published over twenty years
later. In their introduction to *The Food Snob's Dictionary* (2007), David Kamp and Marion Rosenfeld narrate the history of modern food
snobbery as a continual movement of the protagonists from fashion
to fashion in an effort to stay ahead of their growing legion of media-
cued emulators. Doing so has meant learning the subtle differences
among esoteric cooking methods, purchasing professional cookware
and appliances, or sampling new restaurants and foods before others
catch on.[7] As if to demonstrate this point, Sudi Pigott, in *How to Be
a Better Foodie* (2007), devotes a chapter to one-upmanship: "Unusual

Delicacies Others Ignore." In another, entitled "Culinary Fashionability," the author echoes Barr and Levy:

> Instinctively, the committed Foodie yearns to be in the vanguard of the latest culinary trends only just stirring in the highest echelons of cheffy circles, whether they are ingredients that are ripe for a comeback . . . or startlingly esoteric and thrillingly new.[8]

These assessments jibe with the expert market insights of Tom Miner, a representative of the Chicago-based food-service-consulting firm Technomic Inc. In a 2005 reference to the excitement then surrounding vanguard Chicago restaurants Alinea and chef Graham Elliot Bowles's Avenues, he pointed out that a small niche of superfoodies, who thrive on novelty and encourage such chefs to experiment, comprise just 20 percent of cutting-edge restaurants' customers but drive 80 percent of sales. What's more, Miner confirmed this group's significance as tastemakers. "They are the people who lead the mass market," he insisted.[9] In the process, I would add, they've exemplified the constant roaming of nobrow taste.

The fast-paced culture of amateur food bloggers manifests this quality in extremis. In some ways, their situation has been similar to their professional-critic counterparts. Like them, their status has depended on being early to report on any new experience; also like them, the instantaneity of the Internet has brought the pace of doing so to warp speed. But without the cushioning credentials of a newspaper post, amateur bloggers have had to earn respect perpetually anew and at a more breakneck pace. Since their trendsetting status has hinged on their minute-by-minute ranking on search engines, and that has depended in part on the constancy of their output, their authority has been far more precarious.

In Los Angeles, where I live today, the top food bloggers have set a daunting standard of with-it-ry. An exemplary case is Tony Chen, a.k.a. "Sinosoul." When I met him at a pop-up dinner by chef Michael Voltaggio in 2009, he told me that he first made a name for himself by being "FTR," the bloggerati's acronym for *first-to-review*. Having maintained his frenetic output—while developing a cantankerous yet well-informed review style—Sinosoul has been singled out for interviewing by other bloggers in high-profile organs, including the *LA Weekly* and the news website Huffington Post.[10]

Finally, I realize why superfoodies and top chefs have been so symbiotic. In their respective realms, they've been so much alike.

meritorious self-indulgence

I've also noticed that gourmets' nobrow taste has, at every point in my story, been accompanied by an ethic of meritorious self-indulgence. As I argued in the case of open kitchens, signs of play have made work seem more personally gratifying; conversely, exhibitions of admirable work have made play seem more noble.

I posit here that a parallel dynamic has governed the transformation of gourmet cuisine. Gourmet chefs and diners have tried to make pleasure more principled with eco-conscious cuisine; and they've sought to make virtue more permissive by turning ecological correctness into luxury consumption.

That food prohibition is anathema to gourmet adventure, that taste is a food's most important quality—these principles have distinguished contemporary gourmets from, say, groups of food politicos or the health-obsessed. There's a good reason why a film documentary on Alice Waters was named *Alice Waters and Her Delicious Revolution* (2003). For gourmets, politics had better taste good. Similarly, it's no surprise to find Anthony Bourdain's popular TV show entitled *No Reservations* (2005–) or celebrity food critic Jeffrey Steingarten's first collection of essays called *The Man Who Ate Everything* (1997). Exemplary foodies eat everything—or, at least, what they think counts—without reservation.

Steingarten's introduction fleshes out this point. It narrates how he prepared for his post as food critic for *Vogue* by going on a campaign to eradicate his "powerful, arbitrary, and debilitating attractions and aversions" to certain foods. In the name of duty, he confesses to every food he dislikes—a litany spanning kimchi, anchovies, and desserts in Indian restaurants—and he narrates his efforts to rid himself of these biases by seeking out every one of the foods' best examples.[11] In most cases, he succeeded; but it's really the thought that counts.

I'm not the first to see contemporary gourmets as locked in an effort to reconcile their sensualist and novelty orientation with the increasingly respectable demands of eco-friendliness or health consciousness. It's been a recurring theme, in fact, in literature about foodies. In a section of their book entitled "Where a Foodie Meets a Wholefoodie Coming through the Rye," the authors of *The Official Foodie Handbook* comically observe,

> Foodies worry about their health, because they are modern people, but they would never let it get between them and food. They have borrowed a few ideas from that other post-war phenomenon, the Wholefoodies. They are also mad about vegetables, like the Wholefoodies' food-political ally, the vegetarians. But the three groups are marked by mutual disapproval.[12]

In reference to more recent years, Johnston and Baumann made a sustained and empirically based argument to the same effect regarding environmentalism. For their book *Foodies*, they systematically examined issues of *Bon Appétit*, *Gourmet*, *Food & Wine*, and *Saveur* from 2004 through 2008. In 2004, they found no in-depth treatment of environmental, social, or political concerns about food. Over 2007 and 2008, they noted a marked spike in the depth and frequency of attention paid to issues of local, sustainable, and cruelty-free eating. These concerns, however, were consistently resolved by win-win propositions. Claims that local, organic, and humanely raised foods also taste better tended to diffuse any potential conflict between eco-friendliness and epicurean wish fulfillment. Environmentalist concerns were also continually posed as problems to be solved not by collective political action but by individual shopping choices—in other words, consumption.[13]

Michael Serazio notes a similar attempt to reconcile environmentalism with consumerism in "Ethos Groceries and Countercultural Appetites: Consuming Memory in Whole Foods' Brand Utopia" (2011). The purpose of the article is to explain the niche-branding success of Whole Foods Market, "the world's leading retailer of natural and organic foods," from its birth as one store in Austin, Texas, in 1980 through its growth by the end of 2007 into a public company with approximately 265 stores in North America and the United Kingdom.[14] On the shelves at Whole Foods, Serazio notices the persistent provision of both environmentally friendly goods and upscale luxuries such as premium olive oils and chocolates.

In its branding efforts, Serazio finds the Whole Foods blend of morality and materialism embodied in the public persona of its CEO, John Mackey. According to the company's biography, Mackey came to success accidentally while pursuing his love of organics. That point imbues the company's increase in market share with antimaterialist virtue. In public statements, Mackey himself has reinforced that narrative. When Whole Foods went public, Mackey told *Business Week*, "Wall Street isn't going to corrupt Whole Foods Market.... We're going to purify Wall Street."[15]

Serazio's account of the store's success is relevant to the case of gourmets, because the Whole Foods customer demographic has consistently overlapped with foodies'. He reports that the market has tended to attract relatively educated, affluent thirty-five to fifty-five-year-olds residing in liberal-leaning coastal cities and college towns.[16]

As an advocate for meritorious self-indulgence, Whole Foods is no isolated case.[17] It belongs to a pantheon of contemporary brands unrelated to food that have, through marketing, promoted the same combination of ideals. The fusion of competitive professionalism and free play has been central, for example, to the branding of Nike and Apple. The harmonization of conservationism and luxury consumption has marked the messaging of several aspirational cosmetic brands, including the Body Shop, Aveda, and Origins. The market success of such branding efforts is a sign that the cultural ideals of gourmets haven't been theirs alone.

The espousal of virtues in nonculinary industries is surely beyond my purview here. Yet throughout this book, I've tried to show at least that the values of contemporary gourmets have broader cultural roots. Thus, the restaurant trends of recent decades have projected not only the subcultural preoccupations of chefs and foodies but also the collective wishes of a sizable—yet culturally distinctive—elite. Gourmets' expressions of sophisticated taste have also been attempts to resolve some of the same cultural tensions that members of the creative class have felt elsewhere.

Because of the ties between the gourmet subculture and the larger elite culture, I suspect that the next comprehensive change of scene at the gourmet restaurant table will take place just as soon as the broader cultural supports for omnivorous style and taste give way.

acknowledgments

It's true that a good book is the product of hard work, skill, and vision. But it's also the end of a line of lucky breaks and generous people. I've benefited a lot from the latter.

I couldn't see it at the time, but the acceptance of my article "Chef Appeal" for the winter 2007 *Popular Culture Review* first put me on the path to *Smart Casual*. If it hadn't been for the journal's editor, Felicia Campbell, seeing something worthwhile in my work, and if she hadn't organized the American Culture Association/Popular Culture Association conference (2007), where I got feedback on the article as a talk, I wouldn't have been so emboldened in pursuing its implications.

Along the way, I was also fortunate to organize "Food Aesthetics," a panel for the College Art Association conference in February 2010. I have the open minds of Stephanie Bacon and Max Liboiron of the Visual Culture Caucus to thank for accepting my proposal to consider food under visual studies.

I also wish to thank Darra Goldstein, editor of *Gastronomica*, for giving me my first assignment, reviewing a book on restaurant design. These initial steps proved invaluable as I began to cross the disciplinary lines between art and design history—my home fields—and food studies.

I can't see how I would have completed this book in a timely manner without being granted a sabbatical leave from teaching at Cal Poly Pomona. I'm grateful to the Art Department chair of the time, Babette Mayor, and the college dean, Michael Woo—who supported my sabbatical request—and to my dear friend and colleague in art history, Chari Pradel, who carried the program's burdens heroically in my absence. I also tip my hat to Natasha Medvedev, who couldn't have known what she was getting into when she agreed to teach all my classes in my stead, but stuck it out for the full year.

I was overjoyed that another Art Department colleague, Alyssa Lang, introduced me to her husband, sociologist John T. Lang. He invited me to join the stimulating multidisciplinary Food Interest Group he founded at Occidental College. Brainy and resourceful, John led me to invaluable sociology and professional-network sources and gave helpful feedback on my presentation of work in progress to the group. Another of its members, music historian David Kasunic, was also notably forthcoming with response and conversation.

This book wouldn't have had the same depth had not a variety of individuals allowed me to interview them at length. Chef Homaro Cantu, chef Wylie Dufresne, designer Ray Kampf, designer Martin Kastner, restaurateur and designer Pat Kuleto, chef John N. Novi, chef Cindy Pawlcyn, restaurateur Scott Shaw, and restaurateur Rob Wilder took an impressive amount of time out to answer my questions—and, in the case of Rob Wilder, to arrange an otherwise impossible reservation at minibar—when there wasn't anything immediately in it for them. Ray Kampf was particularly instrumental early on, as he introduced me to Scott Shaw, who in turn introduced me to Rob Wilder. Certain interviewees responded to my out-of-the-blue requests to speak with them, and should be commended for their compassion and courage in doing so. Of them, I'd especially like to thank Homaro Cantu and Pat Kuleto for offering me more of their time than anyone had a right to.

I didn't formally interview culinary historian Ken Albala, but he stands out among my debts. I appreciate his willingness to discuss my project, his challenges to my ideas, and his encouragement and support. Such collegiality from a giant in the field of food studies means a lot.

In addition to finding these helpful sources, I tapped the knowledge of countless staff members wherever I dined for research. Much of what I learned about the operational relationships between the "front of the house" and the "back of the house" in gourmet restaurants came from books and articles, but just as much or more was gleaned from talking with restaurant personnel on-site. I'm so thankful for their hospitality and candor.

With some people, I was able to strike up a productive correspondence. I appreciate the willingness of sous-chef Tyler Lyne of Momofuku Ko, pastry chef Ben Roche at Moto, and chef Charlie Trotter of Charlie Trotter's for answering questions via e-mail or Facebook. Rachael Carron was kind enough to photocopy and mail me numerous years of menus from chef Wylie Dufresne's WD-50. Chef Emeril Lagasse couldn't hope for a better public relations manager than Jeff Hinson, who promptly provided me with more than I asked for regarding exact dates and design details for Emeril's restaurant.

Another great twist of fate: through the discussion forum of the Association for the Study of Food and Society, I made contact with food writer Gary Allen. His kind answer to a question I put to the group led me to John Novi, who then led me to key insights about the history of open kitchens and chef's tables not available through the obvious sources. Thank you, ASFS, Gary Allen, and John Novi.

In my search for historical menus, I was aided most of all by the vast resources of the Los Angeles Public Library, in its on-site special collections and online menu collection, and the New York Public Library's Rare Book Division, where Jessica Pigza's expert scanning of old menus saved me countless hours.

For materials other than menus, the libraries I found most useful were those of my own university and also the University of California at Berkeley's Bancroft Library for the Chez Panisse Archives. At Cal Poly Pomona, librarians Bruce Emerton and Nancy Ann Dougherty were especially accommodating. Every day, they set aside carts full of decades of *Gourmet* and *Food & Wine* issues for my convenience during that particular phase of research.

Certain representatives of government and business organizations extended a hand when I had dire need of data or clarification about a statistic. I thank Vera Crain at the Bureau of Labor Statistics for e-mailing me prepublication Consumer Expenditure Survey data from the 1980s and 1990s. I appreciate that Cheryl Russell, editorial director of New Strategist Publications, shared not only then unpublished reports based on CEX data but pointers for interpreting the early surveys. Dorlene Kaplan, editor of Shawguides, Inc., gave me useful figures for recreational cooking programs. *Food Arts* representative Laura Zandi sent me an old issue I couldn't find elsewhere. Yvon Ros of the James Beard Foundation made obtaining the entire history of JBF awards easy by e-mailing me everything to date. Critical points in my book depended on these people's willingness to respond to my inquiries.

Still, the best research and writing in the world won't get a manuscript out of an author's personal computer and into a publisher's. The planets were aligned in my favor when literary agent Malaga Baldi took an interest in this book and agreed to represent it. As with so many other things, this, too, came about through luck and a person's generosity. Creative-nonfiction writer Mary Cappello, a friend and colleague of my father's, took it upon herself to bring my work to Malaga's attention. I'm glad she did. From an agent, I couldn't have wished for more sage and seasoned counsel, stronger representation of my concerns, or a better sense of partnership.

The only thing better than teaming up with Malaga has been also working with University of Chicago Press executive editor Susan Bielstein, and Susan's sharp right hand, Anthony Burton. Having worked with both Susan and Anthony on my last book, *Unpackaging Art of the 1980s* (2003), I was eager to get under the wings of these pros again. My luck got better still when senior manuscript editor Sandra Hazel brought her shrewd and assiduous eye to the manuscript. The opportunity to have a book designed by Isaac Tobin is also a great privilege. With collaborators so supportive, full of integrity, and experienced in publishing, I fear that only I can screw things up now.

From my family, I've also gained so much. It's from them that I first caught the passion for restaurants and cooking. I'm indebted quite literally to my mother and stepfather, Paula and Francis Itaya, who compensated me for many restaurant bills I accrued in research. Their generosity softened the half-salary blow I took as a condition of my sabbatical. It also confirmed, once again, the symbiosis of art and money.

By occasionally sending me links to relevant articles unprompted, both of my stepparents, Sandra Pearlman and Francis Itaya, revealed a shrewdness of news scanning I never knew they possessed. I'd known they were thoughtful.

A lot of what I know about writing I've learned from my father, author Daniel Pearlman. By always taking the time to be my first editor, he's taught me more over the years than I've been able to retain. He's also succeeded in handing down what I'll never lose: a love for the craft and the creative process.

About my boyfriend, Jamisin Matthews: what can I say? It's hard to disentangle the saintly patience and good humor he demonstrated throughout every chapter-writing "crisis" I imposed on our household from all the other advantages I've enjoyed by being with him for so many years.

As a final acknowledgment, I direct a few spirited barks to our dog, Yahiko. His world-weary and skeptical, if ultimately forgiving, glances from across the couch throughout my writing have been nature's reminders not to ascribe too much agency to culture in human affairs. That I clearly didn't heed those hints in drafting a cultural history wasn't his fault.

appendix

What follows is a list of food-service establishments that I visited specifically with the intention of making a study sample for this book. I've listed places first by city, and then in alphabetical order by business name. The date(s) of my visit(s) are in parentheses. Restaurants that belonged to my subsample for studying exhibition kitchens have an asterisk in front of their name.

chicago

Alinea (December 17, 2008)
Avec (February 11, 2010)
*Charlie Trotter's (February 14, 2010)
Graham Elliot (February 13, 2010)
Moto (December 19, 2008; February 12, 2010)
Otom (December 18, 2008)

los angeles

8 oz. (multiple visits over 2009–10)
A-frame (November 20, 2010)

Animal (August 20, 2008)

Bazaar by José Andres (November 28, 2008; February 28, 2009)

BLT (October 7, 2008)

Bottega Louie (June 1, 2010)

Bouchon Beverly Hills (December 15, 2009)

Burger Bar (Las Vegas, August 2009)

California Pizza Kitchen, Hollywood & Highland (September 20, 2008)

Campanile (summer 2009)

*Chinois on Main (June 17, 2010)

Comme Ça (July 7, 2011)

Counter (multiple visits over 2008–10)

CUT by Wolfgang Puck (December 17, 2010)

Delphine at W Hollywood (March 23, 2010)

Enoteca San Marco (Las Vegas, August 2009)

Forage (May 29, 2010)

Foundry on Melrose (April 8, 2010)

Grace (August 5, 2009)

Grill Em All food truck (December 19, 2009)

Hatfield's (May 28, 2010)

Hungry Cat (March 24, 2010, and multiple visits over 2008–10)

Kate Mantilini (September 17, 2009)

Kogi food truck (July 2008)

LA Mill (summer 2009)

LQ@SK "Fooding Around in LA" (pop-up, August 30, 2011)

Lucques (August 26, 2008)

LudoBites at Breadbar, Third Street (pop-up, July 21, 2009)

Marcel Vigneron pop-up restaurant, "Hatchi" Series, Breadbar, Century City
    (December 17, 2009)

Matsuhisa (June 29, 2010)

Michael's Santa Monica (June 22, 2010)

Michael Voltaggio pop-up restaurant, "Hatchi" Series, Breadbar, Century City
    (July 30, 2009)

Oinkster (January 1, 2008)

Ortolan (September 3, 2008)

Providence (May 2008)

Red Medicine (April 22, 2011)

Red O (July 14, 2010)

Saam inside the Bazaar (June 18, 2009; September 11, 2009)

Simon LA (August 11, 2009)

*Spago Beverly Hills (summer 2008)

Susan Feniger's Street (July 3, 2009)

Tar Pit (March 12, 2010)

Tavern (June 15, 2011)

Test Kitchen (October 8, 2010)

Umami Burger (original location, April 25, 2009)

*Urasawa (July 2, 2010)

Water Grill (February 27, 2009)

Waterloo & City (November 9, 2010)

Wurstküche (December 22, 2009)

XIV (May 9, 2009)

new york city

*ABC Kitchen (August 21, 2010)

Aquavit (June 20, 2008)

Babbo (June 17, 2008)

Balthazar (August 17, 2010)

Bar Boulud (August 15, 2010)

Blue Hill (August 18, 2010)

*Breslin (August 9, 2010)

Café Boulud (August 14, 2010)

Craft (August 17, 2010)

Daniel (August 13, 2010)

DB Bistro Moderne (August 14, 2010)

*DBGB Kitchen and Bar (August 18, 2010)

Felidia (June 19, 2008)

Four Seasons (August 16, 2010)

Gramercy Tavern (August 11, 2010)

*L'Atelier de Joël Robuchon (August 12, 2010)

Le Bernardin (August 11, 2010)

Les Halles (June 19, 2008)

Ma Pêche and attached Milkbar (August 21, 2010)

Macbar (August 16, 2010)

Marea (August 20, 2010)

*MASA (August 10, 2010)

*Mercer Kitchen (August 12, 2010)

*Momofuku Ko (August 13, 2010)

*Momofuku Noodle Bar (June 20, 2008; August 23, 2010)

*Momofuku Ssäm Bar (June 17, 2008; August 22, 2010) and attached Milkbar
    (August 23, 2010)

Nobu New York (original Tribeca location, August 22, 2010)

*Nougatine at Jean Georges (August 19, 2010)

Prune (June 18, 2008)

Shake Shack (August 24, 2010)

*Spice Market (August 15, 2010)

*Spotted Pig (August 19, 2010)

Union Square Café (August 10, 2010)

*WD-50 (June 18, 2008; August 20, 2010)

san francisco/bay area/wine country (san francisco, unless otherwise noted)

*A16 (September 4, 2010)

*Chez Panisse (Berkeley, CA, August 31, 2010)

*Commis (Oakland, CA, September 5, 2010)

*Fog City Diner (September 6, 2010)

French Laundry (Yountville, CA, September 1, 2010)

*Incanto (August 30, 2010)

*Morimoto Napa (Napa, CA, September 7, 2010)

*Mustards Grill (Yountville, CA, September 7, 2010)

*OTD (September 2, 2010)

*Saison (September 8, 2010)

*Slanted Door (September 4, 2010)

Ubuntu Napa (Napa, CA, September 7, 2010)

*Wayfare Tavern (September 3, 2010)

*Zuni Café (September 2, 2010)

washington, dc

Art and Soul (August 5, 2010)
*Café Atlantico (August 7, 2010)
*Jaleo (August 8, 2010)
*Michel Richard Citronelle (August 5, 2010)
*minibar (August 6, 2010)

notes

Introduction

1. From the Awards archives of the James Beard Foundation at http://www.jamesbeard.org (accessed June 30, 2012): Chang received Rising Star Chef in 2007, Best Chef: New York City in 2008, and Best New Restaurant for Momofuku Ko in 2009. That Momofuku Ko has maintained two Michelin stars since 2009 is stated on the Momofuku website at http://www.momofuku.com/people/david-chang/ (accessed June 30, 2012). For Momofuku Ssäm Bar honors, see Frank Bruni, "The 10 Best New Restaurants," *New York Times*, December 26, 2007; Paul Wootton, "World's 50 Best Restaurants 2010: The Full List," *Guardian* (London), April 26, 2010; http://www.guardian.co.uk .lifestyle/2010/apr/26/worlds-50-best-restaurants guardian.co.uk.

2. The deluge of coverage mostly followed the first high-profile features on Chang: "Hungry Heart," *Gourmet*, October 2007, 205–15, 252–54; Larissa MacFarquhar, "Chef on the Edge," *New Yorker*, March 24, 2008, 58–67. In 2011, Chang himself joined the fray, launching the magazine *Lucky Peach* with writer Peter Meehan and Zero Point Production. So far, the quarterly has devoted many pages to chronicling Chang's many enthusiasms and globe-trotting. See http://www .mcsweeneys.net/luckypeach.

3. This is the descriptor of the restaurant on the Momofuku Ko Facebook.com page, http://www.facebook.com/pages/Momofuku-Ko/ 130389693707888?v=info (accessed December 14, 2011). It has also been described as such in travel guides. See, for example, Carolyn Galgano, "Top Chef Travels: Momofuku's David Chang on NYC Restaurants," *Fodor's*, October 21, 2009, http://www.fodors.com/news/ story_3680.html.

4. David Chang and Peter Meehan, *Momofuku* (New York: Clarkson Potter, 2009), 28.

5. With regard to food, the mix of "high" and "low" I speak of must be distinguished from a phenomenon in the history of *haute cuisine* whereby chefs sometimes adopted and refined dishes with humble, regional origins, but not to dramatize the contrast of *haute* and humble modes. Stephen Mennell mentions that George Auguste Escoffier had adapted regional dishes in *All Manners Food: Eating and Taste in England and France from the Middle Ages to the Present*, 2nd ed. (Urbana: University of Illinois Press, 1996), 215–16.

6. Patric Kuh, *The Last Days of Haute Cuisine: The Coming of Age of American Restaurants* (New York: Penguin Books, 2001), 92.

7. For details of pre-1980s fine-dining restaurants mentioned in this introduction, I have relied most on Joseph Wechsberg, *Dining at the Pavillon* (Boston: Little, Brown, 1962); Kuh, *The Last Days of Haute Cuisine*; Sirio Maccioni and Peter Elliot, *Sirio: The Story of My Life and Le Cirque* (Hoboken, NJ: John Wiley & Sons, 2004); and Irene Daria, *Lutèce: A Day in the Life of America's Greatest Restaurant* (New York: Random House, 1993). Reviews in *Gourmet* magazine and the *New York Times* over the 1960s and 1970s also provide ample descriptions of décor in the restaurants mentioned and how, if at all, they changed. Many restaurants were reviewed repeatedly. Of these, I sense that Lutèce simplified its décor the most around the time Chef Soltner acquired the restaurant.

8. Daria, *Lutèce*, 27–35.

9. Josée Johnston and Shyon Baumann, *Foodies: Democracy and Distinction in the Gourmet Foodscape* (New York: Routledge, 2010), especially chapter 1, "Foodies, Omnivores, and Discourse," 31–68.

10. Rebecca Spang, *The Invention of the Restaurant: Paris and Modern Gastronomic Culture* (Cambridge, MA: Harvard University Press, 2000); see in particular the chapter "Putting Paris on the Menu," 170–206, especially 172 and 177.

11. Pierre Bourdieu, *Distinction: A Social Critique of the Judgment of Taste*, trans. Richard Nice (Cambridge, MA: Harvard University Press, 1984). Originally published in Paris by Les Éditions de Minuit in 1979.

12. Alan Warde, *Consumption, Food and Taste: Culinary Antinomies and Commodity Culture* (London: SAGE Publications, 1997), 7–21.

13. David Harvey, *The Condition of Postmodernity: An Enquiry into the Origins of Cultural Change* (Oxford: Basil Blackwell, 1989).

14. The 1992 study is discussed in Richard A. Peterson, "Problems in Comparative Research: The Example of Omnivorousness," *Poetics* 33 (2005): 257–82. Further work includes his "Changing Highbrow Taste: From Snob to Omnivore," *American Sociological Review* 61, no. 5 (October 1996): 900–907, and "The Rise and Fall of Highbrow Snobbery as a Status Marker," *Poetics* 25 (1997): 75–92.

15. John Seabrook, *Nobrow: The Culture of Marketing and the Marketing of Culture* (New York: Vintage Books, 2001).

16. Johnston and Baumann, *Foodies*, 198.

17. Max Weber, "Class, Status, Party," in *From Max Weber: Essays in Sociology*, ed. H. H. Gerth and C. Wright Mills (New York: Oxford University Press, 1946), 180–95.

18. Harvey Levenstein, *Paradox of Plenty: A Social History of Eating in Modern America*, rev. ed. (Berkeley: University of California Press, 2003), originally published by Oxford University Press, New York, in 1993; Eric Schlosser, *Fast Food Nation: The Dark Side of the All-American Meal* (New York: Perennial, 2001); and Michael Pollan, *The Omnivore's Dilemma: A Natural History of Four Meals* (New York: Penguin, 2007), originally published by Penguin, 2006.

Chapter 1

1. Michael Bauer, "Is Fine Dining an Obsolete Term?," *San Francisco Chronicle*, May 10, 2010, http://www.sfgate.com/cgi-bin/blogs/mbauer/detail?entry_id=63101; Rachel Forrest, "Where's the Fine in Fine Dining?," SeacoastOnline.com, August 11, 2010, http://www .seacoastonline.com/apps/pbcs.dll/article?aid=20100811/LIFE/; and Kirsten Henri, "From the Magazine: Fine Dining Is Dead, Long Live Fine Dining!," PhillyMag.com, September 27, 2010, http://blogs.phillymag.com/restaurant_club/. Critics and industry leaders have continued to question the relevance of the traditional concept of fine dining. For example, just before this book went to press there was a discussion on the changing meaning of *fine dining* among chefs and restaurateurs at the 2012 Milken Institute Global Conference. James daSilva blogged about it in "From Global Conference: The Evolution of Fine Dining," *SmartBlog on Food and Beverage*, May 17, 2012, at http://smartblogs.com/food-and-beverage/2012/05/17/from-global-conference-the-evolution-of-fine-dining/ (accessed July 3, 2012). Another recent sign of categories reconsidered is the decision at the *Los Angeles Times* to eliminate its star ratings from restaurant reviews. Russ Parsons, reporting on this upset to tradition in "Stars Are Out, at Least for Restaurant Reviews," *LA Times Blogs*, March 8, 2012, at http://latimesblogs.latimes.com/dailydish/2012/03/stars-are-out-at-least-for-restaurant-reviews.html (accessed July 3, 2012), explains that the elimination of star ratings resulted in part from growing complication in the definition of *gourmet dining*: "Star ratings are increasingly difficult to align with the reality of dining in Southern California—where your dinner choices might include a food truck, a neighborhood ethnic restaurant, a one-time-only pop-up run by a famous chef, and a palace of fine dining. Clearly, you can't fairly assess all these using the same rating system."

2. Craig Claiborne, "Elegance of Cuisine Is on Wane in U.S.," *New York Times*, April 13, 1959.

3. Florence Fabricant, "Is New York Worth a Trip? Oui," *New York Times*, November 2, 2005.

4. Diane Cardwell, "2 Stars for Brooklyn Grocery Kitchen," *New York Times*, October 6, 2010, http://www.nytimes.com/2010/10/07/nyregion/07michelin.html?_r=1. For 2012 Michelin-starred restaurants in New York City, see http://www.michelintravel.com/methodology/new-york-city-2012-starred-restaurants/ (accessed July 1, 2012).

5. Kate Krader and Kelly Snowden with portraits by Nigel Parry and food photographs by Anna Williams, "Best New Chefs and Their Simplest Recipes," *Food & Wine*, July 2010, 211–26. The quotation is from page 211.

6. Derrek J. Hull, "Food Trucks Roll into NRA Show 2010"; posted April 22, 2010, on *Floored! The Official Blog of the NRA Show & IWSB*, at http://nrashow.typepad.com/flooredblog2010/04/food-trucks-roll-into-nra-show-2010.html (accessed June 30, 2012).

7. The restaurant's name is all lowercase.

8. LQ@SK refers to the pop-up dinners Chef Quenioux has done for a few evenings each month at Starry Kitchen. See event announcement, "Chef Laurent Quenioux's 18 Course LQ@SK WHITE Truffle Menu on November 14!!," Eventbrite.com, http://18coursetruffledinner.eventbrite.com/ (accessed December 15, 2011).

9. In 2011, Le Bernadin loosened its "jackets required" policy. "Eric Ripert: Keeping a *Grande Dame* Sexy," *Inc.*, October 28, 2011, http://www.inc.com/articles/201110/le-bernardin-eric-ripert-staying-popular-as-times-change_Printer_Friendly.html.

10. Troy Segal, ed., *Zagat Survey 2006: America's Top Restaurants* (New York: Zagat Survey, LLC, 2005), 5.

11. In the 1980s, the term *upscale casual* was applied to dress codes at gourmet restaurants that I will discuss later in this chapter. For instance, in "The Best of San Francisco: The City Where Everyone Loves to Eat," Michael Bauer says this about the Fog City Diner: "Although the name promises diner food, don't kid yourself. Dress is upscale casual" (*Food & Wine*, March 1988, 62).

12. Caroline Bates, "Chez Panisse, Saigon, Swan Oyster Depot," *Gourmet*, October 1975, 11–14, 88–90.

13. Ibid. The quotations are from pages 11 and 12, respectively.

14. Ibid. Both quotations are from page 11.

15. Thomas McNamee, *Alice Waters and Chez Panisse: The Romantic, Impractical, Often Eccentric, Ultimately Brilliant Making of a Food Revolution* (New York: Penguin Books, 2007), 40.

16. Ibid., 44.

17. Ibid., 18.

18. Ibid., 14–15. For reproductions of Chez Panisse menus from 1971 through 1979, see Linda Guenzel, ed., *Beyond Tears: The First Eight Years*, 6 vols. (Berkeley, CA: Chez Panisse Restaurant, 1979).

19. In Jeremiah Tower, *California Dish: What I Saw (and Cooked) at the American Culinary Revolution* (New York: Free Press, 2003), in the book's gallery of plates, Tower provides a photo of himself with writer and gastronome Richard Olney and Stars chef Mark Franz; the caption states, "In front of the restaurant in Paris that inspired me to do Stars." The restaurant was a famous 1920s Montparnasse brasserie-bar.

20. Caroline Bates, "Michael's, Antonio's, Szechwan Palace," *Gourmet*, May 1980, 8–12. The quotation is from page 80.

21. David Kamp, *The United States of Arugula: How We Became a Gourmet Nation* (New York: Broadway Books, 2006), 260.

22. Bates, "Michael's, Antonio's, Szechwan Palace," 10 for both quotations.

23. Notes from my unrecorded conversation in person with Andrew Turner, general manager and sommelier at Michael's Santa Monica, June 22, 2010. In addition, Turner told me that the only variation in servers' attire over the years has been that the shirts were blue at some point. McCarty had also tried the designer Burberry for a time, but then he came back to whatever was the current cut of light-pink, Polo-insignia shirts.

24. Martin E. Dorf, ed., *Restaurants That Work: Case Studies of the Best in the Industry* (New York: Watson-Guptill Publications in association with the Whitney Library of Design, 1992), 88–95.

25. Bryan Miller, "New and French in Lower Manhattan," *New York Times*, June 7, 1985.

26. Bates, "Michael's, Antonio's, Szechwan Palace," 8.

27. Andy Birsh, "Montrachet, Ennie & Michael, City Café," *Gourmet*, July 1990, 33, 126–27.

28. William Grimes, "Easygoing, Not French and Formal," *New York Times*, February 3, 1999.

29. About the remodeling: McNamee, *Alice Waters and Chez Panisse*, 158.

30. Caroline Bates, "Chez Panisse Café, The Elite Café, Ironwood Café," *Gourmet*, June 1982, 8–10, 58. The quotations in this and the following paragraph are from page 8.

31. Ibid. Both quotations are from page 10.

32. Ibid.

33. McNamee, *Alice Waters and Chez Panisse*, 168, 172.

34. From my recorded phone conversation with Cindy Pawlcyn, July 2, 2010.

35. Caroline Bates, "Fog City Diner, 565 Clay, Dynasty," *Gourmet*, March 1986, 18.

36. Stanley Dry, "A New Wave of American Eateries: San Francisco's Fabulous Fog City Diner Leads the Pack," *Food & Wine*, June 1986, 8–10.

37. Although I had been to the restaurant the year it opened, my account of the lighting is based on pictures I took when visiting on September 6, 2010. When I spoke with Pat Kuleto, he confirmed my sense that except for the addition of outdoor seating and a change of lighting to wall-sconce fixtures, the restaurant's design has not changed. Kuleto also informed me that the restaurant was formerly a garage that had housed several failed restaurants over the years. Recorded phone interview, April 13, 2010.

38. Mimi Sheraton, "2 French Choices, Modern and Funky," *New York Times*, November 27, 1981; Jay Jacobs, "Toscana, Odeon, Mrs. J's Sacred Cow," *Gourmet*, June 1981, 10, 50–52. The Jacobs quotation is from page 50.

39. Sheraton, "2 French Choices, Modern and Funky."

40. Benjamin Wallace, "The Restaurant Auteur," *New York*, February 28, 2010, http://nymag.com/restaurants/features/64303/.

41. On the singles bar, T.G.I. Friday's, and Maxwell's Plum: John Mariani, *America Eats Out: An Illustrated History of Restaurants, Taverns, Coffee Shops, Speakeasies, and Other Establishments That Have Fed Us for 350 Years* (New York: William Morrow, 1991), 196–205.

42. Jacobs, "Toscana, Odeon, Mrs. J's Sacred Cow," 10.

43. Ibid.

44. Danny Meyer, *Setting the Table: The Transforming Power of Hospitality in Business* (New York: Harper, 2006), 38, 48, 61.

45. Andy Birsh, "La Caravelle, Union Square Café, Exterminator Chili," *Gourmet*, November 1986, 38–44, 98–104. The quotation is from page 98.

46. Andy Birsh, "La Cité, Union Square Café, Kwong and Wong," *Gourmet*, May 1991, 28–34, 139–40. The quotation is from page 34.

47. Bryan Miller, "Diner's Journal," *New York Times*, May 17, 1985; Penelope Casas, "What's All This We Hear about Tapas?," *Food & Wine*, June 1985, 65–66, 100, 104–5.

48. Meyer, *Setting the Table*, 49.

49. Bryan Miller, "Restaurants," *New York Times*, October 26, 1984, http://www.nytimes.com/1984/10/26/arts/restaurants-036851.html.

50. Stanley Dry, "The Good News about Dining Alone: The Communal Table Has Arrived," *Food & Wine*, February 1986, 8.

51. Frank Bruni, "When Is a Bar Not a Bar?," *New York Times*, February 27, 2008; Michael Bauer, "Is It a Bar or a Restaurant?," "Inside Scoop SF" column, *San Francisco Chronicle*, September 1, 2010, http://insidescoopsf.sfgate.com/blog/2010/09/01/is-it-a-bar-or-a-restaurant/. Also see Devra First, "So a Dish Walks into a Bar . . . ," Boston.com, September 22, 2010, http://www.boston.com/ae/food/restaurants/articles/2010/09/22.

52. Diane Peterson, "Michelin Adopts 3 New Categories," *Press Democrat* (Santa Rosa, CA), October 21, 2009, http://www.pressdemocrat.com/article/20091021.

53. Mary Alice Kellogg, "Dining at the Bar," *Food & Wine*, September 1998, 108–10.

54. Frank Bruni, "Let's Hear It for the Lounge Act," *New York Times*, July 12, 2006, F1.

55. John Mariani, "Eating Out Loosens Up," *Food & Wine*, August 1985, 32.

56. Bates, "Chez Panisse, Saigon, Swan Oyster Depot," 12.

57. Guenzel, *Beyond Tears*, vol. 2.

58. Elizabeth David, introduction to the 1950 edition, in *A Book of Mediterranean Food* (London: Penguin, 1988), n.p. First published by Penguin, 1950.

59. The ad Waters wrote, which attracted Tower, is documented in Kamp, *The United States of Arugula*, 147.

60. Patric Kuh discusses the influence of David and Olney on Chez Panisse's Waters and Tower at length in Kuh, *The Last Days of Haute Cuisine*, 128–36.

61. Richard Olney, *Simple French Food* (Hoboken, NJ: Wiley, 1992). First published by Wiley, 1974. The quotations are from pages 3 and 5.

62. At the time, Caroline Bates mentioned their collaboration in "Stars, Opera House Café, Bentley's," *Gourmet*, April 1985, 20.

63. Specifically, December 11, 12, and 13, 1975, in Guenzel, *Beyond Tears*, vol. 2; March 23–27, 1976, in ibid., vol. 3; and January 23, 1979, in ibid., vol. 6.

64. I found several menus listing pizza before April 1, 1980. The earliest mention I found of pizza at Chez Panisse is in Guenzel, *Beyond Tears*, vol. 2, on a menu dated September 6, 1975. Yet the description of the offering—"provencal 'pizza' made with bread dough, leeks onions [*sic*], olives, fresh herbes [*sic*] and olive oil"—suggests that this was not technically pizza. The quotation marks appeared again in a Provence-themed menu from February 4, 1978, archived in vol. 5. It lists a "Southern French style 'pizza' made with black olives, tomatoes, fresh herbs, anchovies and onion." The first to list *pizza* without quotation marks is in vol. 6 and dated February 9, 1979, but this was for a special dinner, not the regular menu. It was listed as "Pizza Alla Piemontese," and explained as "Little pizzas with anchovies, garlic, tomato and roasted pepper." A "Pizza Provencal," described as "Provencal pizza with artichoke hearts, garlic, niçoise olives and sweet fennel sausage," appears on the regular menu for March 28, 1979, in vol. 6. The menu for July 25, 1979, also in vol. 6, offered "Pizza aux Herbes," described as "pizza baked with provencal herbs and olive oil."

65. Caroline Bates, "Spago, City, Christmas Edibles," *Gourmet*, December 1982, 10–14, 183–88. The quotation is from page 10.

66. Maccioni and Ellliot, *Sirio*, 175–78.

67. A Spago menu from the Los Angeles Public Library online menu collection, archived as "1983," has a section entitled "Pastas" and one entitled "From Our Wood-Burning Pizza Ovens." One reproduced in Jim Heiman, ed., with Steven Heller and John Mariani, *Menu Design in America: A Visual and Culinary History of Graphic Styles and Design 1850–1985* (Cologne: Taschen, 2011), 387–89, has a section entitled "Pastas" and one called "Pizzas." The authors state the menu is from 1981, but that's impossible, since Spago opened in January 1982. The menu is more likely from 1985 or 1986, since that is when Lisa Stalvey, listed on the menu as "Chef," was head chef, according to the website Chefdb.com, http://www.chefdb.com/pl/4872/Spago-Los-Angeles (accessed December 18, 2011). The menu in the LAPL online menu collection doesn't list a chef.

68. Stephanie Curtis, "The Italian Restaurant Circa 1983," *Food & Wine*, September 1983, 4, 6.

69. Jay Jacobs, "Il Nido, Chez Yves, Shun Lee Palace," *Gourmet*, August 1980, 4–8, 43–46.

70. Caroline Bates, "California; Los Angeles Area: Valentino, Saddle Peak Lodge, Manhattan Wonton Company," *Gourmet*, December 1996, 70–78. The quotation is from page 70.

71. Caroline Bates, "Valentino, Rebecca's, Cassis," *Gourmet*, August 1987, 42–46, 75.

72. Mimi Sheraton, "East Side Italian and Vietnamese," *New York Times*, July 31, 1981.

73. Jay Jacobs, "Felidia, Safari Grill, La Petite Auberge," *Gourmet*, December 1985, 22–26, 140–44. The quotations are from pages 24 and 22, respectively.

74. Mimi Sheraton, "The Fun of American Food: Eat American!," *Time*, August 26, 1985, http://www.time.com/time/magazine/article/0,9171,1074755,00.html.

75. On Beard's consulting for RA and on the Four Seasons and Craig Claiborne's review of the restaurant: Kuh, *The Last Days of Haute Cuisine*, 59, 66, 69–70. John Mariani, with Alex von Bidder, documents the first menus of the Four Seasons in *The Four Seasons: A History of America's Premier Restaurant* (New York: Smithmark, 1999), 43–46. The Craig Claiborne review was "Food News: Dining in Elegant Manner," *New York Times*, October 2, 1959.

76. The effort to develop a formalized, high-style American cuisine was led in part by culinary historian James Villas, who published a centennial-themed article under the name Jim Villas: "From the Abundant Land: At Last, A Table of Our Own," *Town & Country*, June 1976, 65–69, 151.

77. The menu is from September 7, 1976, reprinted in Guenzel, *Beyond Tears*, vol. 3, unpaginated.

78. James Beard, *James Beard's American Cookery* (Boston: Little, Brown, 1972), 4.

79. Caroline Bates, "The Union Hotel, Gaylord India Restaurant, Khan Toke," *Gourmet*, April 1982, 14–18, 114–18. The quotation is from page 14.

80. Jay Jacobs, "Le Cygne, Maxwell's Plum, Mary's," *Gourmet*, May 1973, 4–11.

81. Jay Jacobs, "Le Cirque, One if by Land . . . Two if by Sea, Ristorante Il Rigoletto," *Gourmet*, December 1974, 4–6, 132–39. The quotations are from page 6.

82. Jay Jacobs, "Le Cirque, One if by Land . . . Two if by Sea, Ristorante Il Rigoletto," *Gourmet*, December 1974, 4–6, 132–39.

83. Charles Perry, "Los Angeles: Trend-Setting Restaurant City," *Food & Wine*, March 1984, 40.

84. Caroline Bates, "The Kundan, The Golden Eagle, Balboa Cafe," *Gourmet*, December 1983, 14, 110–16. The quotations are from page 116.

85. Tower, *California Dish*, 168. There he mentions a hotdog and hamburger and describes the two dishes I quoted. Caroline Bates mentions a hamburger in her review, "Stars, Opera House Café, Bentley's."

86. Bates, "Fog City Diner, 565 Clay, Dynasty," 18–22, 90, 94. The quotations are from pages 20 and 22.

87. Ron Rosenbaum, "New York Falls in Love with America," *Food & Wine*, October 1985, 40–47, 88–89. The block quotations may be found on page 42. The descriptions of Jams dishes are from page 89.

88. Ibid., 41.

89. Karen A. Franck, "Design on the Plate," in "Food and Architecture," ed. Karen A. Franck, special issue, *Architectural Design* 72, no. 6 (November/December 2002): 61–62.

90. A sure sign of *nouvelle*'s demise among the cognoscenti: Mimi Sheraton, "The Not-So-New Nouvelle Cuisine," *New York Times*, September 5, 1979.

91. Franck, "Design on the Plate," 62.

92. On the derivation of tasting menus from *nouvelle*, from a contemporaneous witness of its recent influence on American cuisine: Mimi Sheraton, "'Tasting' Menu: A Good Idea Sours," *New York Times*, October 10, 1981, 18. On these origins, attested to by chef Daniel Boulud—a chef who should know, because he knew the *nouvelle* chefs—and on the more recent inspirations of American chefs by *kaiseki*, see Leslie Brenner and Michalene Busico, "Eating the Seasons; The World's Most Forward-Looking Chefs Have a New Obsession: A 500-Year-Old Japanese Cuisine Called Kaiseki," *Los Angeles Times*, May 16, 2007.

93. Video interview with chef David Bouley, *Charlie Rose*, August 19, 2011, http://www
.charlierose.com/view/interview/11857 (accessed December 17, 2011).

Chapter 2

1. This is clear from various accounts, including Kuh, *The Last Days of Haute Cuisine*,
25–33; Maccioni and Elliot, *Sirio*, especially 129–140; and Kurt Niklas, as told to Larry
Cortez Hamm, *The Corner Table: From Cabbages to Caviar; Sixty Years in the Celebrity
Restaurant Trade* (Los Angeles: Tuxedo Press, 2000), especially 10–36.

2. A noteworthy history of such "earlier challenges" is Andrew P. Haley's *Turning the Tables: Restaurants and the Rise of the American Middle Class, 1880–1920* (Chapel Hill: University of North Carolina Press, 2011). Haley reveals that around the turn of the twentieth
century, the society elite of the Gilded Age lost its monopolistic influence on the style of
public dining. He argues that the dominance of elite taste was undermined by the growing
market power of the middle class. Haley convincingly establishes that the new restaurant-
goers prompted the proliferation of new restaurant genres and the alteration of old ones
to suit them. Thus, they asserted their own class power in the restaurant marketplace.
Haley also argues that middle-class patrons directly altered elite fine dining. Through their
increasing buying power, they influenced the rise of smaller menus with fewer courses, the
plating of entrées and sides on a single dish, the introduction of more varieties of ethnic
dishes on menus (not just French), and the printing of more menus in English.

Evidently, however, by the time Manhattan's Le Pavillon represented the pinnacle of
American fine dining, between the 1940s and mid-1960s, some of the fashions that Haley
says had largely disappeared by the 1920s—including French-only cuisine, menus in
French, and a socially exclusive *maitre d'*—had made a comeback.

3. Craig Claiborne recalls his objectives as a young journalist in *A Feast Made for
Laughter: A Memoir with Recipes* (New York: Holt, Rinehart and Winston, 1982), 140–55.
The quotation is from page 140.

4. Thomas McNamee, *The Man Who Changed the Way We Eat: Craig Claiborne and the
American Food Renaissance* (New York: Free Press, 2012), 114. Claiborne introduced his
star rating system in the paper on May 24, 1963. Per McNamee (p. 115), in the fall of 1964,
the critic switched from a three-star ranking scale to the four-star one that persists today.

5. From a section entitled "Influence of New Breed of Restaurant Critic," in Y. Blumenfeld, "Gourmet Cooking: Culinary Revolution in America," *Editorial Research Reports
1971*, vol. 1 (Washington, DC: CQ Press, 1971), http://library.cqpress.com/cqresearcher/
cqresrre1971042800.

6. Mimi Sheraton, "Taking the Obfuscation Out of Restaurant Menus," *New York Times*,
April 4, 1981.

7. Ruth Reichl, "How One Place Can Offer Two Contrasting Experiences, Depending on
Who You Are," *New York Times*, October 29, 1993.

8. Kamp, *The United States of Arugula*, 325.

9. From the Zagat website, http://www.zagat.com/About/Index.
aspx?menu=companyHistory (accessed April 18, 2010).

10. In *Turning the Tables: Restaurants from the Inside Out* (New York: HarperCollins,
2005), 121–22, food-blogging pioneer Steven A. Shaw writes about the early history of food
blogging.

11. The panel, "Picturing Food," took place at the Getty Center, Los Angeles, on April 8,
2010. On the tremendous industry influence of Opentable.com, a site that allows diners

to make reservations, see Mark Pastore, "Is OpenTable Worth It?," for his column "Inside Scoop SF," October 18, 2010, http://insidescoopsf.sfgate.com/incanto/2010/10/18/is-opentable-worth-it/.

12. The *New York Times* published a brief announcement of Frank Bruni's new blog: "On the Web nytimes.com/dinersjournal," *New York Times*, April 28, 2006. Another *New York Times* article from the same year explains in more detail the paper's decision to launch blogs in many areas of its coverage. See Byron Calame, "The Times's New Blogs: More Information, Fewer Filters," *New York Times*, April 9, 2006.

13. Bruce Palling, "Have Food Blogs Come of Age?" *Wall Street Journal*, October 22, 2010, http://online.wsj.com/article/SB10001424052748704779704575553973167676514.html.

14. Jane Stern and Michael Stern, *American Gourmet: Classic Recipes, Deluxe Delights, Flamboyant Favorites, and Swank "Company" Food from the '50s and '60s* (New York: Harper Perennial, 1991), 43–45.

15. Kathleen Collins, *Watching What We Eat: The Evolution of Television Cooking Shows* (New York: Continuum, 2009), 79.

16. Kamp, *The United States of Arugula*, 96.

17. Blumenfeld, "Gourmet Cooking."

18. Stern and Stern, *American Gourmet*, 188.

19. Collins, *Watching What We Eat*, 119–20.

20. Linda Bird Francke, with Scott Sullivan and Seth Goldschlager, "Food: The New Wave," *Newsweek*, August 11, 1975, 50–57.

21. The skit by Dan Aykroyd was called "The French Chef," and aired on *Saturday Night Live* on December 9, 1978. The transcript is available at http://snltranscripts.jt.org/78/78hchef.phtml (accessed June 30, 2012).

22. Ann Barr and Paul Levy, *The Official Foodie Handbook: Be Modern—Worship Food* (New York: Timbre Books, 1984).

23. The earliest press on chef celebrity includes Joan Black Bakos, "The Celebrity Chef," *Restaurant Business* 82 (1983): 26; Sheraton, "The Fun of American Food"; and "Chef Celebrities," *Restaurant Business* 85 (May 20, 1986): 197–204. See evidence of magazine circulation increases in CQ Researcher, "Magazine Trends," *CQ Researcher Online*, June 6, 1986, http://0-library.cqpress.com; and Deirdre Carmody, "The Media Business: A Growing Menu of Food Magazines," *New York Times*, July 23, 1990.

24. Michael Ruhlman, *The Reach of a Chef: Beyond the Kitchen* (New York: Viking, 2006), 237.

25. Collins, *Watching What We Eat*, 215. On the increasing popularity of the Food Network, also see my "Chef Appeal," *Popular Culture Review* 18, no. 1 (Winter 2007): 3–24.

26. Michael Hill, Associated Press, "Food Network Spawns Young, Edgy Cooking Channel," Floridatoday.com, April 26, 2010, http://www.floridatoday.com/fdcp/?1273004206694. For more specific information on the ratings associated with cooking-related programs on cable TV in the 2000s, see Andy Fixmer and Sarah Rabil, "Food Is New Real Estate as Cooking Show Ratings Jump," Bloomberg.com, August 20, 2009, http://www.bloomberg.com/apps/news?pid=20670001&sid=awJj6Y1YdCV8.

27. Brian Stelter, "Another Cable Helping for Food Lovers," *New York Times*, February 19, 2010, http://www.nytimes.com/2010/02/19/business/media/19adco.html?_r=2. It's possible, however, that the Food Network became a victim of its own success. Claire Atkinson noted its 10.3-percent decline in viewership in the fourth quarter of 2010 (Atkinson, "Chefs Losing Heat," *New York Post*, January 20, 2011, http://www.nypost.com/f/print/

news/business/chefs_losing_heat_s6K48Z0ZZNMZ6g6QEfs13M). She suggested that the expansion of food-related programming across cable TV was responsible.

28. Hill, "Food Network Spawns Young, Edgy Cooking Channel."

29. Packaged Facts, "Foodies in the U.S.: Restaurant Foodies," advertisement and sneak peak of market survey report, published January 2009, http://www.packagedfacts .com/Foodies-Restaurant-2088291/. I didn't purchase the actual report, as it was several thousand dollars over my budget. Yet I confirmed that the data studied were from 2008 through e-mail correspondence with Claire Caron, customer service representative for Packaged Facts, November 16, 2010. She wrote that "the primary data was compiled by Simmons Market Research Bureau, New York, NY, in its Winter 2007/2008 adult consumer surveys, which is based on the responses of approximately 25,000 adult respondents age 18 or over."

30. Collectively, these articles reveal the Food Network's surge in viewership from the late 1990s through the first years of the 2000s: Dirk Smillie, "Humor Is the Key Ingredi-ent at Lively TV Food Network," *Christian Science Monitor*, July 24, 1997; Katrina Booker, "Selling Cooking to Non-Cooks," *Fortune*, July 6, 1998, 34–35; Jim McConville, "Smaller Nets Spur on Cable: Revamped Channels Boost Ratings," *Electronic Media* 18, no. 50 (De-cember 13, 1999): 1+; Stephanie Thompson, "Extreme Cuisine at Food Network," *Advertis-ing Age* 73, no. 5 (February 4, 2002): 29; Louis Chunovic, "Food Network Is Tweaking Its Recipe," *Electronic Media* 21, no. 5 (February 4, 2002): 7; and "Food Network," *Advertising Age* 74, no. 20 (May 19, 2003): C42.

31. Eric Klinenberg, *Going Solo: The Extraordinary Rise and Surprising Appeal of Living Alone* (New York: Penguin, 2012), 4–5.

32. Levenstein, *Paradox of Plenty*, 105.

33. Harriet B. Presser, *Working in a 24/7 Economy: Challenges for American Families* (New York: Russell Sage Foundation, 2003), 3–4. CQ Researcher, "Magazine Trends."

34. Suzanne M. Bianchi, John P. Robinson, and Melissa A. Milkie, *Changing Rhythms of American Family Life* (New York: Russell Sage Foundation, 2006), 45. The statistic about working mothers in 2000 is also here.

35. Ibid., 107–11, and table 5A.3 in appendix D.

36. Researchers at New Strategist Publications have cross-tabulated data from the Bureau of Labor Statistics Consumer Expenditure Surveys with household data for the years 2001, 2003, 2007, and 2009. Their tables show that the biggest spenders on food away from home in these years have been dual-income households, while singles in high-income, high-education segments have spent a higher percentage of their income on food away from home than other populations.

For 2001 data, see New Strategist Publications, *Who's Buying at Restaurants and Carry-Outs* (Ithaca, NY: New Strategist Publications, 2003), 16, and charts on 28–29 for house-hold data. These charts show that overall, singles and married couples without children spent an especially high proportion of their disposable income on dining out at full-service restaurants, and that married couples without children registered the highest indexed spending on full-service restaurants for lunches and dinners.

For 2003 data, see New Strategist Publications, *The American Marketplace: Demo-graphics and Spending Patterns* (Ithaca, NY: New Strategist Publications, 2005), 433–36, for household data.

For 2007 data, see New Strategist Publications, *Who's Buying at Restaurants and Carry-Outs*, 7th ed. (Ithaca, NY: New Strategist Publications, 2009), 13, which notes that households earning $100,000 or more spent 91 percent as much eating out as on groceries, and that singles spent 79 percent as much on dining out as on groceries. Meanwhile, the average household spent 71 percent as much at restaurants as on groceries.

For 2009 data, see New Strategist Publications, *Who's Buying at Restaurants and Carry-Outs*, 9th ed. (Ithaca, NY: New Strategist Publications, 2011), 13, which notes that households earning $100,000 or more spent 81 percent as much at restaurants as on groceries, and singles spent 72 percent as much of their food dollar eating out as on groceries. Meanwhile, the average household spent 63 percent as much at restaurants as on groceries.

37. Martha Farnsworth Riche, "The Way to a Woman's Heart," *American Demographics* 7, no. 10 (October 1985): 44–47. The quotation is from page 44.

38. National Restaurant Association, *2009 Restaurant Industry Pocket Factbook*, http://www.restaurant.org/search_results.cfm?q=2009+Restaurant+Industry+Pocket+Factbook&x=0&y=0&cx=003254966726427069826%3A94pole1pdsu&cof=FORID%3A10&ie=UTF-8#1100.

39. "New Nuggets for 10/19," *BurgerBusiness* blog post, October 18, 2010, received by e-mail on October 19, 2010: "From research [by] NPD Group comes some interesting data on shifts in what and how Americans eat over the past 30 years. For example, the percentage of at-home meals made from scratch has declined from 72% to 59% over that period. And meals have become simpler: the average number of food items used per meal has decreased from 4.44 in the 1980s to 3.5 now." Also see Milford Prewitt, "Feeding Time-Starved Customers," *Nation's Restaurant News* 41, no. 5 (January 29, 2007): 8–9: "According to NPD statistics, in 1984 consumers went out to dinner roughly 33 times a year. By 2006 that number had dropped to 30 times a year. But the number of meals taken from a restaurant to eat at home or elsewhere doubled in the same time frame from 15 to 30."

For more on this trend toward increasing take-out and prepared meals, especially over the 1990s, see Milford Prewitt, "Takeout Boom Parallels Home-Cooking Inroads," *Nation's Restaurant News* 36, no. 39 (September 30, 2002): 6–7, and Matthew Schifrin, "Crab Rangoon to Go," *Forbes*, March 24, 1997, 124–26.

40. Bill McDowell, "Homeward Bound," *Restaurants & Institutions* 106, no. 6 (March 1, 1996): 60–61.

41. Craig Claiborne, "Colony Host Marks 40 Years," *New York Times*, December 19, 1959.

42. Jay Jacobs, "Le Cirque, One if by Land . . . Two if by Sea, Ristorante Il Rigoletto," *Gourmet*, December 1974, 4–6, 132–39. Vergnes retired in the summer of 1978, according to Jay Jacobs in "Le Cirque, Flower Drum, Restaurant Leslie," *Gourmet*, January 1979, 12, 90–93. The retirement of Vergnes is mentioned on page 12.

43. Donald Aspinwall Allan, "Lutèce, Gino's Restaurant, Benihana Palace," *Gourmet*, September 1970, 10–15.

44. Johnston and Baumann, *Foodies*, 11. Also see "Chefs Cook Up Publicity Feast," *Public Relations Journal* (January 1991): 14; and the American Culinary Federation's website under "About" and "Who We Are," at http://www.acfchefs.org/Content/NavigationMenu2/About/Overview/Default.htm (accessed June 27, 2012).

45. Francke, with Sullivan and Goldschlager, "Food," 52–53.

46. "Modern Living: Hold the Butter! Dam the Cream!" *Time*, March 29, 1976, http://www.time.com/time/printout/0,8816,918178,00.html.

47. Juliette Rossant popularized the term in *Super Chef: The Making of the Great Modern Restaurant Empires* (New York: Free Press, 2004). William Grimes adopts it in *Appetite City: A Culinary History of New York* (New York: North Point Press, 2009), 301–3. Michael

Ruhlman uses the term *branded chef* instead, in *The Reach of a Chef*; see part 4, "The Power of the Branded Chef," 197–270.

48. Rossant, *Super Chef*. One chapter is devoted to Wolfgang Puck. For milestones of Puck's career, see 12–22. For reference to his 1986 appearance on *Good Morning America* and the publication of his first cookbooks, see 17. For reference to when Puck started his line of frozen pizzas, see Michael Barrier, "The Chef as Famous as His Customers," *Nation's Business* 79, no. 7 (July 1991): 29 (3 pp.). For notice that Puck is not the only chef to be listed on the Forbes Celebrity 100 list, see Marcia Layton Turner, *Emeril! Inside the Amazing Success of Today's Most Popular Chef* (Hoboken, NJ: John Wiley & Sons, 2004), 2. For information after 2004, see Pamela Parseghian, "Fine Dining Legend Award Recipient: Wolfgang Puck," *Nation's Restaurant News*, May 21, 2007, http://www.nrn.com/article/fine-dining-legend-award-recipient-wolfgang-puck; and "Wolfgang Puck Worldwide, Inc.," on an investment company website, http://www.fundinguniverse.com/company-histories/Wolfgang-Puck-Worldwide-Inc-Company-History.html (accessed September 15, 2010).

49. Katy Mclaughlin, "Rock-Star Chefs," *Wall Street Journal*, October 2, 2009, http://online.wsj.com/. Regarding the advent of celebrity-chef appearances at charity events in the early 1980s, see Tower, *California Dish*, 210–11.

50. The following sources represent the wide range of the chef-CEOs' activities: Rossant, *Super Chef*; Ruhlman, *The Reach of a Chef*; and Turner, *Emeril!*. On the trend of chefs consulting: John F. Mariani, "What's Hot for 1987," *Food & Wine*, January 1987, 46–55, especially 48. On the advent of celebrity chefs doing live appearances: Ruth Reichl, "Chefs as the Star Ingredients," *Los Angeles Times*, October 8, 1985. Regarding the use of publicists and agents: Laurie Freeman, "Chefs Find a Niche at Hollywood Star Agency," *Restaurant Business* 92, no. 2 (January 20, 1993): 20; and Emily Bell, "A Chef's Primer on Publicists," StarChefs.com, February 2010, http://www.starchefs.com/features/chef-and-restaurant-publicists.shtml.

51. Andy Birsh, "Le Régence, Indochine, Sarabeth's Kitchen," *Gourmet*, July 1986, 28–34, 88–94.

52. Andy Birsh, "Le Cirque, Nick and Eddie, Carmine's," *Gourmet*, December 1991, 32–40.

53. *Café Boulud*, video featuring Daniel Boulud talking about Café Boulud, Savorycities.com, posted March 18, 2010, http://www.savorycities.com/newyork/restaurant/café-boulud/20-e-76th-st (accessed December 11, 2011).

54. My impressions from 2010 are consistent with critics' accounts published at the time of some of the restaurants' opening dates. About Café Boulud: Ruth Reichl, "Daniel Boulud, in a Laid-Back Mood," *New York Times*, December 9, 1998, and Ruth Reichl, "Diner's Journal," *New York Times*, October 9, 1998. On DBGB Kitchen & Bar: Sam Sifton, "Now I Wanna Serve Some Sausage," *New York Times*, October 14, 2009, http://events.nytimes.com/2009/10/14/dining/reviews/14rest.html?.

55. Bret Thorn, "Restaurateurs Assess 'Fine Fast' Food Trend at Aspen Food and Wine Event," *Nation's Restaurant News*, July 9, 2007, http://www.nrn.com/article/restaurateurs-assess-'fine-fast'-food-trend-aspen-food-and-wine-event-0; "Veteran Restaurateur Creates New 'Fast Fine' Restaurant Franchise Concept," FranchiseWorks.com, April 15, 2011, http://www.franchiseworks.com/franchise_news_story.aspx?nid=1058#; Jessica Dukes, "Quality in Quantity: Management Tips for High Volume Restaurants," StarChefs.com, October 2010, http://www.starchefs.com/cook/features/quality-quantity-management-tips-high-volume-restaurants.

56. Dana Thomas explores this phenomenon in *Deluxe: How Luxury Lost Its Luster* (New York: Penguin, 2007).

57. Richard Florida, *The Rise of the Creative Class, and How It's Transforming Work, Leisure, Community and Everyday Life* (New York: Basic Books, 2002), 8; Harvey, *The Condition of Postmodernity*, 156–57.

58. By Richard Florida: *The Rise of the Creative Class*, 9; *The Flight of the Creative Class: The New Global Competition for Talent* (New York: HarperCollins, 2005), 28–29; and *Cities and the Creative Class* (New York: Routledge, 2005), 3–4.

59. Florida, *The Rise of the Creative Class*, 9.

60. On the Higher Education Act of 1965: Victor D. Brooks, *Boomers: The Cold-War Generation Grows Up* (Chicago: Ivan R. Dee, 2009), 136–38. About the tripling of college students between 1965 and 1975: Richard Croker, *The Boomer Century 1946–2046* (New York: Springboard Press, 2007), 57–58. For the growth of institutions of higher learning: David Brooks, *Bobos in Paradise: The New Upper Class and How They Got There* (New York: Simon & Schuster, 2000): 30; and the increasing value of a college degree, 36. On the growth of an education-based meritocratic ideal: Joseph Epstein, *Snobbery: The American Version* (Boston: Houghton Mifflin, 2002), 53–71.

61. Florida, *The Rise of the Creative Class*, 8, for an overview of creative-class values; pages 11 and 235–48, for discussion of data regarding what he calls "the geography of creativity." In *The Flight of the Creative Class*, on page 282, Florida says he uses the same 2000 survey for his regional "creativity index."

62. Bill Bishop, with Robert G. Cushing, *The Big Sort: Why the Clustering of Like-Minded America Is Tearing Us Apart* (New York: Houghton Mifflin, 2008), 50–53, 131–33.

63. Thomas Frank, *The Conquest of Cool: Business Culture, Counterculture, and the Rise of Hip Consumerism* (Chicago: University of Chicago Press, 1997).

64. J. Walker Smith and Ann Clurman, *Generation Ageless: How Baby Boomers Are Changing the Way We Live Today . . . And They're Just Getting Started* (New York: HarperCollins, 2007), 200–203.

65. Florida, *The Rise of the Creative Class*, 117; Sherry Maysonave, *Casual Power: How to Power Up Your Nonverbal Communication and Dress Down for Success* (Austin, TX: Bright Books, 1999), 4.

66. Florida, *The Rise of the Creative Class*, 116–19, for discussion of the new importance of flexibility in the workplace as a symptom of "creative" values; Maysonave, *Casual Power*, 4–6, for discussion of Top Quality Management and the impact of technology on casual work attire.

67. William G. Flanagan, "(Un)dressing for Dinner," *Forbes* 154, no. 6 (September 12, 1994): 256–58; Mariani with von Bidder, *The Four Seasons*, 206; Milford Prewitt, "Ties No Longer Binding: '21' Club Eases Dress Code Permanently," *Nation's Restaurant News* 31, no. 6 (February 10, 1997): 6; William Grimes, "Dress Code: The Last Gasp," *New York Times*, January 28, 1998; Michael DeLuca, "Casual Clothes Point to Larger Trend," *Restaurant Hospitality* (September 1996): 14.

68. Rachel X. Weissman, "Guess Who's Not Coming to Dinner," *American Demographics* 21, no. 6 (June 1999): 30–32.

69. *Gourmet*'s readership in 1983 had a median age of 48.5 and an average household income of $66,000. In 2008, its readers had a median age of 50.3, and an average household income of $81,179. I don't adjust for inflation. *Food & Wine*'s audience in 1983 had a median age of 43 and median individual earnings of $40,000. Its 2009 readers had a median age of 44.7 and a median personal income of $43,614. The higher incomes of *Gourmet* readers probably reflect the difference in median ages, since the sources of these statistics all characterize the magazines' audiences as upscale: Alison W. Heckler, "The Horn of Plenty: Getting a Taste of the Gourmet Food Market," *Target Marketing* 6, no. 7 (July 1983): 1, 4–6, 17–21; Condé Nast, "Condé Nast Media Kit: *Gourmet*," Condé Nast Publications (2009), http://condenastmediakit.com/gou/index.cfm; American Express Company, "*Food & Wine* Media Kit," American Express Company (2009), http://www.fwmediakit.com .index.html. For Food Network data, see my "Chef Appeal," 5, and the following sources: Smillie, "Humor Is the Key Ingredient at Lively TV Food Network"; Booker, "Selling Cooking to Non-Cooks"; McConville, "Smaller Nets Spur on Cable"; Thompson, "Extreme Cuisine at Food Network"; Chunovic, "Food Network Is Tweaking Its Recipe"; and "Food Network."

70. For 1984, there are data on income and education for the biggest spenders on food away from home. On November 12, 2010, Vera Crain, representative of the United States Bureau of Labor Statistics, e-mailed me prepublication data. Table 2, entitled "Average Annual Expenditures of All Consumer Units Classified by INCOME BEFORE TAXES, Consumer Expenditure Survey 1984 Feb 10 92," noted that the top three spenders on dinner "away from home" (there were no data for "full-service restaurants" then) were, by far, the biggest income group they recorded: $50,000 and over, which spent an average of $1,227.89, followed by those making $40,000–49,999, which spent an average of $681.59, and then by those making $30,000–39,999, which spent an average of $644.80. In the same table, education is positively correlated to income, with 77 percent of those making $50,000 and over (the highest bracket listed) having a college education, followed by 62 percent of those making $40,000–49,999, and then by 56 percent of those making $30,000–39,999. One may infer that education is positively correlated with expenditure on food away from home.

For 1988, there are data on income, education, and occupation. On November 12, 2010, Vera Crain of the BLS e-mailed me prepublication data. I consulted table 1200, entitled "Income before Taxes: Average Annual Expenditures and Characteristics, Consumer Expenditure Survey, 1988 July 11, 1991." The top three spenders on dinner "away from home" (there were no data for "full-service restaurants" then) were those making $50,000 and more, at an average of $1057.00, followed by those making $40,000–49,999, at $822.65, and then by those making $30,000–39,999, at $662.77.

Table 1200 also shows a positive correlation between highest income earners and education level. Since income level is positively correlated to spending on dinner "away from home," one may conclude that education had a positive correlation to expenditure on dinner away from home. Noteworthy statistics on education: 78% of the highest income earners ($50,000 and up), 58% of the $40,000–49,999 earners, and 53% of the $30,000–39,999 earners had college educations.

Table 1900 of the 1988 data Crain e-mailed me, entitled "Occupation of Reference Person: Average Annual Expenditures and Characteristics, Consumer Expenditure Survey, 1988 July 11, 1991," showed that the top three spenders on dinner "away from home" (there were no data for "full-service restaurants" then) were "managers and professionals," at an average of $818.70, followed by "construction workers and mechanics," at an average of $612.62, and then by "technical, sales, and clerical workers," at an average of $603.19.

For 1995, there are data on income, education, and occupation. On November 12, 2010, Crain e-mailed me data. Table 1902, entitled "Occupation of Reference Person: Average Annual Expenditures and Characteristics, Consumer Expenditure Survey, 1995 May 8, 1997," shows that the top three spenders on dinner "away from home" by occupation are the same as those having the highest incomes. In other words, the biggest spenders are "managers and professionals." They made an average after-tax income of $55,439 and spent an average of $986.15. "Self-employed" workers, earning an average of $44,407 after taxes, spent an average of $836.40 on dinner away from home. "Construction workers and mechanics," earning an average after-tax income of $36,961, spent an average of $707.08 on dinner away from home.

Table 1902 also reveals a positive correlation between education level and spending on food away from home. The uppermost spenders on dinner "away from home," at an average of $986.15, were "managers and professionals." They also had the highest incomes, and were the most educated. 82% had college educations. The next-best educated, with 58% having college degrees, were "technical, sales, and clerical workers," and they were not among the three top spenders on dinner away from home. The third-best educated, with 54% having college degrees, were the "self-employed," and these were the second-biggest spenders on dinner away from home; they spent an average of $836.40. The third-biggest spenders on dinner away from home were "construction workers and mechanics," and they did not score high in education. The data do not discriminate among types of dining-out destinations. Therefore, one cannot correlate education to specific habits of dining out.

For 2001, there are data on income, education, and occupation in New Strategist Publications, *Who's Buying at Restaurants and Carry-Outs* (Ithaca, NY: New Strategist Publications, Inc., 2004). Page 16 contains income data. The charts on pages 43–44 list education data. Page 16 also gives occupational information relevant to spending on full-service restaurants, and states, "Blue collar workers are big spenders on food from vending machines and mobile vendors while the white collar elite (managers and professionals) are big spenders on full-service restaurant meals." A numeric breakdown of data by occupational type and food-service type is on page 52.

For 2003, there are data on income and education for spending on "food away from home" in New Strategist Publications, *The American Marketplace: Demographics and Spending Patterns* (Ithaca, NY: New Strategist Publications, Inc., 2005). Pages 411–16 give income data. The summary of findings on page 411 notes that households with incomes of $150,000 or more were "the only income group to spend more on restaurant meals than groceries," a fact that could reflect higher restaurant check averages (from pricier meals and/or larger households) or more frequent restaurant dining. Page 413, table 8.5, gives data for the top three household income categories' annual average spending on food away from home. This average was $5,201 for households earning $100,000 or more, $3,703 for those making $80,000–99,999, and $3,195 for households earning $70,000–79,999. Contrast this with spending on food away from home for the bottom three household income categories: $1,105 annually for those earning less than $20,000, $1,691 for households in the $20,000–39,999 bracket, and $2,252 for those earning $40,000–49,999. Page 466, table 8.20, correlates education level to average dollars spent on food away from home per person. Those with a graduate degree spent an average of $3,490 out of an average annual spending of $65,203; those with a bachelor's degree spent $2,967 out of $54,726; and those with an associate's degree spent $2,486 out of $44,547. Consumers with "some college" spent $2,229 out of $37,912. High-school graduates spend $1,715 out of $33,956. Finally, those without a high-school diploma spent $1,173 out of $23,901.

For 2007, there are data on income and education related to spending on food away from home in New Strategist Publications, *Who's Buying at Restaurants and Carry-Outs*, 7th ed. (Ithaca, NY: New Strategist Publications, Inc., 2009). See tables 35 and 11 for income and table 35 for education. Page 13 states that a household making $100,000 or more spent 91 percent as much at restaurants as on groceries.

Finally, for 2009, I found data correlating income and education, average annual spending on food away from home, and average annual total spending. See New Strategist Publications, *The American Marketplace: Demographics and Spending Patterns*, 10th ed. (Ithaca, NY: New Strategist Publications, 2011). Regarding income, in a summary of data on page 478, the report states: "Households with incomes of $150,000 or more . . . spent [an average of] $124,306 in 2009. They are the only income group to spend more on restaurant meals than groceries." On page 480, see table 9.5, "Average Spending by Household Income, 2009." For "food away from home" in the top three income categories, I found spending at an average of $4,525 out of an average annual spending of $82,060 for incomes of $70,000 or more; $2,666 out of $48,900 for incomes $50,000–69,999; and $2,022 out of $39,553 for earnings of $40,000–49,999. For "food away from home" in the bottom three income categories, I noted spending of an average of $1,109 out of an average annual spending of $20,274 for those making less than $10,000; $989 out of $22,720 for incomes $10,000–19,999; and $1,419 out of $29,397 for incomes $20,000–29,999. For education data, see page 533, table 9.20, "Average Spending by Education of Householder, 2009." For "food away from home," consumers having at least a bachelor's degree spent an average of $3,711 out of an average annual spending of $69,389; those with an associate's degree, $2,991 out of $50,444; those with "some college," $2,430 out of $44,697; those with a high-school diploma, $1,987 out of $38,693; those without a high-school diploma, $1,392 out of $30,323.

71. Regarding TV: Croker, *The Boomer Century 1946–2046*, 18–21; Matt Thornhill and John Martin, *Boomer Consumer: Ten New Rules for Marketing to America's Largest, Wealthiest and Most Influential Group* (Great Falls, VA: LINX, 2007), 57; and V. Brooks, *Boomers*, 30. On magazine consumption: Karen Ritchie, *Marketing to Generation X* (New York: Lexington Books, 1995), 65–66.

72. In sources I mentioned earlier, Bill Bishop, Robert Cushing, and Richard Florida have explored the geographic aspect of Americans' self-segregation along the lines of income, education, religion, race, age, tolerance of immigrants, political ideology, and lifestyle. For a discussion of the phenomenon whereby targeted marketing reinforces social segmentation, and for a discussion of the literature on this topic, see my "Interactive Art for a Challenged Democracy," *X-TRA: Contemporary Art Quarterly* 11, no. 3 (Spring 2009): 4–15.

73. Levenstein, *Paradox of Plenty*, 25–39.

74. Ibid., 122–23.

75. Ibid., 113–15.

76. The quotation and these statistics both come from ibid., 117.

77. John A. Jakle and Keith A. Sculle, *Fast Food Roadside Restaurants in the Automobile Age* (Baltimore: Johns Hopkins University, 1999), 50–51. On franchising, see 84–91. The reference to the tripling of fast-food places comes from Levenstein, *Paradox of Plenty*, 233.

78. This theme runs throughout chapters 4–7, pages 83–188, in Richard Pillsbury, *From Boarding House to Bistro: The American Restaurant Then and Now* (Boston: Unwin Hyman, 1990). For reference to McDonald's, see Levenstein, *Paradox of Plenty*, 229.

Chapter 3

1. The foodie buzz about minibar (yes, it's all lowercase) started as soon as it opened. Note the exchange between Buster R. (July 24, 2003) and Joel Wood (July 31, 2003) under

the thread "Has Anyone Tried the Latino minibar at Café Atlantico?" at http://chowhound
.chow.com/topics/168189 (accessed June 30, 2012). Joel Wood described the twenty-four
courses he had there the previous week as "the most exciting dining experience in Washington right now."

   2. That other restaurant was Café Atlantico until July 4, 2011, when it was replaced for
one year by America Eats Tavern, the chef's take on historical cuisine of the United States.
At the time this book went into production, there was no news about what would replace
America Eats Tavern.

   3. Here and the next three paragraphs: Philip Langdon, *Orange Roofs, Golden Arches:
The Architecture of American Chain Restaurants* (New York: Alfred A. Knopf, 1986). For
information on Child's lunchrooms, see pages 19–20; for Howard Johnson's, 50; for 1930s
drive-ins with indoor eating options, 67; and on "Googie" coffee shops of the 1950s and
1960s, 121. In Jakle and Sculle, *Fast Food*, 4–5, the authors personally recall the presence
of food preparation behind lunch counters at the less upscale urban cafés of the later
1940s. They discuss the architectural features of California-style coffee shops on page 53.
On diners: Richard J. S. Gutman, *American Diner: Then and Now* (Baltimore: Johns Hopkins University Press, 2000), originally published by HarperCollins, New York, in 1993. Pictures on pages 86 and 153–54 show variations in the relation of kitchen to dining counter.
A photo of a prewar diner, the Priscilla Candy Shoppe and Tea Room, is in Jim Heimann,
May I Take Your Order? American Menu Design 1920–1960 (San Francisco: Chronicle Books,
1998), 11. Finally, Michael Karl Witzel, *The American Diner* (St. Paul, MN: MBI, 2006), originally published 1999, has photos and discussion of diner layouts on pages 24, 51, and 122.

   4. Jakle and Sculle's *Fast Food* (1999) discusses the 1920s emergence of destination
"dinner houses" featuring steak on pages 266–67.

   5. Andrew Coe, *Chop Suey: A Cultural History of Chinese Food in the United States* (New
York: Oxford University Press, 2009), 220. Coe interviewed Kan.

   6. Benihana is discussed in Jakle and Sculle, *Fast Food* (1999), 284. Jane and Michael
Stern's *American Gourmet* (1991), 270, describes the 1957 Treadway Inn of Niagara Falls,
NY, as having open steak grilling. For discussion and photos of La Fonda del Sol, see
Grimes, *Appetite City*, 278–79.

   7. Regarding Fournou's Ovens, see Caroline Bates, "Fournou's Ovens, Akasaka, Scott's
Seafood Grill and Bar," *Gourmet*, July 1977, 4. For further perspective on the restaurant and
its changes over the following decade, see Caroline Bates, "Fournou's Ovens, Palio d'Asti,
Casa Madrona," *Gourmet*, August 1991, 30–32.

   8. There are earlier examples of serious gourmet establishments with exposed kitchens, but I'm not convinced in these cases that the kitchen's exhibition was anything other
than an architectural compromise. In 1973, Jay Jacobs wrote about one in the downstairs
dining room of a miniscule Manhattan restaurant called Mary's that he declared quite
possibly the best Italian restaurant in the city. "Any one of the five downstairs tables," he
wrote, "provides a good view of the kitchen and its resident cooks, both of whom prepare
all dishes to order." Jacobs's description of the restaurant's utterly bare-bones décor suggests that the open kitchen might have been a necessity. That exhibition kitchens hadn't
yet caught on in the gourmet realm is also evident from the reviewer's comment that while
he enjoyed seeing and smelling the kitchen, others might prefer to sit farther away. Jay
Jacobs, "Le Cygne, Maxwell's Plum, Mary's," *Gourmet*, May 1973, 10.

   9. The article by Craig Claiborne that sparked attention to Novi's is "Restaurant Merits
Three-Hour Drive," *New York Times*, March 6, 1970.

   10. My account of chef John N. Novi's restaurant redesign with open kitchen and chef's

table derives from my interview with the chef, which took place entirely via private Facebook messages between January 28 and 31, 2011.

11. Linda Bird Francke, with Scott Sullivan and Seth Goldschlager, "Food: The New Wave," *Newsweek*, August 11, 1975, 50–57.

12. On the rise in fashion of Japanese sushi bars, see Trevor Corson, "L.A. Story," in *The Zen of Fish: The Story of Sushi, from Samurai to Supermarket* (New York: Harper Collins, 2007), 44–51; Kamp, *The United States of Arugula*, 315–17. On Puck's early Japanese culinary influences in California, see Kamp, *The United States of Arugula*, 250–51. Regarding Puck's hiring of cooks at Chinois on Main and for evidence that before the open kitchen was expanded in 2007, the small open kitchen in front of the dining counter even more closely recalled a sushi bar, see Dorf, *Restaurants That Work*, 96–103.

13. The reference to Spago's taking inspiration from Chez Panisse is in McNamee, *Alice Waters and Chez Panisse*, 158. For the emergence of discussion of California cuisine in the media, see Tower, *California Dish*, 144–45.

14. In an e-mail to me on February 3, 2011, chef Charlie Trotter clarified that the "kitchen table" was instituted and began serving guests in October 1987. The restaurant's "studio kitchen," a dining room featuring its own dedicated kitchen as well as live video feed from the main kitchen, reserved commonly for business special-event dinners, began operations in 1994. Edmund Lawler provides a history of the design and function of these restaurant features in *Charlie Trotter's: An Inside Look at the Famed Restaurant and Its Cuisine* (New York: Lebhar-Friedman Books, 2000), 42–45 and the book jacket, but the text isn't specific about dates.

15. In an e-mail to me of February 3, 2011, Jeff Hinson, public relations manager for Emeril Lagasse, informed me that the original "food bar" at Emeril's opened on March 26, 1990. It was enlarged due to its popularity in 2000. Further description and an account of the food bar's success exist in Turner's *Emeril!*, 52 and 54.

16. Regina S. Baraban and Joseph F. Durocher, PhD, *Successful Restaurant Design* (New York: Van Nostrand Reinhold, 1989), 103–6; and subsequent editions of the book by the same authors and title—the second ed. (New York: John Wiley & Sons, 2001), 160–65; and third ed. (Hoboken, NJ: John Wiley & Sons, 2010), 162–63. The following tout display kitchens as an unceasing and widespread trend: Carol Lally Metz, "Designs That Really Cook," *Lodging Hospitality* 46 (1990): 115–17; Mary Reinholz, "The Post-'80s Open Kitchen," *Restaurant Business* (July 20, 1993): 162–68; Gary Bensky, "The Great White Way: The Display Kitchen Is 'Culinary Broadway,'" *Nation's Restaurant News* 34, no. 34 (August 21, 2000): 29; and Dan Bendall, "Display Cooking," *Food Management* 43, no. 2 (February 2008): 80 (2 pp.). The quotation is from page 80.

17. Highlights in the proclamation of a hot trend in chef's tables—directed to business clients, foodies, travelers, and trade audiences from 1996 to 2010—include Ronald B. Liebner, "Best Seat in the House," *Fortune* 134, no. 5 (September 9, 1996): 196 (2 pp.); "Chef's Tables," *Gourmet*, October 1999, 51–65; Monique R. Brown, "New Spin on Dining," *Black Enterprise* 30, no. 6 (January 2000): 122; Milford Prewitt, "Chefs' Tables Set to Help Ease High-End Doldrums," *Nation's Restaurant News* 37, no. 24 (June 16, 2003): 1; "Chef's Table Creates Cachet," *Lodging Hospitality* 62, no. 12 (August 2006): 16; Dirk Smillie, "Cirque du Sorbet," *Forbes* 178, no. 10 (November 13, 2006): 214–15; Lisa Fickenscher, "Foodies Mob Kitchen," *Crain's New York Business* 23, no. 51 (December 17, 2007): 2; Frank Bruni, "A Celebrity and His Skillet: Dinner at the Chef's Table," *New York Times*, December 24, 2008, http://www.nytimes.com/2008/12/24/dining/24note.html; "Chef's Tables," *Celebrated Living*, Fall 2010, 26; and Cajun Mama, "Carnival Expands Chef's Table Fine Dining Experience on Cruise Ships," blog post, http://travelingmamas.com/carnival-expands-chefs-table-fine-dining-experience-on-cruise-ships/ (undated, but which I accessed January 20, 2011).

18. Lawler, *Charlie Trotter's*, 115.

19. Rajan Chaudhry, "Casual Dining Checks In," *Restaurants & Institutions* 103, no. 26 (November 1, 1993): 18 (6 pp.), focuses on hotel chains and uses the word *upgrade*. Megan Rowe, "Rib Redo," *Restaurant Business* 100, no. 16 (2001): 22–23, doesn't use the word *upscale*, but rather the synonyms *fancy, classy,* and *formal*. The following use the term *upscale*: Bob Sperber, "Going Upscale," *Brandweek* 43, no. 30 (August 19–26, 2002): 1 (2 pp.); Amy Spector, "CPK Founders Launch LA Food Show Concept," *Nation's Restaurant News* 37, no. 23 (June 9, 2003): 1; Leann Cannon, "Kona Grill Imports Island Atmosphere, Flavors to Mainland Units," *Nation's Restaurant News* 38, no. 30 (July 26, 2004): 36; Carolyn Walkup, "Houlihan's Unveils Prototype, Menu Items in New Bid for Elusive Growth," *Nation's Restaurant News* 39, no. 16 (April 18, 2005): 4 (2 pp.); Carolyn Walkup, "Established Concepts Aim to Invigorate Images, Sales," *Nation's Restaurant News* 41, no. 44 (November 5, 2007): 37 (3 pp.); and "Rubio's Opens New Location with Upscale Design," *QSR Magazine* (March 6, 2010), http://www.qsrmagazine.com/news/rubios-opens-new-location-upscale-design.

20. These notes refer to recorded phone interviews I conducted: on April 13, 2010, Pat Kuleto, founder and CEO of Pat Kuleto Restaurant Development & Management Company, mentioned all my cited reasons for why restaurants with open kitchens tend to cost more to install and maintain than those without them. On July 2, 2010, chef and restaurateur Cindy Pawlcyn mentioned the extra expense of attractive materials. On August 25, 2010, Rob Wilder, CEO of ThinkFoodGroup, the umbrella company of chef José Andres's restaurants, cited the costliness of attractive finishes and the more expensive and complicated engineering of HVAC systems. On September 30, 2010, chef and restaurateur Wylie Dufresne, co-owner of WD-50 in Manhattan, said he'd like to think the cost wouldn't be greater. He expressed pride in his professionalism and the high standard to which he would run his kitchen, whether or not it was exposed to diners. Later, though, he unintentionally revealed that there would be a difference when he happened to mention that getting the HVAC right at WD-50 had been tricky.

Numerous print sources confirm the extra costliness of exhibition kitchen design: Reinholz, "The Post-'80s Open Kitchen"; Ed Rubinstein, "Big Apple Operators Make Big Presentation Statements with Kitchens," *Nation's Restaurant News* 32, no. 45 (November 9, 1998): 26 (2 pp.); Lee Simon, "Designing a Feast for Their Eyes," *Restaurant Hospitality* 86, no. 11 (November 2002): 30; and Elaine Martin Petrowski, "The Open Kitchen as Theater," *Architectural Record* 187, no. 9 (September 1999): 171.

21. Sources that mentioned exceptions to the rule of open kitchens costing more include Scott Shaw, founder and CEO of Fishbowl, Inc. In a recorded phone interview on April 10, 2010, he told me that open kitchens are generally more costly, but savings can be found if the elimination of transitional spaces such as service walkways between a BOH kitchen and the dining room enable the restaurant to have a tighter floor plan. This point is reiterated as a possibility in Baraban and Durocher in *Successful Restaurant Design*, 3rd ed. (2010), 162. In Reinholz, "The Post-'80s Open Kitchen," designer David Rockwell states that he was able to cut the expenses of an open kitchen at chef Jean Georges Vongerichten's New York City restaurant, Vong, by "devising a compromised version of the open kitchen: 'We have a special screen in front of the kitchen so you see light and people moving.'"

The following sources confirm the remunerative aspect of chef's tables, owing to their premium cost to the diner: my interview with Pat Kuleto; Prewitt, "Chefs' Tables Set to Ease High-End Doldrums"; Smillie, "Cirque du Sorbet"; and Fickenscher, "Foodies Mob Kitchen."

22. These sources include statements by nonchef restaurateurs, designers, or food-service consultants that identify energetic atmosphere and theatrical entertainment as benefits of display kitchens: Metz, "Designs That Really Cook"; Dorf, *Restaurants That Work*, 65, 150; Larissa Doucette, "Café Centro's Kitchen Takes Center Stage," *Foodservice Equipment & Supplies Specialist* 50, no. 9 (August 10, 1997): 67 (4 pp.); Kate Brennan, "How to Get Guests Hungry for the Hotel Restaurant," *Lodging Hospitality* 56, no. 12 (September 15, 2000): 56; Terence Conran, *Terence Conran on Restaurants* (New York: Overlook Press, 2000), 59; and Baraban and Durocher, *Successful Restaurant Design*, 2nd ed. (2001), 253, 269, and 273. Designer Barbara Lazaroff asserted the sensual benefits of open kitchens in Mary Reinholz's interview with her for "The Post-'80s Open Kitchen," 166. Sources containing assertions that open kitchens give the impression of freshness and cleanliness include Doucette, "Café Centro's Kitchen Takes Center Stage," and Baraban and Durocher, *Successful Restaurant Design*, 2nd ed. (2001), 269.

23. Nonchef restaurateurs, designers, and food-service consultants mention the desirability of emulating a home environment in Dorf, *Restaurants That Work*, 65, and Rubinstein, "Big Apple Operators Make Big Presentation Statements with Kitchens." For claims that open kitchens fulfill a customer need for connection to food preparation, see Baraban and Durocher, *Successful Restaurant Design*, 3rd ed. (2010), 258. In recorded phone interviews with me, Pat Kuleto and Rob Wilder asserted that open kitchens fulfill a customer desire to be close to the chef.

24. Alice Waters, interviewed for McNamee, *Alice Waters and Chez Panisse*, 157, discusses the Chez Panisse Café's installation of an open kitchen for the advantages of having the sensuous "sounds and smells of frying charcoal grilling, and the new pizza oven [that] would drift throughout the dining rooms." Wolfgang Puck mentions the entertainment value of open kitchens in Baraban and Durocher, *Successful Restaurant Design*, 3rd ed. (2010), 162.

25. Brad A. Johnson, "Wolfgang Puck," *Restaurants & Institutions* 105, no. 20 (August 15, 1995): 62; Metz, "Designs That Really Cook"; Dorf, *Restaurants That Work*, 67; my interview with Wylie Dufresne; Chang and Meehan, *Momofuku*, 126.

26. My interviews with John N. Novi and Cindy Pawlcyn, and Prewitt, "Chefs' Tables Set to Ease High-End Doldrums."

27. Florence Fabricant, "In Vongerichten's New Venture, the Kitchen Is on Display," *New York Times*, March 5, 1997; Jack Hayes, "Emeril Lagasse: Bam! This Top-Notch Chef Kicks His Career Up to the Highest Rung of Culinary Fame," *Nation's Restaurant News* 34, no. 5 (January 2000): 108; Brian Spinner, "Ovens Front and Center," *Restaurants & Institutions* 112, no. 14 (June 15, 2002): 69 (2 pp.); and Oliver Strand, "At Eleven Madison Park, Fixing What Isn't Broke," *New York Times*, September 7, 2010, http://www.nytimes.com/2010/09/08/dining/08humm.html.

28. Baraban and Durocher, *Successful Restaurant Design* (1989 ed.), 103–6.

29. Spago Beverly Hills closed for renovation and redesign in the summer of 2012 as this book went to press, so I cannot yet say whether the new design will have the same features I observed during my 2008 visit. See Kat Odell, "End of an Era," *LA Eater*, at http://la.eater.com/archives/2012/05/30/end_of_an_era_spago_done_july_9_reopening_this_fall_with_new_look_new_menu.php (accessed June 30, 2012).

30. Liebner, "Best Seat in the House."

31. Caroline Bates, "Los Angeles and Buellton: Ginza Sushi-ko, Diaghilev, The Hitching Post," *Gourmet*, February 1998, 60–72, 77.

32. Frank Bruni, "Sushi at Masa: It's a Zen Thing," *New York Times*, December 29, 2004; Anthony Bourdain, "Pure and Uncut Luxury," in *The Nasty Bits: Collected Varietal Cuts, Usable Trim, Scraps, and Bones* (New York: Bloomsbury, 2006), 191–94.

33. Smillie, "Cirque du Sorbet."

34. Fickenscher, "Foodies Mob Kitchen."

35. Ruth Reichl, "First Taste: Momofuku Ko," *Gourmet*, March 4, 2008, http://www .gourmet.com/restaurants/2008/03/firsttaste_momofuku?.

36. Frank Bruni, "To Dine at Momofuku Ko, First You Need Nimble Fingers," *New York Times*, May 7, 2008, http://events.nytimes.com/2008/05/07/dining/reviews/07rest.html?.

37. Bourdain, "Pure and Uncut Luxury," 191–94. The quotation is from pages 191–92.

38. Erving Goffman, *The Presentation of Self in Everyday Life* (New York: Anchor Books, 1959). An excellent account of Goffman's theoretical contributions in this work is Ann Branaman, "Goffman's Social Theory," in *The Goffman Reader*, ed, Charles Lemert and Ann Branaman (Malden, MA: Blackwell, 2001), originally published by Blackwell, Malden, MA, in 1997, xlv–lxxxii.

39. Ibid.

40. Harry Blumberg, "The Restaurant Kitchen," *Interiors* (August 1944): 67–68.

41. Baraban and Durocher, *Successful Restaurant Design* (1989), 105; 2nd ed. (2001), 162; 3rd ed. (2010), 163.

42. Reinholz, "The Post-'80s Open Kitchen."

43. Steven Starr, "See-Through Kitchens," *Contract Design* 40, no. 12 (December 1998): 42–43; Bensky, "The Great White Way."

44. Dorf, *Restaurants That Work*, 93–95.

45. Mardee Haidin Regan, "At the New Café Centro, All the World's a Stage," *Food Arts: The Magazine for Professionals* (November 1994): 94–102; Larissa Doucette, "Café Centro's Kitchen Takes Center Stage," *Foodservice Equipment & Supplies Specialist* 50, no. 9 (August 10, 1997): 67 (4 pp.).

46. Grant Achatz and Nick Kokonas, e-mail, from press@nextrestaurant.com, to me as a list subscriber, February 5, 2011.

47. Nicole G. Castagna, "Trends of Steel," *Restaurants & Institutions* 107, no. 21 (September 1, 1997): 73 (4 pp.).

48. Petrowski, "The Open Kitchen as Theater."

49. Dorf, *Restaurants That Work*, 150–51.

50. Metz, "Designs That Really Cook"; Kimberly D. Lowe, "Chefs on Display," *Restaurants & Institutions* 107, no. 16 (July 1, 1997): 78 (2 pp.); Petrowski, "The Open Kitchen as Theater"; Pamela Parseghian, "Enjoy Dining, Close the Door on Open Kitchens," *Nation's Restaurant News* 34, no. 43 (October 23, 2000): 42.

51. Foster Frable Jr., "Planning for Display and Open Kitchens Requires Special Attention to Detail," *Nation's Restaurant News* 32, no. 45 (November 9, 1998): 26 (2 pp.).

52. Dan Bendall, "Display Cooking Equipment," *Restaurant Hospitality* 84, no. 4 (April 2000): 105 (4 pp.).

53. Starr, "See-Through Kitchens."

54. Ibid.

55. Tom O'Brien, "Shoes and Uniforms: Dressing for Success," *Restaurant Business* 108, no. 1 (January 2009): FSB11.

56. Kathleen Collins, "Middle Period (1963–1992)," in *Watching What We Eat*, 69–155.

57. Krishnendu Ray, "Domesticating Cuisine: Food and Aesthetics in American Television," *Gastronomica: The Journal of Food and Culture* 7, no. 1 (Winter 2007): 50–63.

58. Andrew Chan, "'La Grande Bouffe': Cooking Shows as Pornography," *Gastronomica* 3, no. 4 (Fall 2003), as reprinted in Darra Goldstein, ed., *The Gastronomica Reader* (Berkeley: University of California Press, 2010), 139–48.

59. Cheri Ketchum, "The Essence of Cooking Shows: How the Food Network Constructs Consumer Fantasies," *Journal of Communication Inquiry* 29, no. 3 (July 2005): 217–34.

60. Pearlman, "Chef Appeal."

61. The following articles address the shift in the content of popular amateur cooking classes over the mid-1980s: Judy Thorne, "The Craze Is Over, But There Still Is a Market for the Right Kind of School," *Seattle Times*, May 1, 1985; Nancy Jenkins, "At Cooking Classes, a New Seriousness as Boom Days End," *New York Times*, September 11, 1985; and Marilynn Marter, "The Cooking School: Aura of Change," *Philadelphia Inquirer*, September 14, 1986.

62. My figures concerning the Shaw Guides come from an e-mail to me from Dorlene Kaplan, editor of Shaw Guides, Inc., Educational Travel & Creative Careers, on February 14, 2011. At the time of our correspondence, there were 1,206. For further information, see http://cookforfun.shawguides.com.

63. Mary Alice Powell, "Amateur Cooking Classes Get Down to Basics," *Slate Journal-Register* (Springfield, IL), June 22, 1994, p. 16.

64. William Grimes, "Amateur Division: The First Course," *New York Times*, June 24, 1998.

65. Maura Webber, "School Days—And Nights: Interest in All Types of Cooking Classes Continues to Grow; Culinary Classes See Rising Market," *Chicago Sun-Times*, August 13, 2003.

66. Kitty Bean Yancey, "Culinary Getaways Are Tasting Success," *USA Today*, July 8, 2010, http://www.usatoday.com/travel/destinations/2010-07-08-cooking-school-getaways_N.htm.

67. On the luxury chef-for-a-day phenomenon at reputed gourmet restaurants: Suzanne Oliver, "Let's Make Sausage Together," *Forbes* 155, no. 6 (March 13, 1995): 136–37.

68. Carolyn Walkup, "Charlie Trotter: Driven to Excel, This World-Class Chef Vaults to the Top of His Field," *Nation's Restaurant News* 34, no. 5 (January 2000): 180. My mention of the "guest chef" program is in the past tense because Charlie Trotter's closed in August 2012.

69. E-mail announcement, "Just a Little French Feast You Whipped Up," from editor@urbandaddy.com (December 7, 2010).

70. Andrew Parkinson with Jonathan Green, *Cutting It Fine: Inside the Restaurant Business* (London: Jonathan Cape, 2001), 46, later published by Vintage, New York, 2002. The authors describe the various roles on pages 47–63.

71. Gary Alan Fine, *Kitchens: The Culture of Restaurant Work* (Berkeley: University of California Press, 1996), 3, 19, 32, 40–42, 85–87, 88–92, 184, 197, and in the second edition, published with a new preface in 2009, ix–xix. Reports on the working conditions and salaries of chefs from years later have been consistent with Fine's much earlier findings. See Amanda Hesser, "Too Many Cooks? Not Nearly Enough," *New York Times*, October 25, 1998; Erin White, "Reality Bites: Would-Be Chefs Vie for Stardom," *Wall Street Journal*, December 28, 2004; and "Chefs' Salaries: How Do You Stack Up?," *Restaurant Hospitality* (July 19, 2010): unpaginated.

72. Jay Jacobs, *New York à la Carte: Cooking with the Great Chefs* (New York: McGraw

Hill, 1976); Irene Daria, *Lutèce: A Day in the Life of America's Greatest Restaurant* (New York: Random House, 1993); Michael Ruhlman, *The Making of a Chef: Mastering the Heat at the Culinary Institute of America* (New York: Henry Holt, 1997).

73. Daniel Boulud and Peter Kaminsky, *Chef Daniel Boulud: Cooking in New York City* (New York: Assouline, 2002); Eric Ripert, with Christine Muhlke, *On the Line: The Stations, the Heat, the Cooks, the Costs, the Chaos, and the Triumphs* (New York: Artisan, 2008); and Ferran Adrià, Juli Soler, and Albert Adrià, *A Day at El Bulli: An Insight into the Ideas, Methods, and Creativity of Ferran Adrià* (London: Phaidon, 2008).

74. Examples include Anthony Bourdain, *Kitchen Confidential: Adventures in the Culinary Underbelly* (New York: Ecco Press, 2000); Parkinson, with Green, *Cutting It Fine*; Leslie Brenner, *The Fourth Star: Dispatches from Inside Daniel Boulud's Celebrated New York Restaurant* (New York: Three Rivers Press, 2002); Jacques Pépin, *The Apprentice: My Life in the Kitchen* (Boston: Houghton Mifflin, 2003); Doug Psaltis, with Michael Psaltis, *The Seasoning of a Chef: My Journey from Diner to Ducasse and Beyond* (New York: Broadway Books, 2005); Marco Pierre White, with James Steen, *The Devil in the Kitchen: Sex, Pain, Madness, and the Making of a Great Chef* (New York: Bloomsbury, 2008); Bill Buford, *Heat: An Amateur's Adventures as Kitchen Slave, Line Cook, Pasta-Maker, and Apprentice to a Dante-Quoting Butcher in Tuscany* (New York: Alfred A. Knopf, 2006); Dalia Jurgensen, *Spiced: A Pastry Chef's True Stories of Trials by Fire, After-Hours Exploits, and What Really Goes on in the Kitchen* (New York: G. P. Putnam's Sons, 2009); John Delucie, *The Hunger: A Memoir of an Accidental Chef* (New York: HarperCollins, 2009); Jason Sheehan, *Cooking Dirty: A Story of Life, Sex, Love and Death in the Kitchen* (New York: Farrar, Straus, and Giroux, 2009); Grant Achatz and Nick Kokonas, *Life, On the Line: A Chef's Story of Chasing Greatness, Facing Death, and Redefining the Way We Eat* (New York: Gothan, 2011); Gabrielle Hamilton, *Blood, Bones, and Butter: The Inadvertent Education of a Reluctant Chef* (New York: Random House, 2011); Lisa Abend, *The Sorcerer's Apprentices: A Season in the Kitchen at Ferran Adrià's El Bulli* (New York: Free Press, 2011); and Marcus Samuelsson, *Yes, Chef: A Memoir* (New York: Random House, 2012).

75. Some examples: Michael Ruhlman, *The Soul of a Chef: The Journey toward Perfection* (New York: Penguin, 2001); Patrice Johnson, *Uncut: The Inside Story of Culinary School* (Bloomington, IN: AuthorHouse, 2004); Kathleen Flinn, *The Sharper Your Knife, the Less You Cry* (New York: Penguin, 2007); and Katherine Darling, *Under the Table: Saucy Tales from Culinary School* (New York: Atria Paperback, 2009).

76. My ensuing discussion of Matthew B. Crawford's argument refers to his *Shop Class as Soulcraft: An Inquiry into the Value of Work* (New York: Penguin Press, 2009), 1–3, 11, 19–20, 44–62, 68–69, 126, 150.

Chapter 4

1. Josh Ozersky, *The Hamburger: A History* (New Haven, CT: Yale University Press, 2008), 5, 26–27, and 51–58; Andrew F. Smith, *Hamburger: A Global History* (London: Reaktion Books, 2008), 18, 61, and 76.

2. Achatz, *Life, On the Line*, 152–53.

3. Carol Heltosky, *Pizza: A Global History* (London: Reaktion Books, 2008), 63–68; John F. Mariani, *How Italian Food Conquered the World* (New York: Macmillan, 2011), 45–46.

4. I found the dish on a WD-50 tasting menu from September 2007 as "Pizza Pebbles, Pepperoni, Shitake." I am grateful to Rachael Carron at WD-50 for mailing me copies of regular and tasting menus for the fall of every year from 2003 to 2008, which I received on

October 19, 2010. As it was a new dish at the time, Dufresne presented his technique for "Pizza Pebbles" at the Star Chefs International Chefs Congress of 2007. There's documentation at http://chadzilla.typepad.com/photos/star_chefs_icc_2007/star_chefs_126.html (accessed June 30, 2012): under a picture of the dish is the caption, "Another Wylie Dufresne technique that he equated to Pizza Combos." In "Foaming at the Mouth: Wylie Dufresne, Guy Rubino, and the Future of Molecular Gastronomy," blog post, October 11, 2007, http://www.hungryinhogtown.com/hungry_in_hogtown/2007/10/foaming-at-the-.html, blogger Hungry in Hogtown described what it was like to eat the dish: "Pop one of these balls into your mouth and it immediately crumbles into a sandy powder with a texture and taste eerily similar to that of *Combos*, the pretzel snack that 'cheeses your hunger away.'" Brandon Keim published the chef's recipe in "Make Your Own Scientific Super Bowl Snacks," *Wired Science*, January 30, 2009, http://www.wired.com/wiredscience/2009/01/superfoods/.

5. Moto's head chef and founder of the firm Cantu Designs, Homaro Cantu, told me that the restaurant is rigorous in its standards for organic and local sourcing from small farmers in Illinois. Recorded phone interview, December 23, 2009. In a Facebook.com message dated June 2, 2011, Ben Roche, then pastry chef and director of research and development for Moto restaurant and Cantu Designs, told me that Moto began serving "BURGER with cheese" in January 2009.

6. The details of the dish's components and preparation derive from a Facebook.com message from Ben Roche on March 15, 2011.

7. Facebook.com message to me from Ben Roche, March 15, 2011.

8. Mario Batali, *The Babbo Cookbook* (New York: Clarkson Potter, 2002), 8.

9. Ibid., 112.

10. Ibid., 278.

11. At the time the term originally spread, it was not used in a specifically gourmet context. The online edition of *Merriam-Webster Dictionary* identifies its "first known use" in an issue of *Washington Post Magazine* in 1977. See http://www.merriam-webster.com/dictionary/comfort food (accessed June 30, 2012). Some digging brought me to the likely reference: a 167-word paragraph on southern food in "Southern Comfort," *Washington Post Magazine*, December 25, 1977, 30. There, it appears in the first sentence: "Along with grits, one of the comfort foods of the South is black-eyed peas, and to start a new year they are an absolute necessity, at least if you are seeking good luck for the next 365 days." Barry Popik contradicts the dictionary's account in his blog post, "Comfort Food," *The Big Apple*, August 3, 2008, http://www.barrypopik.com/index.php/new_york_city/entry/comfort_food/. He traces the first uses of the term to a May 23, 1966, display ad in the *New York Times* for a book on dieting by Theodore Isaac Rubin, *The Thin Book by a Formerly Fat Psychiatrist*: "Think thin . . . lose weight . . . learn about ammunition foods, comfort foods, and emergency foods."

12. Barry Popik, "Comfort Food" blog post, cites the May 1978 *Bon Appétit* article by M. F. K. Fisher. William Safire discusses the importance of Burros's column in "Miffy Prometheus: Ben Franklin's Comfort Food for Thought," *New York Times Magazine*, July 6, 2003, 12. In it, he advances the idea that Burros was largely responsible for the term's popularization. The Burros article was "Turning to Food for Solace," *New York Times*, March 9, 1985. The following articles, spanning 1985 and 1990, identify restaurants that the authors associate with home cooking and "mom": Bryan Miller, "Diner's Journal," *New York Times*, April 19, 1985; Stanley Dry, "Astonishing Changes Coming Soon! . . . At a Restaurant Near You," *Food & Wine*, July 1985, 15–16; Rosenbaum, "New York Falls in Love with America"; John F. Mariani, "The State of the Art of Eating in America—Menus for the Mid-80's," *Food*

& *Wine*, January 1986, 31–37, 70; Stanley Dry's "Home Cooking Was Never Like This," *Food & Wine*, February 1986, 52–56, 101–3; and John F. Mariani, "What's Hot for 1990: The Good, the Bad—and the Just Plain Silly," *Food & Wine*, January 1990, 44–51.

13. For signs of increased usage, see the February 1999 issue of *Gourmet*, which contains Caroline Bates, "San Francisco and Los Angeles: Comfort Food," 38–44, and David Rosengarten, "New York: Comfort Foods," 52–62.

14. William Grimes, "Critic's Notebook: Into the Mouths of Babes," *New York Times*, January 10, 2001.

15. The *Encyclopedia of Food & Culture* entry on "comfort food," http://www.enotes .com/food-encyclopedia/comfort-food (accessed May 15, 2011). The following assessment of the trend represents its continued relevance to food trends at the end of the decade as well as continued use of the same definition: Andy Battaglia, "Selling Comfort," *Nation's Restaurant News* 45, no. 2 (January 24, 2011): 58.

16. Jane and Michael Stern, *Square Meals: Taste Thrills of Only Yesterday—From Mom's Best Pot Roast and Tuna Noodle Casserole to Ladies' Lunch and the Perfect Living Room Luau* (New York: Alfred A. Knopf, 1985), and *Square Meals: America's Favorite Comfort Food Cookbook* (New York: Lebhar-Friedman Books, 2001).

17. Rita M. Harris, *Comfort Foods: America's Favorite Foods Cooked the Way You Like Them* (Roseville, CA: Prima Lifestyles, 1996); Emily Anderson and Elizabeth Anderson, *All-American Comfort Food: Recipes for the Great Tasting Food Everyone Loves* (Nashville, TN: Cumberland House, 1997); and Gooseberry Patch, *Comfort Food: Homestyle Recipes for Feel-Good Foods Like Mom Used to Make* (Elberton, GA: Gooseberry Patch, 2008).

18. Marian Clark, *The Route 66 Cookbook: Comfort Food from the Mother Road* (San Francisco: Council Oak Books, 2000); Lisa Schroeder, with Danielle Centoni, *Mother's Best: Comfort Food That Takes You Home Again; 150 Favorites from Mother's Bistro & Bar* (Newtown, CT: Taunton Press, 2009).

19. Scotto Family, *Italian Comfort Food: Intensive Eating from Fresco* (New York: Ecco, 2002); Dennis Chan, *Hip Asian Comfort Food: A Tasting of Jacksonville's Blue Bamboo* (Jacksonville, FL: Blue Bamboo, 2009); and Saveur editors, *Saveur: The New Comfort Food; Home Cooking from Around the World* (San Francisco: Chronicle Books, 2011).

20. Mary Dan Eades, MD, Michael R. Eades, MD, and Ursula Solom, *The Low-Carb Comfort Food Cookbook* (Hoboken, NJ: John Wiley & Sons, 2003); Jessie Price and the Editors of *Eating Well*, *Comfort Foods Made Healthy: The Classic Makeover Cookbook* (Woodstock, VT: Countryman Press, 2009); Bette Hagman, *The Gluten-Free Gourmet Cooks Comfort Foods: More than 200 Recipes for Creating Old Favorites with New Flours* (New York: Henry Holt, 2004); and Julie Hasson, *Vegan Diner: Classic Comfort Food for the Body & Soul* (Philadelphia: Running Press, 2011).

21. Kamp, *The United States of Arugula*, 305.

22. Puck's introduction of the smoked-salmon pizza is discussed on Wolfgang Puck's website, at http://www.wolfgangpuck.com/recipes/view/6161/pizza-with-smoked-salmon-and-caviar (accessed June 24, 2011). The full recipe, also there, calls for smoked salmon, dill cream (from a separate recipe), chili and garlic oil, chopped chives, thinly sliced red onion, and Sevruga caviar.

23. Norman Van Aken introduced the term *fusion cooking* as the title and principal subject of a lecture he delivered at a symposium on American cuisine in Santa Fe, New Mexico, in 1988. See http://www.miamidadeculinary.com/professionals_counci105.htm (accessed June 28, 2011). The chef has posted the text of his talk on his own blog site, http://normanvanaken.blogspot.com/2010/02/fusion-cuisine.html (accessed June 28, 2011).

24. William Garry, "Letter from the Editor: Chewing on the Comfort Question," *Bon Appétit* 45, no. 3 (2000): 18.

25. New Strategist Publications, *The American Marketplace: Demographics and Spending Patterns*, 7th ed. (Ithaca, NY: New Strategist Publications, 2005), 359–62. The figures for 2009 come from the tenth edition (Ithaca, NY: New Strategist Publications, 2011), 450–54. Both references to the 1980s rely on Arthur M. Schlesinger Jr., *The Disuniting of America: Reflections on a Multicultural Society*, revised and enlarged edition (New York: W. W. Norton, 1998), 126.

26. Warde, *Consumption, Food and Taste*, 173.

27. Schlesinger, *The Disuniting of America*, especially 11–15, 20–21, 40–49, 71–80, 112–13.

28. Robert Hughes, *The Culture of Complaint: A Passionate Look into the Ailing Heart of America* (New York: Warner Books, 1993), especially 19, 33, 150, 157–58, 168.

29. Bishop, with Cushing, *The Big Sort*, 130–33.

30. Ibid., 45, 47, 50–53.

31. Florida, *The Rise of the Creative Class*, 249–66, and *Cities and the Creative Class*, 129–39.

32. For proof of the existence of the DB Burger in 2001, see William Grimes, "Midtown Playground for an Uptown Chef," *New York Times*, August 22, 2001. Josh Ozersky gives a good narrative of the *haute*-burger wars in *The Hamburger*, 129–30.

33. Boulud speaks of how the idea for the burger originated in Boulud and Kaminsky, *Chef Daniel Boulud*, 158.

34. John Delucie, "Mac & Jeez!," in *The Hunger: A Memoir of an Accidental Chef* (New York: HarperCollins, 2009), 195–201. The quotation is from page 200. Delucie doesn't clarify exactly when he introduced the dish, but it must have been shortly after his arrival at the Waverly Inn. Frank Bruni reviewed the restaurant and mentioned the dish and its fifty-five-dollar price tag in "Dear Graydon . . . ," *New York Times*, January 24, 2007, http://www.nytimes.com/2007/01/24/dining/reviews/24rest/html. By 2009, the price had shot up to ninety-five dollars: "All Hail Mac and Cheese!," *CBS News*, November 21, 2009, http://www.cbsnews.com/stories/2009/11/21/sunday/main5728831.shtml.

35. Chef Pawlcyn told me, in a recorded phone interview of July 2, 2010, that she recalls putting a mac-and-cheese with lobster on the menu in 1986 or 1987. But since the restaurant opened in 1988, she probably meant that the dish existed around the time of the restaurant's opening.

36. Judy Rodgers, *The Zuni Café Cookbook: A Compendium of Recipes & Cooking Lessons from San Francisco's Beloved Restaurant* (New York: W. W. Norton, 2002), 342–46.

37. That the the Breslin's lamb burger was on the menu around the time of the restaurant's opening in October 2009 is clear from the account of food blogger Food in Mouth, "Lamb Burger at the Breslin," blog post, November 6, 2009, http://www.foodinmouth.com/restaurant-reviews/2009/11/lamb-burger-at-the-breslin.html. The specific menu I refer to in discussion of my meal at the Breslin is from August 9, 2010, and in my personal collection.

38. Lauren Collins, "Burger Queen: April Bloomfield's Gastropub Revolution," *New Yorker*, November 22, 2010, 90–103.

39. David Amsden, "The Magician of Meat," *New York*, March 28, 2010, http://nymag.com/restaurants/features/65124/.

40. Recorded in Joshua David Stein, "Pigging Out: April Bloomfield and Fergus Hender-

son at the Breslin," *New York Times Style Magazine*, October 19, 2009, http://tmagazine
.blogs.nytimes.com/.

41. From the Los Angeles Public Library's online menu collection, at http://www.lapl
.org/resources/en/menu_collection.html, I found a menu of July 22, 1955, from the Colony,
New York City. From the Menu Collection of the New York Public Library, special collections, Rare Book Division, Humanities and Social Sciences Library, I located a 1969 menu
of Le Périgord, New York City. Menus from Le Pavillon, Manhattan (one à la carte and one
fixed price), from 1970 are reproduced in Mariani, *America Eats Out*, 148–49. For information about menus at New York City's Four Seasons, see Mariani, with von Bidder, *The Four
Seasons*, 55–60.

42. From the LAPL's Menus special collection, I found a menu labeled "1960s" for
Romanoff's, Los Angeles.

43. Ibid.

44. Kuh, *The Last Days of Haute Cuisine*, 147; McNamee, *Alice Waters and Chez Panisse*, 128; and Tower, *California Dish*, 100–115.

45. On the rise of farmers' markets in the United States: McNamee, *Alice Waters and
Chez Panisse*, 125; Kamp, *The United States of Arugula*, 276–78. The landmark study of the
relationship between alternative food systems and the counterculture in America is Warren J. Belasco, *Appetite for Change: How the Counterculture Took on the Food Industry*,
second updated edition (Ithaca: Cornell University Press, 2007). First published by Pantheon Books, New York, 1989.

46. Kamp, *The United States of Arugula*, 270–71. Closer to the period in question,
Ron Rosenbaum had credited Forgione with this phrase in "New York Falls in Love with
America," 89.

47. All menus I mention here are in my personal collection. The Campton Place menu
is undated. The full description of the dish was "Sauteed Free Range Beef with Blue [*sic*]
Cheese & Port Sauce." I found similar descriptions on two Campton Place menus in the
online archives of the Los Angeles Public Library, both dated 1986. I found a "Roast Free-
Range Chicken with Herbs" on one; on another, a "Grilled Free-Range Chicken with Creamy
Polenta." The listing at L'Atelier de Joël Robuchon was from a dinner menu from August 12,
2010. The menu "Decouverte" included the description "Day Boat Scallop in it's [*sic*] Shell
with a Seaweed Butter; Free-Range Caramelized Quail, Potato Puree." The dish from Gramercy Tavern's lunch menu of August 11, 2010, was called "Pasture Raised Chicken: String
Beans and Sweet Onions." The Comme Ça menu of July 7, 2011, listed a "Free-Range Half
Roasted Chicken."

48. This handwritten menu from Greens in San Francisco was simply archived as
"1980s." Los Angeles Public Library, online menu collection. Chez Panisse soon followed
the example of Greens in growing its own food. In 1982, a decade after the San Francisco
Zen Center began the Green Gulch Farm, Alice Waters began growing her own "garden
lettuces"—Waters's phrase for mesclun leaves for a salad—in the backyard of her home.
For narration of how the garden emerged, see Alice Waters and Friends, *40 Years of Chez
Panisse: The Power of Gathering* (New York: Clarkson Potter, 2011), 107.

49. Stephanie Woodard, "Chef-Gardner: Top Restaurateurs Find Fresh Ideas in Their
Own Backyards and Share Their Gardening Secrets," *Garden Design* 17, no. 1 (1998): 48–57.

50. Caroline Bates, "Chez Panisse, Park Grill, Pane e Vino," *Gourmet*, June 1992, 52–60,
150–51.

51. Lisa Jennings, "Restaurants Bring Farmers to the Table to Connect with Guests," *Nation's Restaurant News* 41, no. 20 (May 14, 2007): 4 (2 pp.).

52. Kate Sekules, "The Conscientious Carnivore," *Food & Wine*, December 2010, 78.

53. From my personal menu collection, Incanto dinner menu from August 30, 2010.

54. From the Incanto website's "Why" page, http://incanto.biz.why.html (accessed July 27, 2010).

55. I draw the following details from ABC Kitchen's lunch menu for August 21, 2010, in my personal collection.

56. My recorded phone interview with chef Cindy Pawlcyn, July 2, 2010.

57. Alice Waters, introduction to Alice Waters, in collaboration with Linda P. Guenzel, *The Chez Panisse Menu Cookbook* (New York: Random House, 1982); all references to this book are from pages ix–xi.

58. Rodgers, *The Zuni Café Cookbook*, 16–19.

59. Suzanne Goin, with Teri Gelber, *Sunday Suppers at Lucques: Seasonal Recipes from Market to Table* (New York: Alfred A. Knopf, 2005), 2–9.

60. Larry Forgione, *An American Place: Celebrating the Flavors of America* (New York: William Morrow, 1996), front jacket flap.

61. Nate Appleman and Shelley Lindgren, with Kate Leahy, *A16: Food + Wine* (Berkeley: Ten Speed Press, 2008), 249.

62. Johnston and Baumann, *Foodies*, 70–71.

63. Rosenbaum, "New York Falls in Love with America," 89.

64. This and subsequent references to Keller's recipes derive from *The French Laundry Cookbook*, which, besides being a definitive statement of the restaurant's approach, is replete with examples of dramatically refined and reimagined variations on common foods. Thomas Keller, with Susan Heller and Michael Ruhlman, *The French Laundry Cookbook* (New York: Artisan, 1999), 407 and 262–63. The recipes are true to how they would have been made in the restaurant. On page 3, Keller states that the recipes in the book are, unlike most other chef cookbooks, exact recipes the restaurant uses, with no shortcuts, adjusted to yield home-style quantities.

65. In 2011, both Chicago chefs opened further modernist venues in that city. Then I could have tried Cantu's iNG as well as Achatz's bar Aviary, or, on occasion, his restaurant Next—which is modernist only part of the time, as it features the cuisine of a different historical moment each season. As of June 2012, I could have sampled the Bazaar by José Andres in Miami's South Beach as well.

66. Harold McGee's foreword to Alicia Foundation elBullitaller, *Modern Gastronomy A to Z: A Scientific and Gastronomic Lexicon* (Boca Raton, FL: CRC Press, 2010), vii–viii, notes that Adrià began his systematic experimentation in 1987. This jibes with the chef's own (foldout) timeline, after page 271, of innovations in Richard Hamilton and Vicente Todoli, eds., *Food for Thought: Thought for Food* (Barcelona: Actar, 2009), which begins in 1987.

67. In-depth self-documentation of innovations and creative processes has been a common trait among the modernists, beginning with the standard-bearer of the movement, Ferran Adrià. The biography of the chef by Colman Andrews, *Ferran: The Inside Story of El Bulli and the Man Who Reinvented Food* (New York: Gotham Books, 2010), highlights Adrià's self-documentation in a chronicle of the chef's own extensive publication history, pages 201–2.

In Grant Achatz and Nick Kokonas, *Alinea* (Berkeley, CA: Ten Speed Press, 2008), Achatz contributes an elaborate exegesis of how he generates new ideas. See "Where It Comes From," 27–35. Achatz also maintains a website related to his restaurant Alinea entitled "Alinea Mosaic," at http://alineamosaic.com. It was established in 2008 at the time of the *Alinea* book's publication as a discussion forum where members of the public can ask questions about the kitchen's methods and concepts and receive answers from the relevant Alinea staff members. Achatz and his business partner, Nick Kokonas, have also emphasized the chef's creative progress throughout their memoir, *Life, On the Line* (2010).

Heston Blumenthal's *The Fat Duck Cookbook* (New York: Bloomsbury, 2008), reprinted with less deluxe binding in 2009, is another example of exhaustive self-documentation. Pages 17–127 comprise "History," an autobiography that chronicles every stage of Blumenthal's food consciousness as a child through each threshold in his thinking and discoveries about cooking, cooking science, cooking aesthetics, and restaurant development.

The modernists have also been particularly fond of presenting their work at global chefs' congresses. For a chronicle of their rapid rise since 1999, see Anya von Bremzen, "Where Chefs Go to See the Future," *Food & Wine*, May 2010, 58–63.

Perhaps no more comprehensive documentation of modernist invention exists to date, however, than that of Nathan Myhrvold, with Chris Young and Maxime Bilet, *Modernist Cuisine: The Art and Science of Cooking*, 6 vols. (Bellevue, WA: Cooking Lab, 2011). This approximately 2,400-page, six-volume compendium of cooking history, fundamentals, seminal figures and philosophies, ingredients and their properties, and cooking techniques encompasses the classical methodologies and those recently developed by molecular gastronomy and modernist chefs.

68. My recorded phone conversation with Wylie Dufresne, September 30, 2010. For especially informative accounts of vanguard chefs' relationships to industrial food labs and food scientists, see Betty Hallock, "Molecular Mealtime," *Brand X* 1, no. 3 (April 29, 2009): 10–11, and, best of all, Myhrvold, with Young and Bilet, *Modernist Cuisine*.

69. Achatz narrates the beginning of his collaboration with Kastner in *Life, On the Line*, 156–59.

70. My recorded phone interview with Martin Kastner, founder of the Crucial Detail design company (1998–), January 29, 2010.

71. My recorded phone interview with Homaro Cantu on December 23, 2009.

72. Ibid.

73. Ibid.

74. "BURGER with cheese" and "RED Bull" are from the Moto restaurant GTM (Grand Tour Moto) menu of February 12, 2010, in my personal collection.

75. I had the "Philly Cheesesteak: Airbread filled with cheese and topped with Kobe beef" at the Bazaar, November 28, 2008, and the same dish, simply called "Philly Cheese-steak," at minibar, August 6, 2010. I had the popcorn dish at Saam on June 18, 2009. All menus for these dates are in my personal collection.

76. My recorded phone interview with Wylie Dufresne, chef and co-owner of WD-50, September 30, 2010.

77. Bob Krummert, "Chicago: New Epicenter of Eats," *Restaurant Hospitality* 89, no. 5 (May 2005): 26.

78. Sidney W. Mintz, "Cuisine: High, Low, and Not at All," in *Tasting Food, Tasting Freedom: Excursions into Eating, Culture, and the Past* (Boston: Beacon Press, 1996), 92–105.

79. Johnston and Baumann, *Foodies*, 14–15.

80. Paula Tarnapol Whitacre, Peggy Tsai, and Janet Mulligan, Rapporteurs (Food and Nutrition Board, Board on Agriculture and Natural Resources, Board on Population Health and Public Health Practice) for the Institute of Medicine and National Research Council of the National Academies, *The Public Health Effects of Food Deserts: Workshop Summary* (Washington, DC: National Academies Press, 2009), 1 (from which the quotation is taken), 8, 12–13. A study using census data from 2000 found that the availability of food stores was markedly skewed toward middle- and upper-income neighborhoods. Another study, which looked at changes in the availability of food stores across the nation between 1997 and 2008, discovered that overall, lower-income neighborhoods had the smallest growth in access to food stores and the largest decrease in grocery stores.

81. Rosenbaum, "New York Falls in Love with America," 89.

82. About the trend's influence on American chefs, see Julia Moskin, "New Nordic Cuisine Draws Disciples," *New York Times*, August 23, 2011, http://www.nytimes .com/2011/08/24/dining/new-nordic-cuisine-draws-disciples.html? I take issue only with Moskin's implication that the aesthetics of this new style of cuisine are naturalistic compared with the style of modernists such as Ferran Adrià from El Bulli. One look at the many pictures of dishes in René Redzepi's *Noma: Time and Place in Nordic Cuisine* (New York: Phaidon, 2010) reveals that this naturalism Moskin finds—in the tendency of the Nordic-style chefs to plate elements, as she put it, "whorled, piled and clustered on the plate as if by waves or wind"—is the height of artificial style. The dishes look as if the smallest elements—of flower, roots, etc.—have been placed with micro-tweezer precision.

83. July issues of *Food & Wine*.

84. Colin Sterling, "2011 James Beard Awards: Restaurant, Chef Semifinalists Announced," *Huffington Post* (first posted February 17, 2011; updated May 25, 2011), at http://www.huffingtonpost.com/2011/02/17/2011-james-beard-awards-restaurants-chefs_n_824501.html (accessed June 30, 2012).

85. October issues of *Gourmet*.

86. Andrew Abbott, *The System of Professions: An Essay on the Division of Expert Labor* (Chicago: University of Chicago Press, 1988). Keith M. Macdonald strongly criticizes Abbott's idea of interprofessional competition in *The Sociology of Professions* (London: Sage Publications, 1999), originally published by Sage, 1995. On page 16, Macdonald argues that professions "are competing in a marketplace where they may or may not impinge on each other and where they also compete, conflict and collaborate, in a quite non-systematic way with non-professionals, with their clients and with the state." While this criticism is valid in cases where the impingement of one profession on another is of no concern, I believe that Abbott's theory is relevant to the particular case of gourmet chefs. In this case, there is little real threat of the loss of professional ground to amateurs, since Americans have proved that they do so little cooking. Yet the loss of professional distinction between gourmet and nongourmet chefs has been a possibility.

Conclusion

1. Joseph Epstein made the rise of meritocratic ideals a centerpiece of *Snobbery*. On pages 126–27, he points out an important symptom of that cultural shift. The increased emphasis on an applicant's Standardized Achievement Test scores, as opposed to family legacy, helped chip away at the WASP elite's privileged access to prestigious cultural institutions.

2. Seabrook, *Nobrow*, especially 25–29, 64–71, 171.

3. Here I part company with Seabrook, who suggests that intellectuals' propagation of the concept of camp in the 1960s was just a "temporary measure" for staving off low culture's encroachments on high: ibid., 69. I hold the view of many camp theorists that its currency persists. A recent critical anthology on camp, which explores the concept's application well beyond the 1960s, is Fabio Cleto, ed., *Camp: Queer Aesthetics and the Performing Subject; A Reader* (Ann Arbor: University of Michigan Press, 2002).

4. Susan Sontag, "Notes on Camp" [1964], in *Against Interpretation and Other Essays* (New York: Anchor Books, 1990), 275–92. The quoted phrases are from pages 280 and 288, respectively. Originally published by Farrar, Straus and Giroux, New York, 1966. For a critique of the incoherence of Sontag's famous essay, see Mark Booth, "Campe-Toi! On the Origins and Definitions of Camp," in *Camp* (London: Quartet, 1983), 11–41. A good overview of the immediate mass-media popularization of Sontag's essay is in Fabio Cleto, "Section IV: Pop, Camp, Surplus Counter-Value, Or the Camp of Cultural Economy; Introduction," in *Camp: Queer Aesthetics*, 302–7.

5. Epstein, *Snobbery*, 227–38.

6. Barr and Levy, *The Official Foodie Handbook*, 7.

7. David Kamp and Marion Rosenfeld, *The Food Snob's Dictionary: An Essential Lexicon of Gastronomical Knowledge* (New York: Broadway Books, 2007), xiii–xix.

8. Sudi Pigott, *How to Be a Better Foodie: A Bulging Little Book for the Truly Epicurious* (New York: Viking Studio, 2007), 94, 134.

9. Virginia Gerst, "A Trend That Bites Back," *Crain's Chicago Business* 28, no. 33 (August 15, 2005): 31, 34.

10. The pop-up dinner at which I met Sinosoul was Breadbar, Century City location, Los Angeles, on July 30, 2009. High-profile interviews with him include Erica Zora Wrightson, "Meet Your Food Blogger: Tony Chen of Sinosoul," *LA Weekly*, October 29, 2009, http://blogs.com/squidink/2009/10/meet_your_food_blogger_tony_ch; and Lien Ta, "SinoSoul's Tony Chen: L.A.'s Most Controversial Food Blogger," *Huffington Post*, May 3, 2011, http://www.huffingtonpost.com/2011/05/03/sinosouls-tony-chen-la_n_857173.html?.

11. Jeffrey Steingarten, "Introduction: The Man Who Ate Everything," in *The Man Who Ate Everything* (New York: Vintage Books, 1997), 3–15. The quoted passage is from page 3.

12. Barr and Levy, *The Official Foodie Handbook*, 33.

13. Johnston and Baumann, *Foodies*, 138–52.

14. Michael Serazio, "Ethos Groceries and Countercultural Appetites: Consuming Memory in Whole Foods' Brand Utopia," *Journal of Popular Culture* 44, no. 1 (February 2011): 158–77. The quotation is from page 159.

15. Ibid., 164.

16. Ibid., 159, 165.

17. If this characterization of foodies and their Whole Foods consumer counterparts seems familiar to readers of *Bobos in Paradise: The New Upper Class and How They Got There* (New York: Simon & Schuster, 2000), that's because the gourmet ethic of meritorious self-indulgence I've identified rhymes with the "bourgeois bohemian" ethos that author David Brooks describes as a core trait of affluent and educated adult baby boomers. But I don't bring Brooks's book to bear on my argument here, because I find his characterization of baby boomers and their tastes monolithic. Also, unlike mine, his argument pertains only to one generation.

selected bibliography

Abbott, Andrew. *The System of Professions: An Essay on the Division of Expert Labor*. Chicago: University of Chicago Press, 1988.

Achatz, Grant, and Nick Kokonas. *Alinea*. Berkeley, CA: Ten Speed Press, 2008.

———. *Life, on the Line: A Chef's Story of Chasing Greatness, Facing Death, and Redefining the Way We Eat*. New York: Gotham Books, 2011.

Adrià, Ferran, Juli Soler, and Albert Adrià. *A Day at El Bulli: An Insight into the Ideas, Methods, and Creativity of Ferran Adrià*. London: Phaidon, 2008.

Andrews, Colman. *Ferran: The Inside Story of El Bulli and the Man Who Reinvented Food*. New York: Gotham Books, 2010.

Bakos, Joan Black. "The Celebrity Chef." *Restaurant Business* 82 (1983): 26.

Baraban, Regina S., and Joseph F. Durocher, PhD. *Successful Restaurant Design*. 3rd. ed. Hoboken, NJ: John Wiley & Sons, 2010. Originally published by Van Nostrand Reinhold, New York, 1989. 2nd ed., New York: John Wiley & Sons, 2001.

Barr, Ann, and Paul Levy. *The Official Foodie Handbook: Be Modern—Worship Food*. New York: Timbre Books, 1984.

Beard, James. *James Beard's American Cookery*. Boston: Little, Brown, 1972.

Belasco, Warren. *Appetite for Change: How the Counterculture Took on the Food Industry*. 2nd updated ed. Ithaca, NY: Cornell University Press, 2007. Originally published by Pantheon Books, New York, 1989. First updated by Cornell Paperbacks, Ithaca, NY, 1993.

Bianchi, Suzanne M., John P. Robinson, and Melissa A. Milkie. *Changing Rhythms of American Family Life*. New York: Russell Sage Foundation, 2006.

Bishop, Bill, with Robert G. Cushing. *The Big Sort: Why the Clustering of Like-Minded America Is Tearing Us Apart*. Boston: Houghton Mifflin, 2008.

Booker, Katrina. "Selling Cooking to Non-Cooks." *Fortune*, July 6, 1998, 34–35.

Boulud, Daniel, and Peter Kaminsky. *Chef Daniel Boulud: Cooking in New York City*. New York: Assouline, 2002.

Bourdain, Anthony. *A Cook's Tour: In Search of the Perfect Meal*. New York: Bloomsbury, 2001.

———. *Kitchen Confidential: Adventures in the Culinary Underbelly*. New York: Ecco Press, 2000.

———. *The Nasty Bits: Collected Varietal Cuts, Usable Trim, Scraps, and Bones*. New York: Bloomsbury, 2006.

Bourdieu, Pierre. *Distinction: A Social Critique of the Judgment of Taste*. Translated by Richard Nice. Cambridge, MA: Harvard University Press, 1984. Originally published by Les Éditions de Minuit, Paris, 1979.

Chang, David, and Peter Meehan. *Momofuku*. New York: Clarkson Potter, 2009.

"Chef Celebrities." *Restaurant Business* 85 (May 20, 1986): 197 (8 pp.).

Collins, Kathleen. *Watching What We Eat: The Evolution of Television Cooking Shows*. New York: Continuum, 2009.

Crawford, Matthew B. *Shop Class as Soulcraft: An Inquiry into the Value of Work*. New York: Penguin Press, 2009.

Daria, Irene. *Lutèce: A Day in the Life of America's Greatest Restaurant*. New York: Random House, 1993.

Dorf, Martin E., ed. *Restaurants That Work: Case Studies of the Best in the Industry*. New York: Watson-Guptill Publications in association with the Whitney Library of Design, 1992.

Epstein, Joseph. *Snobbery: The American Version*. Boston: Houghton Mifflin, 2002.

Fine, Gary Alan. *Kitchens: The Culture of Restaurant Work*. 2nd ed. Berkeley: University of California Press, 2009. Originally published 1996.

Florida, Richard. *Cities and the Creative Class*. New York: Routledge, 2005.

———. *The Flight of the Creative Class: The New Global Competition for Talent*. New York: HarperCollins, 2005.

———. *The Rise of the Creative Class and How It's Transforming Work, Leisure, Community, and Everyday Life*. New York: Basic Books, 2002.

Gerth, H. H., and C. Wright Mills, eds. *From Max Weber: Essays in Sociology*. New York: Oxford University Press, 1946.

Goffman, Erving. *The Presentation of Self in Everyday Life*. New York: Anchor Books, 1959.

Grimes, William. *Appetite City: A Culinary History of New York*. New York: North Point Press, 2009.

Guenzel, Linda, ed. *Beyond Tears: The First Eight Years*. 6 vols. Berkeley, CA: Chez Panisse Restaurant, 1979.

Gutman, Richard J. S. *American Diner: Then and Now*. Baltimore: Johns Hopkins University Press, 2000. Originally published by HarperCollins New York, 1993.

Harvey, David. *The Condition of Postmodernity: An Enquiry into the Origins of Cultural Change*. Oxford: Basil Blackwell, 1989.

Heiman, Jim, ed., with Steven Heller and John Mariani. *Menu Design in America: A Visual and Culinary History of Graphic Styles and Design 1850–1985*. Cologne: Taschen, 2011.

Jakle, John A., and Keith A. Sculle. *Fast Food: Roadside Restaurants in the Automobile Age*. Baltimore: Johns Hopkins University Press, 1999.

Johnston, Josée, and Shyon Baumann. *Foodies: Democracy and Distinction in the Gourmet Foodscape*. New York: Routledge, 2010.

Kamp, David. *The United States of Arugula: How We Became a Gourmet Nation*. New York: Broadway Books, 2006.

Kamp, David, and Marion Rosenfeld. *The Food Snob's Dictionary: An Essential Lexicon of Gastronomical Knowledge*. New York: Broadway Books, 2007.

Kuh, Patric. *The Last Days of Haute Cuisine: The Coming of Age of American Restaurants*. New York: Penguin Books, 2001.

Langdon, Philip. *Orange Roofs, Golden Arches: The Architecture of American Chain Restaurants*. New York: Alfred A. Knopf, 1986.

Levenstein, Harvey. *Paradox of Plenty: A Social History of Eating in Modern America*. Rev. ed. Berkeley: University of California Press, 2003. Originally published by Oxford University Press, New York, 1993.

———. *Revolution at the Table: The Transformation of the American Diet*. Berkeley: University of California Press, 2003.

Maccioni, Sirio, and Peter Elliot. *Sirio: The Story of My Life and Le Cirque.* Hoboken, NJ: John Wiley & Sons, 2004.

McNamee, Thomas. *Alice Waters and Chez Panisse: The Romantic, Impractical, Often Eccentric, Ultimately Brilliant Making of a Food Revolution.* New York: Penguin Books, 2007.

Mariani, John. *America Eats Out: An Illustrated History of Restaurants, Taverns, Coffee Shops, Speakeasies, and Other Establishments That Have Fed Us for 350 Years.* New York: William Morrow, 1991.

Mariani, John, with Alex von Bidder. *The Four Seasons: A History of America's Premier Restaurant.* New York: Smithmark, 1999.

Maysonave, Sherry. *Casual Power: How to Power Up Your Nonverbal Communication and Dress Down for Success.* Austin, TX: Bright Books, 1999.

Meyer, Danny. *Setting the Table: The Transforming Power of Hospitality in Business.* New York: Harper, 2006.

Mintz, Sydney W. *Tasting Food, Tasting Freedom: Excursions into Eating, Culture, and the Past.* Boston: Beacon Press, 1996.

New Strategist Publications. *American Incomes: Demographics of Who Has Money.* Ithaca, NY: New Strategist Publications, Inc., 2001.

——. *The American Marketplace: Demographics and Spending Patterns.* Ithaca, NY: New Strategist Publications, Inc., 2005 (7th ed.) and 2011 (10th ed.).

——. *Who's Buying at Restaurants and Carry-Outs.* Ithaca, NY: New Strategist Publications, Inc., 2003 and 2009 (7th ed.) and 2011 (9th ed.).

Niklas, Kurt, as told to Larry Cortez Hamm. *The Corner Table: From Cabbages to Caviar; Sixty Years in the Celebrity Restaurant Trade.* Los Angeles: Tuxedo Press, 2000.

Parkinson, Andrew, with Jonathan Green. *Cutting It Fine: Inside the Restaurant Business.* New York: Vintage, 2002. Originally published by Jonathan Cape, London, 2001.

Pearlman, Alison. "Chef Appeal." *Popular Culture Review* 18, no. 1 (Winter 2007): 3–24.

Pépin, Jacques. *The Apprentice: My Life in the Kitchen.* Boston: Houghton Mifflin, 2003.

Peterson, Richard A. "Changing Highbrow Taste: From Snob to Omnivore." *American Sociological Review* 61, no. 5 (October 1996): 900–907.

——. "Problems in Comparative Research: The Example of Omnivorousness." *Poetics* 33 (2005): 257–82.

——. "The Rise and Fall of Highbrow Snobbery as a Status Marker." *Poetics* 25 (1997): 75–92.

Pigott, Sudi. *How to Be A Better Foodie: A Bulging Little Book for the Truly Epicurious*. New York: Viking Studio, 2007.

Presser, Harriet B. *Working in a 24/7 Economy: Challenges for American Families*. New York: Russell Sage Foundation, 2003.

Reichl, Ruth. "Chefs as the Star Ingredients." *Los Angeles Times*, October 8, 1985.

Rosenbaum, Ron. "New York Falls in Love with America." *Food & Wine*, October 1985, 40–47, 88–89.

Rossant, Juliette. *Super Chef: The Making of the Great Modern Restaurant Empires*. New York: Free Press, 2004.

Ruhlman, Michael. *The Making of a Chef: Mastering the Heat at the Culinary Institute of America*. New York: Henry Holt, 1997.

——. *The Reach of a Chef: Beyond the Kitchen*. New York: Viking, 2006.

——. *The Soul of a Chef: The Journey toward Perfection*. New York: Penguin, 2001.

Seabrook, John. *Nobrow: The Culture of Marketing and the Marketing of Culture*. New York: Vintage Books, 2001.

Sheraton, Mimi. "The Fun of American Food: Eat American!" *Time*, August 26, 1985. http://www.time.com/time/magazine/article/0,9171,1074755,00.html.

Smith, Andrew F. *Eating History: 30 Turning Points in the Making of American Cuisine*. New York: Columbia University Press, 2009.

Sontag, Susan. "Notes on Camp" [1964]. In *Against Interpretation and Other Essays*, 275–92. New York: Anchor Books, 1990. Originally published by Farrar, Straus & Giroux, New York, 1966.

Spang, Rebecca. *The Invention of the Restaurant: Paris and Modern Gastronomic Culture*. Cambridge, MA: Harvard University Press, 2000.

Stern, Jane, and Michael Stern. *American Gourmet: Classic Recipes, Deluxe Delights, Flamboyant Favorites, and Swank "Company" Food from the '50s and '60s*. New York: Harper Perennial, 1991.

Tower, Jeremiah. *California Dish: What I Saw (and Cooked) at the American Culinary Revolution*. New York: Free Press, 2003.

Turner, Marcia Layton. *Emeril! Inside the Amazing Success of Today's Most Popular Chef*. Hoboken, NJ: John Wiley & Sons, 2004.

Warde, Alan. *Consumption, Food and Taste: Culinary Antinomies and Commodity Culture*. London: SAGE Publications, 1997.

Waters, Alice, and Friends. *40 Years of Chez Panisse: The Power of Gathering*. New York: Clarkson Potter, 2011.

Wechsberg, Joseph. *Dining at the Pavillon*. Boston: Little, Brown, 1962.

Witzel, Michael Karl. *The American Diner*. St. Paul, MN: MBI, 2006. Originally published 1999.

index